D1108958

CONGRESS AND THE NEW POLITICS

The
Study of
Congress
Series

CONGRESS
AND THE
NEW POLITICS

JOHN S. SALOMA III
Massachusetts Institute of Technology

LITTLE, BROWN AND COMPANY · BOSTON

HIEBERT LIBRARY
FRESNO PACIFIC UNIV.-M. B. SEMINARY
FRESNO, CA 93702

COPYRIGHT © 1969 BY LITTLE, BROWN AND COMPANY (INC.)

ALL RIGHTS RESERVED. NO PART OF THIS BOOK MAY BE REPRODUCED
IN ANY FORM OR BY ANY ELECTRONIC OR MECHANICAL MEANS IN-
CLUDING INFORMATION STORAGE AND RETRIEVAL SYSTEMS WITHOUT
PERMISSION IN WRITING FROM THE PUBLISHER, EXCEPT BY A
REVIEWER WHO MAY QUOTE BRIEF PASSAGES IN A REVIEW.

LIBRARY OF CONGRESS CATALOG CARD NO. 71-76615

FIRST PRINTING

PUBLISHED SIMULTANEOUSLY IN CANADA
BY LITTLE, BROWN & COMPANY (CANADA) LIMITED

PRINTED IN THE UNITED STATES OF AMERICA

For Tom Curtis

*who taught a young political scientist
the power of principle
in congressional politics*

Foreword

The Study of Congress is sponsored by the American Political Science Association with the support of a generous grant from the Carnegie Corporation. The project was first conceived by a small group of scholars and congressmen (the latter led by Chet Holifield, D-Calif., and Thomas B. Curtis, R-Mo.) who held a series of discussion meetings on Congress with financial aid from the Philip Stern Family Fund. These discussions led to an agreement to seek support for a comprehensive study of Congress. A formal proposal was prepared by Evron M. Kirkpatrick, Executive Director of the American Political Science Association, and Donald G. Tacheron, Associate Director, which resulted in the grant by the Carnegie Corporation.

The Study of Congress gave political scientists an opportunity to cover ground in one concerted thrust which they might individually inch over in a decade. Such an opportunity was unprecedented, and it increased the urgency and importance of the basic questions: What should be the target of the study? Who should do it? How should it be done?

Reform of Congress is always in the air. Congress is criticized, even by its own members, because, as a representative body, it mirrors the weaknesses as well as the strengths of the represented. Moreover, it is powerful; almost alone among the national legislatures, it has withstood domination by the Executive and has remained the coordinate branch the Founding Fathers meant it to be. What Congress does matters very much, here and abroad, and for that reason one is tempted to try to change it, to alter some procedure or structural arrangement in order to increase one's influence on the legislative product.

Nevertheless, reform is not the target of this research project.

Congress does change, but slowly, adaptively in things that matter, and seldom according to blueprint. Structure and procedure are not neutral; they are used to work the will of those who control them. Moreover, alterations in them often have unforeseen consequences. This is more likely to be true when structure and rules, and to whose benefit they work, are imperfectly understood. The Study of Congress began, therefore, with a modest admission and an appropriate resolution: there are large gaps in what political scientists know about Congress and the Study would try to fill in as many as it could.

Each of the studies which make up the Study of Congress has been undertaken by a scholar already deeply immersed in the subject. The research in each case promises to produce a book, a monograph, or one or more scholarly articles. Each man is free to recommend changes in the organization and procedures of Congress, but there will be no "official" list of recommendations by the Study of Congress itself. The purpose of the Study is to produce original research studies of Congress. Like other research enterprises, the usefulness of this one will be determined by the people who use it.

The Study of Congress Series presents associated studies designed to tell interested people as much as possible about how Congress works. It provides analytical descriptions of Congress, its subsystems, and its relations with its environment. The series fills in research blanks and suggests relevant variables for future research. It provides some basis for stating the functions performed by Congress for the political system, evaluating the performance, and pointing out alternative structural arrangements and modes of action which realistically seem to be open to Congress. Until these tasks are completed, our lists of congressional reforms are little more than statements of personal preference.

What kind of a job is Congress doing in the mid-twentieth century? How can our national Legislature be made more effective in the decades ahead? John S. Saloma III confronts these questions in the third book in the Study of Congress Series. He begins by setting forth several alternative approaches to the evaluation of Congress. Adopting an integrative strategy, Saloma examines various models for organizing power, both within the Legislature and vis-à-vis the Executive branch. The body of the book consists of chapters evaluating six major functions performed by contemporary Congresses: representation of diverse interests, law-making, oversight and control of administration, investigation, education and information, and constituent service. In his judgment, Congress has demonstrated considerable vitality, innovative response and adaptation; yet, it still exhibits significant slack in virtually all its functions. The author concludes with imaginative speculation about Congresses of the future, especially how members might best adapt to the informational revolution with its ubiquitous computers amid the changing context of American politics.

Ralph K. Huitt
Robert L. Peabody

Preface

This book in the Study of Congress Series began as a study of congressional effectiveness. In developing tests for the evaluation of congressional performance, we found that a logical starting place was the literature of congressional reform, replete with its criticisms of the contemporary Congress and its criteria, stated and unstated, for constructing new congressional orders. The literature of reform, however, with its emphasis on prescription and the future, often passed over the excitement and significance of incremental change and institutional adaptation. For this, a second source seemed particularly valuable — some of the historical interpretations and analyses of the development of American political institutions. Once Congress was viewed in a temporal dimension, the temptation arose to extend an analysis of institutional development and performance into the future. One aspect of "futurism," as the current enthusiasm in studies of the future has been popularly described, appeared to have significance for the effectiveness of Congress in the future — the application of the modern digital computer to decision making in government.

To these academic perspectives on the present and future effectiveness of Congress were added two further personal bases of knowledge. The Congressional Fellowship Program of the American Political Science Association afforded an introduction to the House and Senate through the kind offices of Congressman Thomas B. Curtis (R-Mo.) and Senator Leverett Saltonstall (R-Mass.) and a continuing association with a community of scholars and congressmen interested in understanding and updating the United States Congress. Finally, a growing interest in, and exposure to, the changing politics of the 1960's, particularly those changes relating to the American party system, provided greater awareness of what has been called the "new politics" and its implications for the future of Congress.

These disparate materials on congressional reform and change have been organized in this book, in three fairly distinct sections, as a series of evaluations of congressional performance. The plural use of the word is important; throughout, alternative evaluations rather than a particular evaluation are suggested and developed.

In Part One, "Congress in Context," some general problems of evaluating Congress are examined from a theoretical perspective. Chapter One deals with the problem of defining standards or criteria for evaluation. Chapter Two further develops alternative normative views on the problem of organizing power in the American system. A series of models or frameworks for evaluating performance are defined for legislative-executive relations and the internal organization of power within Congress.

Part Two comprises a series of evaluations of the functional performance of the contemporary Congress. Chapter Three examines the representative function of Congress; Chapter Four, the legislative; Chapter Five, the control, or "oversight," and investigative functions; and Chapter Six, the informative and constituency service functions.

Part Three extends the analysis of congressional performance to Congress in the future. A central dimension of change, described as the "information revolution," is developed in Chapter Seven, with particular attention given to the prospects for congressional adaptation of a possible information technology of 1975. The final chapter examines Congress and the new politics of the 1970's, emphasizing the future political environment of Congress. The book concludes with a personal evaluation of the contemporary Congress and its prospects for the future.

Among the many individuals who have contributed directly or indirectly to the preparation of this volume, several deserve a special word of appreciation. Robert L. Peabody, Frederick H. Sontag, Miss Terry A. Knopf, and William Schneider had the patience to read and comment upon the entire manuscript. Harvey Mansfield, Sr., Arthur Maass, Don K. Price, Joseph A. Cooper, Roger Davidson, Joel M. Fisher, and Alton Frye offered helpful suggestions on the introductory chapters. Miss Mary McInnis and Ralph B. Earle, Jr., contributed invaluable assistance to the congressional office survey and analysis included in the chapter on constituency service. Robert

Chartrand, Ralph Earle, Kenneth Janda, and Donald D. Kummer-feld provided the most extensive and useful commentary on the draft chapter on Congress and information systems. Mrs. Eileen Mason of Little, Brown and Company followed the manuscript through publication with great patience and helpful editorial advice. Finally, the finished manuscript would not have been possible without the dedicated editorial and typing assistance of Miss Judith R. Lang and Miss Susan B. LeVine.

John S. Saloma III

Table of Contents

List of Tables

CONGRESS AND THE NEW POLITICS

PART ONE

Congress in Context

CHAPTER ONE

Evaluation: Developing Standards for Congressional Performance

It is impossible to judge Congress, therefore, without a clear idea of what is expected of it. Creating an "effective" or "better" Congress is a case of applied science, like medicine and psychiatry, or social work and business management, or steering a boat and setting up an international conference. It is probably more complicated than all of these. Without ends in mind, discussion of congressional performance must be largely meaningless, just as would be teaching navigation without regard to directions of the compass, or arguing the installation of a computer in a business without knowing the direction which the business is to follow.[1]

The evaluation of congressional performance is not a new intellectual concern. It is part of a broader charge embodied in the fundamental documents of American independence and political constitution. The Declaration of Independence tells us,

Whenever any Form of Government becomes destructive of these [of life, liberty and the pursuit of happiness], it is the Right of the People to alter or to abolish it, and to institute new Government, laying its Foundation on such Principles and organizing its Powers in such Form, as to them shall seem likely to effect their Safety and Happiness.

As the demands of self-government have become ever more exacting, high standards of congressional performance have become both a necessity and an ideal. How close are we today to such a level of congressional excellence?

This volume examines the performance of the contemporary Con-

[1] Alfred de Grazia, *Republic in Crisis: Congress Against the Executive Force* (New York: Federal Legal Publications, 1965), pp. 18–19.

3

gress from several perspectives, including reform and change. What kind of a job is Congress doing? How adaptive is it as a political institution? How has it redefined its roles in the rapidly changing context of American politics? And what can we say of the future? How do the challenges of information technology and the "new politics" bear specifically on the Congress?

Attempting to answer these questions is an ambitious task. Some political scientists would argue that our understanding of American political processes and institutions is so imperfect as to make any evaluation of them worthless. The problems are admittedly formidable, and we should realistically expect only partial answers. The serious study of congressional behavior dates from World War II, and a new generation of scholars — some of them perhaps because they were exposed to the inner workings of Congress through the Congressional Fellowship Program of the American Political Science Association — has come of age only in this decade.[2]

But the issue has been forced by events. The frustrations of a young and charismatic President with the Congresses of the early 1960's raised anew questions of congressional performance. The fact that President Kennedy's constituency included many members of the national press corps and articulate representatives of the academic community only added to the public sentiment for congressional reform. The decision of Congress to establish a Joint Committee on the Organization of the Congress in the Eighty-ninth Congress — some twenty years after the Monroney-LaFollette Committee which drafted the Legislative Reorganization Act of 1946 — indicated that Congress was willing to join in the evaluation of its performance.

In these past few years there has been an unprecedented increase of literature on congressional operations and reform.[3] Much of it has been highly sophisticated but limited in scope, following the counsel

2 See John C. Wahlke and Heinz Eulau (eds.), *Legislative Behavior: A Reader in Theory and Research* (Glencoe, Ill.: The Free Press, 1959); and Heinz Eulau (ed.), *Political Behavior in America: New Directions* (New York: Random House, 1966). For a general discussion of the behavioral approach in the study of American politics see Albert Somit and Joseph Tanenhaus, *The Development of American Political Science: From Burgess to Behavioralism* (Boston: Allyn & Bacon, 1967), Chap. XII; and Robert A. Dahl, "The Behavioral Approach," *American Political Science Review (APSR)*, December 1961, pp. 763–72.

3 James A. Robinson includes one of the most extensive bibliographies on Congress in his *Congress and Foreign Policy-Making: A Study in Legislative Influence and Initiative* (rev. ed.; Homewood, Ill.: The Dorsey Press, 1967), pp. 215–45. His bibliography from 1962–66 alone accounts for roughly 40 per cent of the total citations.

of Ralph K. Huitt that political scientists cannot offer really useful advice to Congress until they fill in some of the gaps in knowledge of how Congress works.[4] A few monumental works, such as Richard Fenno's study of the House Appropriations Committee and the Harold Green–Alan Rosenthal analysis of the Joint Committee on Atomic Energy, have examined committee "sub-systems" within Congress.[5] The discussion of congressional reform has gradually shifted from polemic to a more subtle approach incorporating congressional attitudes toward reform (the "reform market") and the probable political consequences of reform.[6] Yet with few exceptions the evaluation of congressional performance has been fragmentary and disappointing. Several understandable reasons for this are discussed below.

The public evaluation of Congress is general, ambivalent, and indirect with little attention given to specific aspects of congressional performance. A recent assessment of the public's image of Congress suggests that most Americans evaluate Congress in the most general and often contradictory terms.[7] The public's attitude toward Congress is one of "general ambivalence." On the one hand Americans evaluate their governmental and political institutions much more favorably than do citizens in other countries. In a cross-national survey some 85 per cent of Americans cited their government as an object of pride, compared with 46 per cent of British respondents.[8] Yet another sur-

[4] "Congressional Reorganization: The Next Chapter," paper presented at the annual meeting of the American Political Science Association, Chicago, September 1964, p. 1.

[5] See Richard F. Fenno, Jr., *The Power of the Purse: Appropriations Politics in Congress* (Boston: Little, Brown & Co., 1966); and Harold P. Green and Alan Rosenthal, *Government of the Atom: The Integration of Powers* (New York: Atherton Press, 1963).

[6] For an excellent introduction to the politics of Congressional reform, see Roger H. Davidson, David M. Kovenock, and Michael K. O'Leary, *Congress in Crisis: Politics and Congressional Reform* (Belmont, Cal.: Wadsworth Publishing Co., 1966), esp. pp. 163–76. Another example of the new literature on congressional reform is Aaron Wildavsky, "Toward a Radical Incrementalism: A Proposal to Aid Congress in Reform of the Budgetary Process" in Alfred de Grazia (ed.), *Congress: The First Branch of Government, Twelve Studies of the Organization of Congress* (Washington, D.C.: American Enterprise Institute, 1966), pp. 115–65.

[7] For an extended discussion, see Davidson, Kovenock, and O'Leary, *op. cit.*, Chap. II, "The Public Looks at Congress," pp. 38–66.

[8] Gabriel A. Almond and Sidney Verba, *The Civic Culture: Political Attitudes and Democracy in Five Nations* (Boston: Little, Brown & Co., 1965), p. 64. *The Civic Culture* data suggest the limitations of assessing American political institutions on a non-comparative basis. Almond and Verba conclude that the attachment of Americans to their political system includes "both generalized system affect as well as satisfaction with specific governmental performance" (pp. 313–14).

vey suggests that among various governmental institutions Americans
rate the Supreme Court and the Executive branch ahead of Congress
(although all three ahead of the two major political parties).[9] Perhaps
most significant was the finding that most of the public evaluates Congress by *first* assessing the President. The public expects Congress "to
cooperate with the President and to expedite major aspects of his legislative program." [10]

Some additional considerations based on public opinion polls and
voting studies suggest how little *direct* evaluation the public makes
of Congress. A national Gallup poll in 1965 found that 57 per cent of
Americans did not know the name of their congressman and that 70
per cent did not know when he next came up for election. Only 19
per cent could identify their congressman's vote on any major bill that
year.[11] Americans find it easier to identify with the personal leadership
of the President than with the corporate performance of Congress.
The President is an early object of political socialization, the symbol
of national unity.[12] Later the political party becomes the major refer-
ent or guide to political decisions for the American voter.[13]

For most Americans, then, the intricacies of congressional organiza-

[9] Davidson, Kovenock, and O'Leary, *op. cit.*, p. 50.

[10] *Ibid.*, pp. 59–64. The authors suggest, "Supporters of the President's party
tend to view Congress more favorably than do members of the 'out' party,
whether or not the presidential party also controls one or both houses of
Congress."

[11] *Washington Post*, November 7, 1965, p. A2.

[12] Easton and Dennis note that the initial symbolization of government as the
person of the President and the strong affect this permits the child may make
possible a "subsequent overflow of this feeling to cold and impersonal institutions
and norms." They also found that by the middle grades the child is both "increasingly prone to identify Congress as the chief source of law-making as well
as a more representative symbol of our government than the President." David
Easton and Jack Dennis, "The Child's Image of Government," *The Annals of
the American Academy of Political and Social Science*, September 1965, pp. 40–
57. Alfred de Grazia finds that the childlike affinity to the President persists in
the adult world: "His mail is full of the most outlandish requests; he is Santa
Claus, Batman, 007, Big Brother, Smoky the Bear, and a host of other wonder
workers. He is human, comprehensible; his complications, which are never
allowed to appear excessive, are better understood than those of the impersonal
bureaucracy or the Congress." Arthur M. Schlesinger, Jr., and Alfred de Grazia,
Congress and the Presidency: Their Role in Modern Times (Rational Debate
Seminars; Washington, D.C.: American Enterprise Institute, 1967), pp. 42–43.

[13] See the discussion of party identification in Fred I. Greenstein, *The American Party System and the American Voter* (Foundations of Modern Political
Science Series; Englewood Cliffs, N.J.: Prentice-Hall, 1963), pp. 30–36; and
Angus Campbell *et al.*, *The American Voter* (New York: John Wiley & Sons,
1960), Chaps. VI–VII.

tion and procedure hold little meaning. Newspaper and television reports leave the average citizen with fragmentary impressions of the progress of legislation and occasionally vivid portraits of legislative personalities. (Some recent evidence, however, suggests that the public tends to discount mass media communication about Congress and that general attitudes toward Congress and congressmen are both more stable and more favorable than has generally been recognized.) [14]

Elite discussion of congressional performance has been based on inadequate information about Congress and an incomplete understanding of how Congress functions. Public inattention to congressional performance may not be surprising. Unfortunately the quality of elite discussion has done little to alter the situation. We may distinguish three elite groups that share responsibility for advancing the public understanding and criticism of Congress: political scientists, the national press, and congressmen themselves.

The political science profession has exhibited a generally pro-executive bias in its analysis and criticism of national political institutions, a bias only recently countered by the renewed research interest in Congress.[15] For example, Lewis Dexter notes the absence of a "relevant contemporary development" of the doctrine of checks and balances. "Most people in the United States today have no clear notion as to why there should be a Congress which is separate from and independent of the other two branches of government." [16] If political

---

[14] See the summary of some unpublished research by Dr. Franklin P. Kilpatrick, Milton C. Cummings, Jr., M. Kent Jennings, and Edwin E. Olson at the Brookings Institution, in U.S. House Committee on Standards of Official Conduct, *Hearings: Standards of Official Conduct,* 90th Congress, 1st Session, 1967, pp. 18–23. The public rated congressmen as a group in highly favorable terms, stressing the qualities of being service oriented, of good personal character, capable, well educated, and personable. Dr. Kilpatrick noted, "Our interviews with legislators showed that many of them feel — and I would add the majority of them feel — that the stream of unfavorable comment shows a low public regard for Congress as an institution. It is more likely that the reverse is true. High regard gives rise to high standards, and departures from these standards are reacted to all the more strongly. In a viable democracy, there is in the electorate an always latent and frequently active capacity to criticize officeholders, and to do so in such ways and on such occasions that a positive image of our political institutions is sustained and even enhanced." *Ibid.,* p. 21.

[15] See Davidson, Kovenock, and O'Leary, *op. cit.,* "The Professional Kibitzers," pp. 39–47.

[16] " 'Check and Balance' Today: What Does it Mean for Congress and Congressmen?" in Alfred de Grazia (ed.), *Congress: The First Branch of Government,* pp. 83–113.

theorists and philosophers have not articulated the rationale for a Congress separate from the other political institutions in the American system, Dexter concludes, congressmen should speak for themselves. Partly because they have not, "there is no general climate of opinion or informed public support to back Congress when, on occasion, it does carry out its job of checking — and sometimes blocking — the programs of the executive departments." [17]

National columnists and editorial writers, with some exceptions, have helped to influence a public sympathetic to the President in preference to the Congress.[18] The natural advantages that the President enjoys over the Congress in media coverage have been discussed elsewhere.[19] They provide powerful support to the mode by which the public assesses Congress. The increasingly important congressional function of overseeing the executive bureaucracy is rarely communicated to the public. When Congress does receive inordinate attention, it is frequently due to the notoriety of individuals such as former Senator Joseph McCarthy, Senator Thomas Dodd, or Congressman Adam Clayton Powell — instances of public controversy that only lower the public and elite esteem for Congress as an institution.

The cumulative effect has been that "much exaggeration and misinformation about Congress passes for intelligence." [20] When we bear in mind V. O. Key's injunction that "opinion . . . results from the preachings of the influentials" and that the quality of debate in a democratic society is an elite responsibility, the need for a more objective and precise discussion of congressional performance is obvious.[21]

The evaluation of congressional performance is complicated by the cyclical nature of the legislative process and the American party system. Public assessments of congressional performance vary widely with time and subject. The Harris survey, for instance, registered a shift from a 27 per cent to a 62 per cent favorable rating of Congress between December, 1963 when most Kennedy programs were tied up in

17 *Ibid.*, p. 84.
18 Davidson, Kovenock, and O'Leary, *op. cit.*, includes a brief survey of press corps' attitudes toward Congress. An extended analysis will be published separately by the Dartmouth Public Affairs Center.
19 See, for example, Douglass Cater, *The Fourth Branch of Government* (Boston: Houghton Mifflin, 1959); and Elmer E. Cornwell, Jr., *Presidential Leadership of Public Opinion* (Bloomington, Ind.: Indiana University Press, 1965).
20 Arthur Maass, *Washington Post*, March 3, 1963, p. E3, cited in Davidson, Kovenock, and O'Leary, *op. cit.*, p. 41.
21 *Public Opinion and American Democracy* (New York: Alfred A. Knopf, 1961), pp. 556–58.

Congress and December, 1965 when President Johnson had secured most of his major legislative goals in the new 89th Congress.[22] Over the course of each legislative session and each Congress, press evaluations of Congress will similarly vary.

Much of the criticism of Congress overlooks the cyclical nature of the legislative process. Particular legislation, notably the appropriations bills and annual authorizations from certain legislative committees, goes through an annual cycle of committee hearings, reports, floor actions, and conference. Major new legislation may require two sessions of a full Congress to complete congressional deliberation. Still a third class of legislation will not be completed for two or more Congresses, either because it is controversial and lacks sufficient support for congressional passage or because it is lower in priority on a congested congressional schedule. Because of these cycles, our legislative and representative systems appear to work unevenly, in fits and starts. Points of resistance and delay, such as the House Rules Committee or the Senate filibuster, receive more public attention than the ongoing processes of building and maneuvering legislative majorities.

This failure to understand the legislative process, especially the time and political support required, has led many critics of Congress to overemphasize the importance of structural and procedural reform. Thus former Senator Joseph Clark forecast in 1964 that substantial portions of President Johnson's programs are "foredoomed to failure unless Congress is reformed." [23] Within a few months a generally astute political analyst observed, "One-party dominance on a vast new scale has been established." [24]

Clearly, Congress functions in a broader political setting. Its decisions are subject to the play of political forces and party fortunes in the society at large — as they should be for a representative assembly. The periodic tests of parties, candidates, and issues at the polls give political direction to American government. It is meaningless to consider Congress apart from the ebb and flow of political reform that has characterized American politics. If there is public or, more likely, elite dissatisfaction with the legislative pace of Congress, it might be

[22] See Davidson, Kovenock, and O'Leary, *op. cit.*, p. 53, for a tabularization of "Public Evaluations of Congressional Performance, 1943–1965."

[23] Clark, *Congress: The Sapless Branch* (New York: Harper & Row, 1964), pp. 243–44.

[24] Samuel Lubell, *The Future of American Politics* (3rd ed., rev.; New York: Harper & Row, 1965), p. 18. For an analysis of the cyclical formation of party majorities, see V. O. Key, "Dualism in a Moving Consensus," in *Politics, Parties and Pressure Groups* (5th ed.; New York: Thomas Y. Crowell Co., 1964), pp. 222–27.

directed, at least in part, to the degree of public support for congressional action.

The evaluation of congressional performance is complicated by the changing nature of congressional roles in the American system. The critic of Congress is following a performance where the script is never finished. Political scientists have only recently begun to write about the "silent constitutional revolution" that has produced fundamental changes in the relationships between the Executive and Legislature. Richard Neustadt reminds us that we are now ending only "our first generation of experience with an executive establishment in modern dress." [25] In the twenty-five years between 1940 and 1965 the context of congressional performance has been altered dramatically: population has increased 47 per cent; gross national product, 660 per cent; the federal budget, 1,000 per cent; defense spending, 3,500 per cent; and federally sponsored research and development, 5,000 per cent.[26] The impact of change, however, has been seen much more clearly on the Presidency and the executive bureaucracy than it has on the Congress. The efforts of Congress to perfect new techniques of oversight, or surveillance, have gone largely unnoticed, and after twenty years of legal usage the term "oversight" is so little understood by the public at large that the draft Legislative Reorganization Act of 1967 has renamed it "legislative review." [27]

There is no reason to expect the silent constitutional revolution to end shortly. It is more likely that Congress will continually need to redefine its role. It follows that the problem of developing standards for evaluating congressional performance is a dynamic one. The pat formulas and prescriptions for Congress that are so common in the literature of American government are already outdated. They offer even less guidance in assessing the congressional future.

The lack of any broad consensus on the roles Congress should perform makes any single comprehensive evaluation of Congress almost

[25] "Politicians and Bureaucrats," in David B. Truman (ed.), *The Congress and America's Future* (Englewood Cliffs, N.J.: Prentice-Hall, 1965), p. 114. See also Neustadt's articles "Presidency and Legislation: The Growth of Central Clearance," *APSR*, September 1954, pp. 641–71; "Presidency and Legislation: Planning the President's Program," *APSR*, December 1955, pp. 980–1021; and Don K. Price's discussion *The Scientific Estate* (Cambridge, Mass.: The Belknap Press, 1965).

[26] Arthur D. Little, Inc., *Management Study of the U.S. Congress*, commissioned by NBC News for the special report, "Congress Needs Help," 1965, pp. 36–37.

[27] An exception is the testimony of Professor Arthur Maass before the Joint Committee on the Organization of Congress, *Hearings: Organization of Congress*, 89th Congress, 1st Session, 1965, pp. 941–57.

impossible. If we assume that the previous limitations have been met (i.e., that an informed elite sensitive to the contingencies of the legislative process and the dynamic context of congressional roles is leading public discussion of the performance of Congress), one fundamental problem remains. Each observer or critic will have a *different* perspective on, and hence a different evaluation of, the job Congress is doing. In analyzing individual evaluations, we might ask the following questions:

1. What procedural and substantive values does the observer hold? (These may not be explicit in his evaluation.)

2. What are his personal policy objectives and expectations from the political process? (What quantity and quality of decisions does he consider "adequate" or "good" for the political system?)

3. What are his perceptions of other people's demands on the political system? What are his perceptions of the general needs of society that require public action (i.e., what is his view of the "public interest")? What are his perceptions of the resources available to the political system and the capacity of the system to use them?

4. Within his general perspective on American politics and his value framework, what expectations does he have of the Congress? Should Congress initiate legislation? Ratify laws? Oversee the executive agencies? Follow the leadership of the President? Serve constituents?

5. How much importance does he attach to each of these facets of the job of Congress in arriving at an overall estimate of the job Congress is doing?

We can be sure that the problem of "evaluation" is complex. And we have not raised the problem of "comparability" (i.e., how to reduce the evaluations of different people to a general evaluation). What possibilities remain for evaluating congressional performance?

First, we can examine several approaches that have been attempted or suggested in the literature. Several are partial, and none is altogether satisfactory, but an examination of them should help to clarify the problem. Second, we can select the most promising approaches, note any inherent limitations, make explicit our operating assumptions, and proceed.[28]

[28] One possibility for a more comprehensive evaluation within this framework would be for a panel of expert judges to rate Congress according to various specific performance criteria and to state their preferences for the alternative models defined below. This would permit further analysis of performance ratings in relation to the value premises of the observer.

SOME APPROACHES TO EVALUATING CONGRESS

The problem of developing standards for congressional performance
is not new. The literature of congressional reform, with its heavily
prescriptive emphasis, has dealt with the problem in several ways.
Some of the approaches have been explicit, others much more implicit in their values and premises.

*Policy outcomes or legislative output as a measure of congressional
performance.* In its most general form, this standard of congressional
performance means the *quantity* of legislation enacted by Congress.
Most commonly, assessment is based on the "reasonable promptness"
with which Congress acts on the legislative recommendations of the
President.[29] Congress retains a legitimizing role, but the President
normally provides exuberant leadership in the legislative process, sets
the national priorities and congressional agenda, and in effect defines
the standards against which congressional performance will be
measured. This perception of congressional performance, as we saw
earlier, is an important aspect of the public's image of Congress. The
President's record with Congress is tallied as a kind of presidential
"box-score" on which Congress is rated as well.[30]

Legislative output need not imply subservience to the President.
The legislative record of the 80th Congress was quite impressive, although not from President Truman's point of view. Alternative assessments that also qualify as policy-outcome based are: (1) that
Congress should function to *restrain* presidential demands for new
legislative authority and to provide a forum for complaints against
bureaucratic decision; and (2) that Congress, through log-rolling and
political favors to special interests, legislates and appropriates public
funds much too freely.

Taking the more common definition of the criterion, we may note
several major limitations in its application:

1. The legislative-output standard requires a previous definition of
policy goals or needs. These legislative targets are frequently based on
an assumed social-utility function. They are defined by the President
with the assistance of the executive bureaucracy. Congress frustrates
these policy needs when it does not respond positively and coherently

29 Clark, *op. cit.*, p. 106.
30 See, for example, "Legislative Scores 1954–1967," in *Congressional Quarterly Almanac 1967*, p. 161.

to presidential leadership. But what if the President and the policy elites are sharply divided about priorities in public policy? This standard for evaluating Congressional performance assumes that the President and the evaluator share roughly the same policy views (i.e., a "liberal" orientation in domestic policy issues and an "international-ist" one in foreign policy).[31] But this approach is always open to the possibility that the Congress may become the defender of these very values against a President who is less acceptable to the policy elites. A case in point is Arthur Schlesinger's conclusion that "something must be done to assure the Congress a more authoritative and continuing voice in fundamental decisions in foreign policy." [32]

2. The legislative-output standard implies an excessively mecha-nistic view of the legislative process and of a Congress that sacrifices the *quality* of legislation. Congressmen frequently complain that Congress has become "a rubber-stamp" to executive proposals. In a parallel criticism, former Congressman Thomas B. Curtis (R-Mo.) contrasts the "conduit" and "deliberative" theories of the legislative process:

> The legislative process under the conduit theory is reduced to a system whereby the decisions, wherever they are made, would be forced through the Congress by whatever methods may be necessary. These methods in practice bypass the tech-niques of appealing to facts and fair argument. The great fault of the conduit theory for reaching decisions is that it does not permit Congress to avail itself of the greatest amount of knowledge and wisdom within the society.[33]

A large number of legislative successes does not necessarily mean good legislation. In spite of the acclaim of the President and most liberals,

[31] See, for example, James MacGregor Burns' contrast of "executive impetus" and "legislative tendency," in *The Deadlock of Democracy: Four-Party Politics in America* (Englewood Cliffs, N.J.: Prentice-Hall, 1963), pp. 259–64. Burns' conclusion is typical: "No political system is neutral — certainly not the con-gressional and presidential. Power is inseparable from structure. . . . The stronger the exertion of presidential power, the more liberal and internationalist it will be because of the make-up and dynamics of the presidential party. The stronger the exertion of congressional power, the more conservative and isola-tionist will be our national policy because of the structure of congressional forces" (p. 264).

[32] Schlesinger and de Grazia, *op. cit.*, p. 28.

[33] In Mary McInnis (ed.), *We Propose: A Modern Congress. Selected Proposals by the House Republican Task Force on Congressional Reform and Minority Staffing* (New York: McGraw-Hill Book Co., 1966), p. viii.

one impartial review of the highly productive 89th Congress concluded:

> Except on a partisan basis its performance cannot be judged excellent simply because it passed his programs. In its internal decision-making methods it was subject to the same weaknesses as the 88th, 87th, and many preceding them, and it suffered from the same difficulties, shortcomings, and need to improve its decision-making facility.[34]

3. The emphasis on decision and effective action may have negative side effects on the overall performance of the political system. Apart from maintaining the quality of legislation, there is the problem of building a public consensus behind major new legislation. The more doubtful the nature and extent of existing public support for a legislative proposal, the longer Congress may want to study and refine it. The President for his part may use legislative proposals to "educate" the Congress and the public about a new legislative "need," as did Truman in his 1945 message on Medicare to the Congress. The legislative-output criterion ignores Congress' function as an aggregator and accommodator for the whole political system.

A related problem of the legislative-output standard is its tendency to further "judicial monopolism" — the view that only the Judiciary is fit to or should consider constitutional questions. Donald G. Morgan observes, "Policy defines action, and action requires abundant power. Small wonder that the leisurely committee discussions and floor debates which lawyers had once conducted on constitutional restraints now appeared irrelevant or even obstructive." [35] President Roosevelt once advised congressmen to leave constitutional questions to the courts — to separate policy and constitutionality. Morgan argues, however, that such a course invites public ignorance of constitutional issues, congressional neglect, and early Supreme Court invalidation or Supreme Court self-restraint. More important, in the end, the theory "tends to weaken the standing of the Court and thereby of the Constitution and democracy itself. It postpones to the Judiciary the whole task of achieving accommodation of interests as these concern constitutional power." [36]

---

[34] Philip Donham and Robert J. Fahey, *Congress Needs Help* (New York: Random House, 1966), p. 153.
[35] *Congress and the Constitution: A Study of Responsibility* (Cambridge, Mass.: The Belknap Press, 1966), p. 334. See also pp. 3–15, 331–62.
[36] *Ibid.*, p. 338.

4. The legislative-output standard, by focusing on policy decisions, neglects other congressional roles such as overseeing administration and serving constituents. One frequently finds reform proposals that congressmen grant broad operating mandates to executive agencies and relieve themselves of constituent casework, together with the proposal that congressmen be required to act on all executive requests for major legislation within a specified period of time.[37]

"Efficiency" or "effectiveness" as a standard of congressional performance. As we have seen, the legislative-output standard usually suggests a pro-executive bias and a limited role for Congress. In attempting to define a more neutral standard of evaluation, some observers have adopted the criterion of "efficiency" or "effectiveness." The terms are used interchangeably by congressmen and in most of the literature on Congress. Organization theory makes a more precise distinction. Efficiency is primarily a criterion of the *internal* life of an organization, of the economic and technical costs of converting inputs to the organization to outputs. Effectiveness is the ability of the organization to realize or attain its formal objectives and intentions in its general environment.[38] For example, congressional hearings may be efficient in scheduling witnesses or in the use of a congressman's time; they may be effective in helping Congress to understand a particular problem or to enact legislation that will accomplish the intent of Congress.

A representative example of this approach to evaluation is the *Management Study of the U.S. Congress.* The report sought to:

> 1. Appraise congressional effectiveness and efficiency in terms of the role assigned Congress by the Constitution, and the extent to which Congress can, and does, make use of modern management practices and techniques;

[37] See Davidson, Kovenock, and O'Leary, *op. cit.*, p. 31; and *Final Report of the Twenty-Sixth American Assembly: The Congress and America's Future* (New York: The American Assembly, Columbia University, 1964).

[38] Katz and Kahn observe, "Efficiency is primarily a criterion of the internal life of an organization." They define effectiveness as "the maximization of return to the organization, by economic and technical means (efficiency), and by political means." Daniel Katz and Robert L. Kahn, *The Social Psychology of Organizations* (New York: John Wiley & Sons, 1966), pp. 161–65. Barnard makes the classic distinction of effectiveness as the attainment of the formal objectives of the organization and efficiency as the maintenance of cooperation in the social system. C. I. Barnard, *The Functions of the Executive* (Cambridge, Mass.: Harvard University Press, 1938).

2. Identify operating problems in Congress;

3. Recommend ways in which Congress can improve its effectiveness in adopting modern management practices and techniques.[39]

The study was intended to be as "nonpolitical" as possible, avoiding "issues that are primarily partisan in their consequences or that relate fundamentally to revising the existing power structure within the Congress." [40] The efficiency criterion was also explicitly adopted by a bipartisan study group of congressmen, headed by Congressman Chet Holifield (D-Cal.) and former Congressman Thomas B. Curtis, that met from 1961 to 1963,[41] and by the Joint Committee on the Organization of the Congress established during the 89th Congress.[42]

The standard should be defined so as to exclude efficiency as maximizing desired policy outcomes, although it is often used in that sense. The National Committee for an Effective Congress, while concerned with improving congressional performance, does so by supporting the election of liberal members of both parties to the Congress.[43] The standard should also be defined in a broader sense than that of economizing, although it is frequently used in that sense as well.

The efficiency-effectiveness criterion implies rather that Congress should be strengthened to make *its* will realized. A careful reading of

[39] Arthur D. Little, Inc., *op. cit.*, p. 9.

[40] *Ibid.*, p. 11.

[41] A joint memorandum and working outline position paper circulated by Congressmen Curtis and Holifield in the fall of 1961 was prefaced by the following statement: "It is intended merely to point out some of the key areas in which changes may be necessary to increase efficiency, expedite the business of the House, streamline its functions to meet present-day demands, and otherwise improve the operation of the Legislative branch of the Federal government."

[42] For a representative sample of the attitudes of members of the Joint Committee see *Hearings: Organization of Congress*, 89th Congress, 1st Session, 1965, pp. 1–17.

[43] NCEC describes itself in promotional literature as "an experienced citizens' action group founded in 1948 on the belief that today's Congress bears a responsibility transcending local or special interests; and the recognition that the growing imbalance in leadership between the Legislative and Executive branches can best be redressed by the election of outstanding men to Congress." See also Donald J. Lambro, "Liberalism's Little-Known Sugar Daddy: How the National Committee for an Effective Congress Uses Its Vast Resources to Push Both Parties Leftward," *Human Events*, July 1, 1967, pp. 8–9; and Harry M. Scoble, *Ideology and Electoral Action: A Comparative Case Study of the National Committee for an Effective Congress* (San Francisco: Chandler Publishing Co., 1967).

the companion volume to the *Management Study of the U.S. Congress* suggests the full implication of the criterion:

> To be effective, Congress must be decisive. . . . Congress asserts its most basic constitutional authority and discharges its legislative duties by making decisions as a body. Congressional decision-making is the heart of all Congressional action and effectiveness. . . . Congress is most effective when it addresses itself thoughtfully and in timely fashion to the current important public problems and issues.[44]

It follows that the effective Congress must have leadership, internal order and rules — it must be organized as a working body.

The efficiency-effectiveness criterion is inadequate for three reasons:

1. The efficiency standard applied within the existing power structure of Congress is clearly not neutral in its definition or consequences. It excludes by our definition responsiveness to presidential direction (the policy-outcome criterion). More important, effectiveness is defined in terms of Congress' own definition of its role, assuming that consensus can be achieved on that definition. But simply strengthening Congress by giving it, for example, more staff resources may introduce important qualitative changes in congressional operations. To state the problem another way, while there may be a greater consensus among congressmen about the proper role of Congress than there is among the public at large, there is no single will of Congress.[45] Accordingly, reforms to improve congressional effectiveness or strengthen Congress will have different effects on different congressmen and may well alter both the power structure and roles of Congress in a manner not foreseen by the efficiency reformers.

2. The efficiency standard avoids the problem of evaluation by passing it back to the Congress. This is clearly not satisfactory to many of the critics of Congress both within and without the Legislature. The Senate debate on the terms of reference of the Joint Committee on the Organization of the Congress is a vivid example. The new committee was barred from making recommendations for changes in House or Senate rules, according to former Senator Joseph Clark (D-Pa.), because such broad authority "might conceivably overthrow

---

[44] Donham and Fahey, *op. cit.*, pp. 147–49.
[45] See Davidson, Kovenock, and O'Leary, *op. cit.*, Chap. III, "Congressmen View Congress and Reform."

the balance of power in the Senate." [46] The efficiency criterion may have much utility in a strategy of incremental congressional reform, but as a comprehensive standard for evaluation it provides only a partial perspective on congressional performance.

3. The efficiency approach, like the legislative-output approach, assumes that the subject of congressional performance is basically a mechanistic one. It exhibits little understanding for the underlying political determinants of congressional operation. Its view of the congressional world can be considered dynamic only in a severely limited sense.

General criteria or "process values" as standards of congressional performance. Some "process values" used in evaluating congressional performance are "representativeness," "constitutionality," "legitimacy," "quality," and "rationality." Much of the critical literature on Congress takes this approach.[47] For example, a recurrent theme in the critique of congressional handling of the federal budget is its lack of rationality. The 1966 CED (Committee for Economic Development) policy statement on *Budgeting for National Objectives* cites "failure to debate and decide national fiscal policy on broad, over-all terms" and "a piecemeal approach to appropriations" as major dissatisfactions shared by most observers and by many congressmen.[48] Due process standards in legislative procedure and standards of integrity when conflicts of interest enter also fall within this category.

The general-criteria approach has three limitations or qualifications:

1. The approach is limited to a consideration of the *means* of congressional action, not ends or objectives. Process values are at best guidelines for congressional behavior. They provide no ultimate cri-

[46] See *Congressional Record*, 89th Congress, 1st Session, March 8, 1965, *passim.*

[47] See Harvey Mansfield, "Introductory Address: Criteria for Congressional Reform," *Final Report of the Seventh Air Force Academy Assembly: The Congress and America's Future* (Colorado Springs: U.S.A.F. Academy, 1965). Efficiency may also be considered a process value, although we prefer to discuss it separately.

[48] Research and Policy Committee, Committee for Economic Development, *Budgeting for National Objectives: Executive and Congressional Roles in Program Planning and Performance* (New York: CED, 1966), p. 42. See also John S. Saloma III, *The Responsible Use of Power: A Critical Analysis of the Congressional Budget Process* (Washington, D.C.: American Enterprise Institute, 1964), Chap. II, "Common Criticisms of the Congressional Budget Process." The general criterion of "rationality" overlaps with the standard of efficiency or effectiveness defined in terms of decision-making capacity. Both posit a system of rational, intelligent decision making, although the "rationality" criterion assumes a perspective external to Congress.

teria for determining how far or in which direction Congress should move. In this sense, procedural criteria also avoid making general evaluations. They are only useful for a limited kind of evaluation.

2. Process values or criteria require careful definition before they can be applied. "Rationality" may be used in a comprehensive or limited sense, depending on one's views of the possibilities for social calculation.[49] "Representativeness" poses special problems for the analysis of the American political process because of the presence of separate representational systems for the selection of President and Congress, unlike the unitary representational system of parliamentary governments. "Constitutionality" provides important guidelines but is limited by the built-in ambiguity of the Constitution, especially with regard to shared functions.

3. Whether clearly or vaguely presented, some process values can be used to introduce different and conflicting value criteria, depending on the values of the evaluator employing them. Whose definition of representativeness is to be used? Process values not only are of limited help in solving the problem of evaluation but are also major complicating factors. A related problem is which process values are relevant. "Rationality" may indicate wide executive discretion in administration; "representativeness," a corresponding need for congressional intervention through its oversight role.[50] The dilemma, except in an arbitrary sense, is not resolved by making one standard dominant.

Functional performance as a standard for evaluating Congress — the perspective of systems analysis. A fourth general approach to the evaluation of congressional performance adopts the conceptual framework of systems analysis or particular derivatives like structural-functional analysis.[51] The concept of system, first developed in biology

[49] See Charles E. Lindblom, "The Science of 'Muddling Through,'" *Public Administration Review,* Spring 1959, pp. 79–88.

[50] See Theodore J. Lowi's discussion of the "inconsistency between *representation* and *government* or synonymously, participation and decision," *Legislative Politics U.S.A.* (2nd ed.; Boston: Little, Brown & Co., 1965), pp. vii–xxi.

[51] An excellent review and critique of the application of general systems theory to political analysis (including derivative systematic approaches, i.e., structural-functional analysis and input-output analysis) may be found in Oran R. Young, *Systems of Political Science* (Foundations of Modern Political Science Series; Englewood Cliffs, N.J.: Prentice-Hall, 1968), pp. 13–48. A comprehensive introduction to the functional analysis of legislative systems is provided in Malcolm E. Jewell and Samuel C. Patterson, *The Legislative Process in the United States* (New York: Random House, 1966), pp. 5–27. See also Roland Young, *The American Congress* (New York: Harper & Bros., 1958); and Joseph Cooper, "The Importance of Congress," *Rice University Studies,* Summer 1968, pp. 53–68, as examples of this approach in the analysis of Congress.

and the physical sciences, may be generally defined so as to include the idea of "a group of objects or elements standing in some characteristic structural relationships to one another and interacting on the basis of certain characteristic processes." [52] We encounter familiar examples in the solar system, the human nervous or circulatory systems, the convention system of presidential nomination, and the international monetary system. General systems theory has been of particular interest to social scientists as a source of concepts and working models for application in systematic empirical analysis, for example, in the comparative study of economic and political development and stability. In what ways is it relevant to a normative analysis of congressional performance?

In a general sense, systems analysis provides only a method of specifying, clarifying, and applying other sets of evaluative criteria, such as system output and process values. It is primarily an analytical construct for explaining relationships. Yet, in the very process of defining conceptual frameworks, new perspectives to analysis are introduced and with them new value assumptions. The congressional system may be analyzed in terms of several groups of systems concepts: (1) descriptive concepts that outline the *basic structure and processes* of Congress (the degree to which the system and its subsystems are open or closed; hierarchical levels of Congress; internal organization, integration, differentiation, interdependence; interaction of Congress with its environment, including boundary definitions and inputs and outputs; systems paths over time); (2) concepts relating to the *regulation* and *maintenance* of Congress as a system in the broader political system; (3) dynamic concepts dealing with *non-disruptive change*, adaptation, learning, growth, system goal-achievement; and (4) concepts that relate to *systemic crisis* and *breakdown* such as overload and decay.[53]

One derivative of systems analysis that has been utilized in the

[52] Oran Young, *op. cit.*, p. 15. For a broader theoretical development of the concept of "legislative system," see John C. Wahlke *et al.*, *The Legislative System: Explorations in Legislative Behavior* (New York: John Wiley & Sons, 1962), pp. 3–28, 377–83.

[53] This list is adapted from Oran Young, *op. cit.*, pp. 17–18. An alternative approach, which analyzes system performance in terms of capabilities, conversion processes, and maintenance and adaptation functions is suggested by Gabriel A. Almond and G. Bingham Powell, Jr., *Comparative Politics: A Developmental Approach* (Boston: Little, Brown & Co., 1966), pp. 16–41. See also Katz and Kahn, *op. cit.*; and Lewis A. Froman, Jr., "Organization Theory and the Explanation of Important Characteristics of Congress," *APSR*, June 1968, pp. 518–26.

study of congressional performance is structural-functional analysis, particularly in studying the phenomena of system maintenance and regulation.[54] The term "function" in the broadest sense may be defined as the observed *consequence*(s) of a pattern of action for the system (which may be perceived as objectives, processes, or results). The term "structure" refers to the patterns of action and resultant institutions of the system themselves. Functions are performed by structural arrangements. Structural-functional analysis, then, involves both a definition or classification of the functions of a given system and the variety of structural arrangements that do or can perform them. As an approach to analysis it has been applied most often to analytical problems in comparative politics and political development. We can analyze, for example, the functions performed by a given structure such as the cabinet in parliamentary and presidential systems or, alternatively, we can examine a specific function such as judicial review to determine which institutional structures perform it in different systems.

Congress as an institutional structure performs a number of readily identifiable, specific functions in the political system: it represents people, passes laws, oversees executive agencies, investigates through the committee process basic social and economic problems, informs the public, and services the requests of constituent localities and interests.

Congress, in attending to these specific functions, also performs more general functions for the political system as a whole.[55] It manages conflict through bargaining and compromise. In representing demands or interests in the formulation of legislation and the control of administration, it serves to integrate the political system. It enhances the legitimacy of governmental decisions by ensuring that decisions are reached through publicly accepted procedures and implemented by responsible agents. It helps to form the opinion of a democratic electorate and enhance popular participation in the com-

---

[54] Oran Young, *op. cit.*, pp. 28–33.

[55] Two levels of functions have also been suggested by Robert K. Merton, who defines *manifest functions* as "those objective consequences contributing to the adjustment or adaption of the system which are intended and recognized by participants in the system; *latent functions*, correlatively, being those which are neither intended nor recognized." *Social Theory and Social Structure* (rev. ed.; New York: The Free Press, 1957), p. 51. Katz and Kahn differentiate between *intrinsic functions* referring to "the immediate and direct outcome of a system or subsystem in terms of its major project" and *extrinsic functions*, "the system outcomes as they affect other systems or subsystems to which the structure in question is related." *Op. cit.*, p. 62.

plicated processes of government. In defining public policy, it adapts the structure of governmental institutions to a steadily changing political environment. An extended list of these specific and general functions of Congress is outlined below.[56]

I. Specific functions
   A. Major
      1. Representative (articulation, aggregation, and communication of constituency demands or interests).
      2. Legislative (passage of laws, resolutions, etc., in constitutionally specified fields, especially revenue and appropriation).
      3. Control of Administration (oversight or review of administration of legislation, appropriations, investigation).
      4. Investigative (research into basic social and economic problems, probable consequences of legislation, evaluation of existing programs).
      5. Informative (informing and educating the public, communicating information to constituents).
      6. Constituent Service (answering constituent requests, servicing specific constituent interests).
   B. Other
      1. Judicial (impeachment; judging elections, returns, and qualifications of members).
      2. Executive Counsel (treaties and confirmation of appointments).
      3. Constituent (developing amendments to the Constitution).
      4. Leadership (election of President when electoral college fails to produce a majority, determining the order of presidential succession).
      5. Internal Organization (determining own rules and procedure).

[56] For alternative classifications of congressional functions see Jewell and Patterson, *op. cit.*, pp. 8–15, 23–25; George B. Galloway, *The Legislative Process in Congress* (New York: Thomas Y. Crowell Co., 1953), pp. 3–24; Arthur D. Little, Inc., *op. cit.*, pp. 13–21; William J. Keefe and Morris S. Ogul, *The American Legislative Process: Congress and the States* (Englewood Cliffs, N.J.: Prentice-Hall, 1964), pp. 8–26; Davidson, Kovenock, and O'Leary, *op. cit.*, pp. 34–37; and Rowland Egger and Joseph P. Harris, *The President and Congress* (Foundations of American Government and Political Science Series; New York: McGraw-Hill Book Co., 1963), pp. 62–66.

II. General functions

1. Conflict Management (adjustment of interest demands through bargaining and compromise).
2. Integration (relating popular policies to governmental performance).
3. Legitimation (ratification of governmental decisions through constitutional procedure, delegation of authority to other governmental agents).
4. Participation (affording multiple access to decision making, maximizing opportunities for expressing interest and public review).
5. Recruitment and development of political leadership (for higher elected positions including the Presidency).
6. Education of a democratic electorate (clarifying policy, identifying and publicizing issues, forming opinions).
7. Adaptation (response to changed requirements for government which facilitates changes in the political system).

Structural-functional analysis may be utilized as an approach to evaluation in a more limited or specific sense. The functions of an institution such as Congress may also be defined as the *expectations* or *purposes* conceived for it by the framers of the institution, by members or participants, or by outside observers. Congressional performance can accordingly be evaluated by comparing observed behavior with a given set of functions defined in this normative sense. This approach is also useful in broadening analysis to include other structures of institutions that may compete with or complement Congress in performing a specific function. The President, for example, exercises representative, legislative, control, and informative functions; the bureaucracy and private institutions, representative and investigative functions; the courts and mass media, the control function. The functions Congress performs and their relative importance may also change substantially over time.

Finally, systems analysis and its derivatives provide a new perspective on institutional reform. This perspective stresses the dynamic aspects of systems development and adaptation to environmental change. Over a period of time such systemic change may be far more significant than conscious internal organization change, a point many advocates of congressional reform have overlooked.[57]

---

[57] Katz and Kahn, *op. cit.*, pp. 446–49.

In sum, systems analysis suggests a comprehensive, dynamic, multi-faceted approach to the evaluation of congressional performance. It asks what functions Congress performs in the American political system both as a task-oriented institution and as a component of the larger system. Given this conceptual framework, the evaluator can then ask how well Congress performs specific functions (in terms of process values) or raise the crucial normative question — what functions *should* Congress perform? As a standard for evaluation itself, however, functional analysis has several limitations:

1. Functional analysis provides a framework for explanation and description rather than prescription. Once the evaluator begins to define functions in terms of expectations or purposes, the problem of whose value preferences will be adopted reappears.

2. An uncritical application of functional analysis may introduce a conservative bias to the problem of evaluation.[58] System goals may be assumed as given or fixed when significant disagreement actually exists, especially between those inside and outside the system. Or it may be assumed that certain functional behaviors are necessary. Analysis of system maintenance and adaptation functions may imply a positive valuation to organizational "survival." The distinction between functions which enhance the adaptation and adjustment of a given system and dysfunctions which lessen them is a case in point.

3. The concepts of "system" and "function" lack precision. System boundaries are ambiguous. It may be difficult to define the specific functions that clarify the operation of the system. New functions may not be perceived. Considerable overlap may exist in any definition of functions. As a result, it is not surprising to find such a wide variety of functional definitions of Congress.

4. What is functional for a given social system may be dysfunctional for another, related system; i.e., certain functional behaviors may serve organizational goals at the expense of other parallel organizations, and subordinate or superordinate systems.

5. Finally, as a technique of analysis, systems theory and the

---

[58] Merton argues that functional analysis involves *no intrinsic* ideological commitment, citing examples of conservative and radical interpretations. *Op. cit.*, pp. 37–42. The bias in the literature on the United States Congress has tended to be conservative. See, for example, Aaron Wildavsky's critique of comprehensive budgeting in *The Politics of the Budgetary Process* (Boston: Little, Brown & Co., 1964).

structural-functional approach are of limited use in analyzing power and influence or goal formation.[59] Its conceptual richness does not extend to some critical problem areas for normative analysis, such as the choice among alternative methods for organizing power or decision-making procedure.

Comparative analysis of legislative performance. A final approach to the evaluation of congressional performance that is also implicit in systems analysis is the comparative analysis of legislative systems. How does congressional performance compare with the performance of state legislatures or the legislatures of other countries? Most of the literature on Congress ignores the great variation among legislative bodies. For example, what may appear in isolation to one observer to be a decline in congressional power relative to the Executive may not appear so from a comparative perspective.[60]

Robert Dahl has projected a new potential for systematic studies in political evaluation based on "an extraordinarily great and rapid growth in the amount of empirical data and measures bearing on a wide variety of aspects of national political systems." [61] The political scientists will be able to derive relevant indicators to measure various selected "criteria of value" and compare performance cross-nationally. One such study has already been completed comparing ten countries on critical criteria of democratic performance: electoral equality, effectiveness of citizen control over elected leaders, and freedom of political competition.[62]

The potential for computer-assisted analysis of political systems with cross-national data is enormous. Explicit and systematic analysis will introduce a new sophistication to political evaluation. Yet the element of judgment would not be reduced. The evaluator would still have to order or select from a multiplicity of different and often conflicting value criteria.

[59] See Oran Young, *op. cit.*, pp. 24–26, 33–37.

[60] See Kenneth C. Wheare, *Legislatures* (New York: Oxford University Press, 1963), Chap. 9, "The Decline of Legislatures?"

[61] Dahl, "The Evaluation of Political Systems," in Ithiel de Sola Pool (ed.), *Contemporary Political Science: Toward Empirical Theory* (New York: McGraw-Hill Book Co., 1967), p. 168.

[62] Dean Neubauer, "On the Theory of Polyarchy: An Empirical Study of Democracy in Ten Countries," unpublished Ph.D. dissertation, Yale University, 1966. See Dahl's summary, "The Evaluation of Political Systems," pp. 170–74.

AN INTEGRATED STRATEGY FOR EVALUATION

From these various approaches to evaluation we can begin to develop guidelines for a more meaningful assessment of Congress. First, from functional analysis we shall adopt the conceptual framework of Congress as a multifunctional institution. It will not be possible to analyze in detail each of the functions defined. Of the specific functions of Congress, we shall consider only the six which we defined as major: representative, legislative, control, investigative, informative, and constituent service. Of the general functions of Congress, we shall consider only adaptation in our discussion of the future of Congress. Although selective, this approach should illuminate central facets of congressional performance.

Second, we shall introduce several alternative models for legislative-executive relations and the internal organization of Congress in order to make more explicit various normative perspectives that have been common in evaluations of congressional performance. Both the legislative-output and efficiency-effectiveness approaches, as they have commonly been used, make assumptions about the "proper" roles and functions of Congress, especially in its relationship with the Executive branch. The two approaches assume two quite different roles for Congress in the legislative process — one responsive to executive leadership, the other based on an independent leadership capacity for Congress.

In one sense these alternative models represent different normative definitions of the functions Congress *should* perform in the American political system. To the extent that Congress has functioned, or does actually function, in accordance with these models (and each has *some* historical basis for its definition), they also suggest a more complete description of Congress and a number of frameworks for the analysis of congressional performance.

Third, within our analysis of specific functions performed by Congress we shall consider alternative evaluations that have been made of the contemporary Congress. It is our purpose to introduce the reader to a number of relevant value criteria and to pose major issues in the evaluation of Congress, not to argue the validity of particular criteria. We shall consider both general criteria (process values) and the value expectations of the relevant alternative models where appropriate. (The authors' personal assessment of Congress is discussed in the final chapter.) A logical extension of this approach, which is not attempted in this volume, is a comparative assessment of functional performance in terms of specific value criteria.

Thus our analysis is a series of partial and often opposing evaluations of Congress. The approach adopted, by focusing on certain critical functions and by explicitly defining different value assumptions for Congress, may advance public understanding of the Congress and the debate on Congress and America's future.

Organizing Power:
Some Alternative Solutions

Overshadowing the numerous problems of evaluating congressional performance is a central and continuing theme of American politics — how power should be organized in the American political system. Arthur Schlesinger, Jr., has observed: "The relationship between the Congress and the presidency has been one of the abiding mysteries of the American system of government. . . . [I]n discussing how these two branches of government are supposed to work together, the sacred texts are relatively reticent and enigmatic." [1]

For Congress, the problem of organizing power has two related aspects. In a "government of separated institutions sharing powers [or functions]," [2] what should the relationship between Congress and the Executive be? Moreover, how should power be organized *within* the Congress? How should Congress structure itself to fulfill its constitutional role (or its perception of that role) in the broader system? [3] The problem has gained new urgency and complexity with the growth of a central executive bureaucracy or "permanent government," in

[1] Arthur M. Schlesinger, Jr., and Alfred de Grazia, *Congress and the Presidency: Their Role in Modern Times* (Rational Debate Seminars; Washington, D.C.: American Enterprise Institute, 1967), p. 1.

[2] The description is Richard E. Neustadt's, *Presidential Power: The Politics of Leadership* (New York: John Wiley & Sons, 1960), p. 33.

[3] Wilfred E. Binkley says defining the relationship between the Executive and the Legislature was "the chief structural problem of the Constitutional Convention." For his discussion of the convention debate as well as the Federalist and Jeffersonian solutions to the twofold problem of organizing power, see *President and Congress* (New York: Alfred A. Knopf, 1947), Chaps. I–III. For a contemporary analysis of legislative-executive relations in the legislative and administrative processes, see the statement of Professor Arthur Maass, U.S. Senate, Subcommittee on Separation of Powers, Committee on the Judiciary, *Hearings: Separation of Powers*, 90th Congress, 1st Session, 1967, pp. 185–201.

theory subject to the control of the political branches but in actuality exercising political initiative on its own.[4]

The delineation of power in American politics has, according to Schlesinger, taken the form of a "permanent argument about the power of the presidency" — and, by implication, about the power of the Congress as well — that has preoccupied American historians and political scientists. At the public level the argument is translated into the vivid spectacle of "permanent guerilla warfare" between the two branches of government, each actively recruiting partisans through competing, overlapping, yet separate elections.[5]

Given the characteristic elements of the Constitution, the problem of power has no determinate solution. It remains one of the open questions of the American practice of government. The frequently confused, inconsistent, and repetitive arguments characteristic of the debate have led many observers to discount it. They hold that the continuing disregard for doctrinal consistency, beginning with the Federalists, proves conclusively "the lack of serious intellectual content in the debate." [6] Policy preferences rather than principles have determined the political tactics as well as the outcome of various contests. From another perspective, that of political development, Samuel P.

[4] See Richard E. Neustadt, "Politicians and Bureaucrats," in David B. Truman (ed.), *The Congress and America's Future* (Englewood Cliffs, N.J.: Prentice-Hall, 1965). See also David B. Truman's discussion of the competition between the President and Legislature for control of the operating agencies of the Executive branch. "In consequence of alternative lines of access available through the legislature and the executive and of divided channels for control of administrative policy, many nominally executive agencies are at various times virtually independent of the chief executive. Although some of these lines of access may operate in series, they are not arranged in a stable and integrated hierarchy." *The Governmental Process: Political Interests and Public Opinion* (New York: Alfred A. Knopf, 1951), p. 508.

[5] Schlesinger and de Grazia, *op. cit.*, pp. 2–10. Interestingly, much of the literature on the American Presidency is concerned with Presidential power or "greatness" while the literature on Congress lacks a comparable focus. See James MacGregor Burns' analyses "The Presidency and the Historians" and "The Presidency and the Political Scientists," in *Presidential Government: The Crucible of Leadership* (Boston: Houghton Mifflin Co., 1966), pp. 78–97.

[6] Schlesinger and de Grazia, *op. cit.* Schlesinger admits, however, that "a dimension of substantive difference remains, based on the efficacy of each branch as a means of resisting or advancing change. . . . This means that as the anxieties of American life have tended to speak through the Congress, so the urgencies have tended to speak through the presidency. . . ." Neustadt uses a parallel analogy of congressional-executive relations as a "great game," much like collective bargaining. "It is a game played catch-as-catch can, case by case. And everybody knows the game, observers and participants alike." *Presidential Power*, p. 37.

Huntington finds the American polity "quaintly old," our central institutions retaining much of their traditional form and substance in a culture otherwise characterized by a positive orientation toward change.[7] However, the implications of these statements — that the problem of organizing political power has been solved by expedients or that the form of the solutions has been relatively archaic and static — need careful examination and qualification.

Three factors have had an important bearing on the problem and the solutions that have evolved.

Dualism in the American political culture. The establishment and preservation of *two* primary centers of initiative and decision in the American political system have given the Congress actual and potential powers unequaled by any other legislative body. President and Congress stand at the respective apexes of *two* representational systems, which by their very existence divide sovereignty. The contrasts with the parliamentary model, with Legislature and Executive joined by a unitary cabinet, and one national constituency, are instructive. The dualism of the American system, embodied in the constitutional settlement and supported by the political culture, ensure that *both* the President and Congress will have powerful stakes in decision making at the national level.[8] From this perspective, the rumors of the death of Congress are clearly premature, and comparisons with the trend of legislatures elsewhere, particularly in parliamentary systems, highly misleading.

Such a dual system of representation and decision making builds into our form of government both permanent conflict and the continuing necessity for cooperation between the different centers of power. It has fundamentally affected bureaucratic organization and political parties as they have evolved in the United States.[9] We need

[7] Huntington, "Political Modernization: America vs. Europe," *World Politics*, April 1966, pp. 378–414.

[8] On numerous occasions both President and Congress have violated the constitutional limits on guerilla warfare, but none came so close to repealing the constitutional settlement as the impeachment of Andrew Johnson. Binkley concludes that, by a single vote, the system established by the Constitution was saved from "suspension if not destruction." *Op. cit.*, Chap. VII, "The Reaction Against the Executive."

[9] See Norton E. Long, "Power and Administration," *Public Administration Review*, Autumn 1949, pp. 257–64. The most comprehensive discussion of the decentralization of the American governmental system and the nature of American political parties is Morton Grodzins' in Daniel J. Elazar (ed.), *The American System by Morton Grodzins: A New View of Government in the United States* (Chicago: Rand McNally & Co., 1966), Chap. X, "American Parties and the American System."

not concern ourselves here with the origins of this dualistic approach to politics but should simply note that it has persisted in American political literature, institutions, and behavior.[10]

American political scientists, starting at least with Woodrow Wilson, have viewed this duality as an irrational and inefficient form of government. "Political modernization," according to Huntington, involves: (1) the *rationalization* of authority (replacing a large number of traditional, religious, familial, and ethnic political authorities by *one* secular, national political authority); (2) the *differentiation* of new political functions and the development of specialized structures to perform those functions; and (3) increased *participation* in politics by social groups throughout society and the development of new political institutions, such as political parties and interest associations, to organize this participation.[11] The American system, with its diffusion of authority and its continued belief in fundamental law (and the institution of judicial review), has never been fully rationalized. Moreover, in spite of the separation of powers (i.e., functions) which implies differentiation, functions were blended or fused through the complex of checks and balances. Only in participation has America become politically modernized, Huntington concludes. Sovereignty was and remains divided; power, separated; and functions, combined in many different institutions — most immediately the President and Congress.

The economic and political development of "the first new nation" permitted a complicated system of political decision making during the nineteenth century.[12] However, when the United States emerged as a world power and the American economy was nationalized, the

[10] See Robert G. McCloskey's discussion of the "ambivalence" of American political values, "The American Ideology," in Marian D. Irish (ed.), *Continuing Crisis in American Politics* (Englewood Cliffs, N.J.: Prentice-Hall, 1963), pp. 10–25. On the origins of American political ideas, see David W. Minar, *Ideas and Politics: The American Experience* (Homewood, Ill.: The Dorsey Press, 1964), esp. Chap. II, "Backgrounds to American Political Consensus."

[11] Huntington, *op. cit.*, p. 378.

[12] Huntington, citing Louis Hartz' thesis of *The Liberal Tradition in America* (New York: Harcourt, Brace & World, 1955), says that the absence of feudal social institutions in America made the centralization of power unnecessary. "The combination of an egalitarian social inheritance plus the plentitude of land and other resources enabled social and economic development to take place more or less spontaneously." *Ibid.*, p. 405. See also Lucian W. Pye's typology of the "crises in political development," in *Aspects of Political Development* (The Little, Brown Series in Comparative Politics; Boston: Little, Brown & Co., 1966), pp. 62–67; and Seymour Martin Lipset, *The First New Nation: The United States in Historical and Comparative Perspective* (New York: Basic Books, 1963), esp. Chaps. I–II.

American political system experienced further rationalization and differentiation *within* the dualistic framework of presidential and congressional power, a point to which we shall return shortly.

The ideological perspectives on organization. The definition of two centers of authority within American politics has both limited and expanded the possible solutions to the problem of organizing congressional power. The final solution of a single authority — the evolution of a parliamentary-cabinet form of government — has been rejected historically. Thus the choice has been confined to a number of other alternatives or combinations of alternatives — a choice that still remains open.

It is possible to discern in American political history a number of perspectives on organizing power — both between President and Congress and within the Congress. Some of these have ideological content. They may, for example, be based on doctrines of party responsibility or legislative independence.[13] Four alternative models of legislative-executive relations and a similar number of models for internal legislative organization have been abstracted for further analysis below.

An open choice among alternative forms has not precluded the development of ideological content in the historical debate about the organization of power. While American party politics have been largely pragmatic and actors have shifted positions to suit their interests, important continuities persist both of position and interest. George Galloway traces the historical struggle over the powers of the House Committee on Rules to control the flow of legislation and finds two consistently opposed principles: "Whether legislative action should be controlled by a majority of the entire House or whether the majority party should control through its nominal agent." [14] Both the Progressives in 1910 and the "conservative coalition" after 1937 took the former position in support of quite different legislative ends, although in quite different legislative contexts. Continuities of interest also add content to the debate. James MacGregor Burns sees these interests coalescing into two political systems, the congressional and the presidential. The congressional party system is unified by a com-

13 See James A. Robinson, *The House Rules Committee* (Indianapolis, Ind.: The Bobbs-Merrill Co., 1963), pp. 111–27.

14 Galloway, *History of the House of Representatives* (New York: Thomas Y. Crowell Co., 1962), p. 62. See also Arthur N. Holcombe, *Our More Perfect Union: From Eighteenth-Century Principles to Twentieth-Century Practice* (Cambridge, Mass.: Harvard University Press, 1950), Chap. VI, "Majority Rule in the House of Representatives," pp. 149–90.

mon ideology which Burns describes as conservative, isolationist, and "intrinsically negative." But, Burns argues, congressional party ideologists are articulate and *positive* in their defense of the congressional party system:

> States' rights, local elections, restricted franchise, minority rights, rural overrepresentation, checks and balances, congressional power, the danger of majority or "mass" rule, judicial review (at least in the old days), powerful committees, the seniority system, the filibuster — in short, the Madisonian system in all its ramifications — arouse their stout support. And the ideologists in Congress are buttressed outside it by able political thinkers like James Burnham, by perceptive journalists like William S. White and David Lawrence, and by a host of newspapers, magazines, and commentators.[15]

From another perspective the debate has been obscured by a rigid and sterile American political theory. Daniel Boorstin characterizes Americans as being uninterested in political theory.[16] Americans have a sense of "givenness" about their institutions. The Constitution embodies a "preformed original theory" given by the Founding Fathers, perfect and eternally valid. Thus there is no need to debate the role of our basic political institutions. Yet while Americans are intensely conservative about political philosophy, they are flexible, pragmatic, and innovative in their interpretation of the Constitution through government and law. They combine an implicit theory of politics, offered by experience, with an explicit, unexperimental constitutional orthodoxy. Only a consideration of both elements will reveal the dynamic character of American political institutions.

This tendency of Americans not to make explicit their theory of politics has increased the confusion and contradiction in the debate. It is not uncommon for participants to take positions on the organiza-

---

[15] Burns, *The Deadlock of Democracy: Four Party Politics in America* (Englewood Cliffs, N.J.: Prentice-Hall, 1963), pp. 247–48. Another example of the relationship between political interest and the organization of power is the post-Reconstruction southern influence in the Democratic party and the nation. See Ralph M. Goldman, *The Democratic Party in American Politics* (Government in the Modern World Series; New York: The Macmillan Co., 1966), pp. 134–36.

[16] *The Genius of American Politics* (Chicago: The University of Chicago Press, 1953), Chap. I, "How Belief in the Existence of an American Theory Has Made a Theory Superfluous." While Boorstin argues that we have no philosophy, Louis Hartz traces the "cult of constitution worship" to a fixed dogmatic liberalism that has permeated American politics. *Op. cit.*

tion of power that are inconsistent in their assumptions or practical effects. Former Senator Joseph Clark, one of the more articulate spokesmen for congressional reform, supports strong national parties and strong party leadership in Congress (reforms that would give party leaders control of legislation) and, at the same time, democratization of congressional procedure to permit a majority of the House or Senate to work its will (reforms that would facilitate decision making by fluctuating bipartisan majorities).[17]

The changing power equilibrium — innovation and adaptation. A third factor has influenced the organization of power in the American system. We have noted the structural limits imposed by the Constitution, especially the formal commitment to a dual system of representation and decision making. Within these outlines we have argued that there are important continuities of ideological position and interest — continuities that can be abstracted for the purpose of constructing alternative models for organizing power. Both considerations must be placed within a broader context — incessant change.

American political institutions have been anything but static or archaic. Although some striking parallels may exist between the contemporary American system and earlier forms of the English polity, the author does not agree with the assertion that after independence the American political system "did not undergo any revolutionary changes at all." [18] Many of the constitutional outlines for the organization and powers of the three branches remained to be filled in, not to mention the extraconstitutional mechanisms that developed rapidly beside them. Some of these innovations were uniquely American, others anticipated political developments that later became widely characteristic of the modern democracies. The American facility for

17 Joseph Clark, *Congress: The Sapless Branch* (New York: Harper & Row, 1964). David Truman points out that "a considerable number of suggestions, especially some that are urged in the name of democratizing the House or Senate, would have the effect of further weakening the power of the central elective leadership, the Speaker and the floor leaders." A reduction in the number of signatures required for discharge "would transfer control from one minority to another (and shifting) one equally inaccessible to control by the elective leaders." *The Congress and America's Future,* p. 179.

18 Huntington, "America vs. Europe," p. 380. Among parallels with Tudor England, the Presidency is depicted as a Tudor monarch, the only survival in the contemporary world of the constitutional monarchy of medieval Europe. Huntington takes a generally pessimistic view of the capacity of Congress to adapt to major changes in American society. See "Congressional Responses to the Twentieth Century," in Truman, *The Congress and America's Future,* pp. 5–31.

political experimentation and engineering, the pragmatic spirit of American politics, could, even before the advent of the modern Presidency, claim such impressive innovations as judicial review, American federalism, modern political parties, the convention system for party nominations, the urban machine, and the direct primary. Within the Congress itself, experimentation and change occurred in the development of rules and procedure and the standing committee system.[19] More than a century after Jefferson's Presidency, Congress experienced "the revolution of 1910," which destroyed the accumulated powers of the speakership of the House, the second most powerful office in the national government.[20] Similarly, the Constitution, which limits the powers of the political branches and the subordinate levels of the federal system, has been interpreted differently under different Courts. The shift of the Court's position in the reapportionment cases— between *Colegrove* v. *Green* (1946) and *Baker* v. *Carr* (1962) — provided "the impetus for an institutional revolution of the deepest significance." [21] Except in British constitutional history it is hard to find parallels of such extensive "peaceful revolution" or change in other political systems. But that is one of the strengths of the American system — it has been able to accommodate revolutionary change while giving the appearance of continuity.[22]

The President and Congress, as central institutions in the American political system, have been an important part of this revolutionary change. Together they form a kind of moving power equilibrium, adapting to the increasing demands for central political decision, both essential to the equilibrium and neither able to innovate its power structure or decision-making procedures without affecting the other.

Two images of this power equilibrium are helpful. When there is

[19] See Joseph Cooper, "Jeffersonian Attitudes Toward Executive Leadership and Committee Development in the House of Representatives 1789–1829," *The Western Political Quarterly*, March 1965, pp. 45–63.

[20] Galloway summarizes some contemporary evaluations of the dramatic transition from "Czar" Cannon to "King" Caucus. *Op. cit.*, pp. 136–39.

[21] Gordon E. Baker, *The Reapportionment Revolution: Representation, Political Power, and the Supreme Court* (Studies in Political Science; New York: Random House, 1966), p. 4.

[22] See Hubert H. Humphrey's description of reapportionment as "that special brand of American revolution which seeks to redress wrongs and to correct injustices within the framework of law and through the legal processes of democracy. It is part of the never-ending process of growth and change which has characterized our political and governmental systems from their inception." Foreword to Royce Hanson, *The Political Thicket: Reapportionment and Constitutional Democracy* (Englewood Cliffs, N.J.: Prentice-Hall, 1966), p. vi.

little need for central decision making, the power relationships between President and Congress may be characterized by the cyclical alternation of power between the two institutions, as during the nineteenth century. The national government operated without a central budget mechanism, was only marginally concerned with foreign policy after the War of 1812, and assumed little responsibility for the broader social and economic costs of industrialization. Either the President *or* the Congress could operate the system and both at various times did.

Economic, political, and social change gradually upset the equilibrium of the nineteenth century. Theodore Roosevelt's excursions in international waters and the demand for governmental rationalization imposed by the financial burdens of World War I required a new equilibrium with a major reallocation of roles between President and Congress. The passage of the Budget and Accounting Act of 1921 creating the executive budget was the first of several revolutionary changes in legislative-executive relations that have led to the "modern" or "institutionalized" Presidency and to "executive-centered" government.[23] Rationalization and centralization of authority under the American Presidency have made new advances in the 1960's with presidential application of the "new economics" in fiscal and monetary policy and with a government-wide adoption of the Planning, Programming, Budgeting System (PPBS) developed in the Department of Defense.[24] Congress has constantly innovated or attempted to innovate new roles and powers in keeping with the changing equilibrium of decision making. The establishment of the General Accounting Office; the development of a new oversight, or surveillance, capacity using such instruments as the legislative veto, annual authorization, and investigatory staff; the reform of the standing committee system and the addition of professional staff for commit-

[23] For an elaboration of the term "executive-centered" government, see Theodore Lowi, *Legislative Politics U.S.A.* (2nd ed.; Boston: Little, Brown & Co., 1965), pp. xii–xxi. A historical analysis of the changing roles of President and Congress in the budget process is included in John S. Saloma III, *The Responsible Use of Power: A Critical Analysis of the Congressional Budget Process* (Washington, D.C.: American Enterprise Institute, 1964), pp. 1–21. For a parallel treatment of legislative and executive roles in foreign policy, see James A. Robinson, *Congress and Foreign Policy-Making* (rev. ed.; Homewood, Ill.: The Dorsey Press, 1967).

[24] See Walter W. Heller, *New Dimensions of Political Economy* (The Godkin Lectures at Harvard University 1966; Cambridge, Mass.: Harvard University Press, 1966), and David Novick (ed.), *Program Budgeting: Program Analysis and the Federal Government* (Cambridge, Mass.: Harvard University Press, 1965).

tees are all congressional responses to the twentieth century. The creation of a Joint Committee on Atomic Energy, which shares an unusual degree of decision-making authority with the Executive branch, "probably the most powerful Congressional committee in the history of the nation," is one of the most radical innovations.[25]

Friends and critics of Congress alike have been impatient with the pace of congressional adjustment to reform in the Executive. But much contemporary commentary on Congress misses the point — Congress *is* adapting itself to a new power equilibrium and is defining new complementarities and tensions with the Presidency. How well Congress is performing these new roles will be discussed at some length in Part II of this volume.

The concept of a moving power equilibrium embracing the historic paradox of the constitutional settlement is not only useful in interpreting the history of legislative-executive relations but also suggests that the equilibrium will change in the future. The recommendation of the Joint Committee on the Organization of the Congress, in its report of September, 1966, that a Joint Committee on Congressional Operations be established to make a "continuing study of the organization and operation of the Congress, and to recommend improvements designed to strengthen Congress" (especially with regard to automatic data processing and information retrieval systems) is a clear indication that Congress is aware of the changing power equilibrium in the American system.[26]

FOUR MODELS OF
LEGISLATIVE-EXECUTIVE RELATIONS

The organization of power has important implications for policy outcomes in a political system: it is instrumental in reinforcing certain values which may or may not be explicit. For example, in the United

[25] For a discussion of the unique relationship of the Joint Committee on Atomic Energy to the Executive branch, see Harold P. Green and Alan Rosenthal, *Government of the Atom: The Integration of Powers* (New York: Atherton Press, 1963), pp. 25–30, 71–114, 266–73. "What makes the JCAE stand out is that its involvement in executive processes and its domination of certain areas of the atomic energy program have become thoroughly institutionalized and accepted — the *modus operandi* and not merely an occasional occurrence" (p. 112).

[26] U.S. Senate, "*Legislative Reorganization Act of 1966*," Senate Report No. 1629, 89th Congress, 2nd Session, 1966, pp. 38–40.

States, the decision to separate powers was based on a belief in the liberty of the individual.[27]

How Congress should organize itself and what functions it should perform in the American system are questions that have received differing answers, depending on the values and policy objectives of the spokesman. When we ask the question, "How well is Congress doing its job?" we invite as many answers as there are different points of view about the job Congress *should* be doing. Before we can say anything about congressional performance or the desirability of various congressional reforms, we must first specify our perspective on Congress.

For this study and to simplify analysis, four models, or conceptual frameworks, for organizing power between the Legislature and Executive have been developed. Four additional models have been selected for organizing power within Congress.[28] Although unified models embracing both theories of legislative-executive organization and internal congressional organization might have been constructed, our preference is to treat these two aspects of organizing power separately at first and then in relation to each other. In the real world of American politics, and even in the ideal world of the political scientist, elements from several of these models are usually combined.

The presidential-responsible party model. Usually referred to as the "responsible two-party model," this perspective of Congress is the one most frequently taken by academic critics outside of Congress. It is derived from the doctrine of responsible party government and finds its prototype in some variation of the British parliamentary system.

---

[27] For a discussion of theory of the division of power, see Arthur Maass (ed.) et al., *Area and Power: A Theory of Local Government* (Glencoe, Ill.: The Free Press, 1959). Also see M. J. C. Vile, *Constitutionalism and the Separation of Powers* (Oxford, Eng.: Clarendon Press, 1967).

[28] Alfred de Grazia has attempted to develop theoretical models based on Executive and Republican Force respectively. See *Republic in Crisis: Congress Against the Executive Force* (New York: Federal Legal Publications, 1965); "Toward a New Model of Congress," in Alfred de Grazia (ed.), *Congress: The First Branch of Government, Twelve Studies of the Organization of Congress* (Washington, D.C.: American Enterprise Institute, 1966), pp. 7–22; and Schlesinger and de Grazia, *op. cit.*, pp. 33–102. The most comprehensive attempt to relate theories of the proper functions of Congress to specific reform positions is the work of Roger H. Davidson, David M. Kovenock, and Michael K. O'Leary, *Congress in Crisis: Politics and Congressional Reform* (Belmont, Cal.: Wadsworth Publishing Co., 1966). Davidson, Kovenock, and O'Leary develop three theoretical models: literary, executive-force, and party-government. In our study the approach taken of developing four separate models for both legislative-executive relations and internal legislative organization should solve some of the logical problems left unresolved by both efforts.

Perhaps its closest approximation in congressional history is found in the Democratic Congresses under Woodrow Wilson.[29] The title "responsible party" is somewhat misleading since the model is more complicated in the American presidential system than in the parliamentary one. The President is assigned the primary leadership role supported by a powerful party leadership in Congress. The model values presidential policy leadership highly.

The presidential-responsible party model assumes a distinctive theory of democracy. The essence of democracy is established by "the popular choice between and control over alternate responsible parties; for only such parties can provide the coherent, unified sets of rulers who will assume collective responsibility to the people for the manner in which government is carried on. Only in the alternation in office of such parties can the popular will be translated into governmental action."[30] Policy, then, should be defined in periodic election contests between two "programmatic" parties.

The presidential-responsible party model links President and Congress by a *national*, presidentially oriented party.[31] The role of the President as chief of party takes precedence over the constitutional role of the Congress as an independent critic of the Executive. The party in Congress is controlled and takes leadership from *outside* the Congress. The President as chief of party and chief legislator dominates the legislative process. Congress enacts his legislative program and accords him, as chief executive, maximum discretion in adminis-

[29] For a summary of the literature on responsible party government, see Austin Ranney, *The Doctrine of Responsible Party Government: Its Origins and Present State* (Illinois Studies in the Social Sciences; Urbana, Ill.: The University of Illinois Press, 1954), XXXIV, 3. Note especially his discussion of Woodrow Wilson as "the first American exponent of the doctrine of responsible party government," *ibid.*, pp. 25–47. The classic contemporary statement of the doctrine is found in the Committee on Political Parties of the American Political Science Association, "Toward a More Responsible Two-Party System," *American Political Science Review* (APSR), XLIV, Supplement (September 1950). A more recent and modified statement of this perspective is given by James MacGregor Burns, *Deadlock of Democracy*. Burns argues that a form of responsible party government functioned under Jefferson, although most observers would hold that national political parties based on the presidential nominating convention and popular election of the President did not develop until the Jacksonian era. Although Congress has at times been highly responsive to presidential leadership, these periods would appear to be the exception, when popular presidential mandates (with large congressional majorities) have temporarily superseded existing machinery.

[30] Ranney, *op. cit.*, p. 12.

[31] See Burns, *Deadlock of Democracy*, Chap. XIV, "Strategy for Americans."

tration, subject only to broad policy oversight or surveillance. Congress retains roles of policy clarification and representation.[32]

In summary, the presidential-responsible Party model is basically a *programmatic* model. Program is the dominant consideration; the majority principle, qualified by party, the means to its enactment. Congress, from this perspective, is an archaic and unrepresentative institution which has thwarted and delayed necessary legislation. The underlying assumption is that Congress is anti-majoritarian in its procedures and legislative decisions. Only the failure to offer the American electorate the opportunity to express its majority opinion on various programs has prevented their enactment as law. The general direction of reform is clear — greater responsiveness to presidential leadership and majority rule through cohesive parties.

The presidential-pluralist or pluralist model. The pluralist perspective views government in general and the Legislature in particular as an arena of interest group activity characterized by group conflict and bargaining. In America, "social pluralism makes bargaining necessary and basic agreement makes it possible." [33] The pluralist perspective is not new. Both Madison and Calhoun, two of America's greatest political theorists, took an essentially pluralist view of government as a bargaining system with varying veto powers available to the participants, although both added anti-majoritarian prescriptions to their writings.[34]

[32] See Davidson, Kovenock, and O'Leary, *op. cit.*, pp. 34–37. "According to the party-government conception, Congress (as well as the Executive) would be set in motion by a strong and lucid party structure, serving chiefly as a forum for the staged confrontation of party ideologies."

[33] Robert A. Dahl and Charles E. Lindblom, *Politics, Economics, and Welfare: Planning and Politico-Economic Systems Resolved into Basic Social Processes* (New York: Harper & Bros., 1953), Chap. XII, "Bargaining: Control Among Leaders." One leading exponent of this perspective is David B. Truman. See *The Governmental Process*, esp. Chap. XII, "Techniques of Interest Groups in the Legislative Process." Lindblom shifts the emphasis from interest groups to "proximate policymakers" who are "always signalling, persuading, influencing each other in innumerable informal ways" to achieve mutual adjustment. See *The Policy-Making Process* (Foundations of Modern Political Science Series; Englewood Cliffs, N.J.: Prentice-Hall, 1968), p. 93.

[34] Madison assumed that the function of government was to moderate interest conflict. He accordingly relied on a wide representation of interests in government and on the complexity of the constitutional system itself to prevent "too rapid" formation of, or permanence to, a majority coalition of interests. Party, however, provided the basis for a stable majority coalition, negating much of Madison's theory. Calhoun added the formal requirement of decision by "concurrent majority" (unanimous consent) to ensure that every major interest would have some voice in the outcome. See Burns, *Deadlock of Democracy,*

The pluralist model, however, has acquired increasing relevance since the 1920's when the decline of party as a unifying force in the Legislature became evident. The strict limitation placed on the Speaker's power after 1910 had a long-term debilitating effect on party.[35] Leadership and coherence in the legislative process gradually broke down, a trend that was reinforced by other progressive-era, anti-party reforms, such as the direct primary, and by the increasing diversity in congressional districts caused by industrialization and urbanization. The vacuum in the legislative system was filled in turn by a return to the "disintegrate ministry" of the individual committee chairmen (Woodrow Wilson's description of the House *before* Reed and Cannon) and by the rise of the professional lobbyists and new interest organizations.[36]

The increasing importance of interest groups in the legislative process began to attract the attention of a new group of American political scientists. The "group theorists" — men such as Arthur Bentley, Pendleton Herring, and David Truman — refined and elaborated the pluralist model to its current form.[37]

Chap. I, "Madison and the Strategy of Checks"; also further references, pp. 343–45. For an excellent contrast of Madisonian theory with the political perspectives of Jefferson and Adams, see Samuel P. Huntington, "The Founding Fathers and the Division of Powers," in Maass *et al., op. cit.,* Chap. VII. Calhoun's theory of the "concurrent majority" is developed in C. Gordon Post (ed.), *"A Disquisition on Government" and Selections from the "Discourse"* (New York: The Liberal Arts Press, 1953).

[35] Joseph Cooper concludes that "party unity and coherence did in fact ultimately decline" after the emasculation of the Speaker's powers, citing the growing power of blocs in Congress, especially after 1919. He also traces the increased power and scope of operations of the Rules Committee to this cause. See Joseph Cooper, "Congress and Its Committees: An Historical and Theoretical Approach to the Proper Role of Committees and the Legislative Process," unpublished Ph.D. dissertation, Harvard University, 1961, pp. 99–103.

[36] See E. Pendleton Herring, *Group Representation Before Congress* (Institute for Government Research: Studies in Administration; Baltimore: The Johns Hopkins Press, 1929). By 1929 Robert Luce could baldly assert that "Senators and Representatives are merely conduits, the means of transmission, and for very many [legislative proposals] they are not even endorsers to the extent of guaranteeing more than perfunctory interest. The true source may usually be found in some administrative official, or in some organization, or in some constituent with a grievance, an ambition or a hope. Congress is not to any material extent an originating body." *Congress: An Explanation* (Godkin Lectures, Harvard University, 1925; Cambridge, Mass.: Cambridge University Press, 1926), p. 3.

[37] Bentley, *The Process of Government* (Chicago: University of Chicago Press, 1908); Herring, *op. cit.;* Truman, *The Governmental Process.* For a critique of the "group theorists," see Harmon Zeigler, *Interest Groups in Ameri-*

While the pluralist model has generally been presented in empirical terms, it has clearly normative assumptions and implications. It rejects the conception of a popular will or a national interest standing apart from, or superior to, the interests of the groups within the polity. American pluralism, with its normative emphasis on private association, self-government, self-regulation, and individual liberty, is firmly within the liberal tradition. The pluralist defense of private groups and associations has led, according to Grant McConnell, to "a system of responsibility which rivals the system embodied in the formal structure of government." [38] It is a "positivist" model at heart.

With regard to legislative-executive relations, the pluralist perspective emphasizes the complexity and indeterminacy of relationships among different political actors or interests. Party may provide some organizational control and political leverage, but it is not effective for producing coherent, reliable, legislative majorities. Constitutional boundaries and prescriptions between President and Congress hold little intrinsic meaning when the institutions of government are seen as centers of interest-based power. Truman emphasizes the fact that the political process

> rarely, if ever, involves a conflict between the legislature and the executive viewed as two monolithic and unified institutions. The actual competing structures on each side are made up of elements in the legislature and in the executive, reflecting and supported by organized and unorganized interests.[39]

Thus, resolution of the legislative-executive debate is not a primary concern to the pluralists.

From the pluralist perspective, the President, if he chooses to use the vantage points his office affords, can be the most powerful interest represented in the legislative process. Accordingly, we can distinguish

---

can Society (Englewood Cliffs, N.J.: Prentice-Hall, 1964), Chap. I, "Interest Groups in the Literature of Political Science," and Joseph La Palombara, "The Utility and Limitations of Interest Group Theory in Non-American Field Situations," *Journal of Politics*, February 1966, pp. 29–49.

[38] *Private Power and American Democracy* (New York: Alfred A. Knopf, 1966), pp. 1–8, 119–65. "The problem posed here," McConnell observes, "is not irresponsible government versus responsible government; responsibility exists in either system. The difference lies in the different constituencies to which responsibility is owed and paid" (p. 164). A classic pluralist critique of an inclusive "national" or "public interest" is given in Truman, *The Governmental Process*, pp. 49–52.

[39] *The Governmental Process*, p. 433.

two variants of the model, depending on whether or not a strong Executive is assumed.[40] Both interpretations, however, see internal leadership in the congressional system as plural and weak. Power in Congress is dispersed, affording and requiring presidential initiative. Congress, its committees, and individual members tend to react to public (interest group) pressure rather than to lead public opinion. The representative owes his allegiance to his constituency, since his re-election depends primarily on his maintaining the support of a majority of interests in his district. The Legislature is thus a Congress of Ambassadors with each of its members an agent or delegate of external interests.

In summary, the presidential-pluralist or pluralist model is basically a *bargaining* model with the President enjoying superior or inferior bargaining advantages depending on his skill and upon the perspective of the viewer. The harmonizing and adjustment of group demands is the model's primary characteristic. As Truman notes, it is a "means of reaching a closer conformity between governmental policies and deep-seated expectations about the political process." [41] In the face of dispersed leadership and multiple points of control within both the Legislature and Executive, the pluralist tends to accept presidential leadership as necessary and even to favor reforms that would strengthen the President's bargaining position. However, in general, the pluralist implicitly defends the existing system of decentralized decision making and the political values it helps to foster.[42]

[40] See Neustadt, *Presidential Power*, pp. 35, 36–37. James MacGregor Burns in his sequel to *Deadlock of Democracy* has found it necessary to add a third model, the Hamiltonian, to his original contrast of Madisonian (pluralist) and Jeffersonian (presidential party) models in order to interpret the Presidency of Lyndon Johnson. The Hamiltonian model implied "a federal government revolving around the Presidency, and depending on energy, resourcefulness, inventiveness, and a ruthless pragmatism in the executive office"; the Madisonian model implied "a prudent, less daring and active government, one that was balanced between the legislative and executive forces and powers." These two are actually on a continuum. Burns' argument is that the Johnsonian Presidency absorbed all the checks that previously balanced the system and that only vigorous national parties can now infuse purpose into the power of the Presidency. See *Presidential Government*, esp. pp. 312–51. Robert Dahl makes a similar distinction between an "executive-centered 'grand coalition of coalitions' " and a "coalition of chieftains," but notes that the difference is only one of degree. *Who Governs? Democracy and Power in an American City* (New Haven: Yale University Press, 1961), Chap. 15, "Five Patterns of Leadership," pp. 184–89.

[41] Truman, *The Governmental Process*, p. 393.

[42] Dahl defines the fundamental axiom in the theory and practice of American pluralism as follows: "Instead of a single center of sovereign power there *must be* multiple centers of power, none of which is or can be wholly sovereign" (emphasis added). Robert A. Dahl, *Pluralist Democracy in the United States:*

The constitutional balance model. A third perspective of Congress stresses constitutional balance in the roles of President and Congress.[43] It accepts the executive reforms of recent years that have led to executive-centered government but also sees need for the full development of corresponding congressional roles, especially in appropriations and in administrative oversight or supervision. It also expects Congress to assume greater initiative in legislation in areas where the President has not acted. The constitutional balance model, then, sees Congress assuming important institutional roles to complement the modern Presidency. It is the perspective adopted by many, if not a majority, of the members of Congress today.[44]

The constitutional balance model (referred to hereafter simply as the constitutional model) assumes a strong but independent President *and* Congress. Separate but overlapping constituencies are preserved; i.e., President and Congress are *not* linked by a cohesive party organization. Party roles are secondary to constitutional-institutional roles. Ernest Griffith describes the idealized constitutional synthesis as the "institutionalized mutual responsibility of coequals." [45] Roles may shift between the Executive and Legislature, but balance is preserved. The President may assume responsibilities for an executive budget, legislative clearance, administrative reorganization, and delegated legislation; but the Congress develops corresponding responsibilities: audit, administrative oversight through authorization and appropriation, the legislative veto. The constitutional model is not static but,

---

Conflict and Consent (Chicago: Rand McNally & Co., 1967), p. 24. If anything, the presidential-pluralist may oppose changes in congressional organization that consolidate congressional power versus presidential power. See, for example, Don K. Price's reservations about the consolidated power of the Joint Committee on Atomic Energy in *The Scientific Estate* (Cambridge, Mass.: Belknap Press, 1965), pp. 224–26.

[43] Davidson, Kovenock, and O'Leary treat both the constitutional and Whig models (see definition below) as the "literary" model of Congress. *Op. cit.*, pp. 17–25. The literary theory is essentially a "restatement of the constitutional formulation of blended and coordinate powers." Admittedly, the constitutional and Whig models shade into one another, but the Whig model rejects "executive-centered" government, i.e., the twentieth-century power equilibrium between President and Congress. The distinction is critical in any discussion of congressional performance.

[44] Davidson, Kovenock, and O'Leary found that 31 per cent of their respondents in the House of Representatives accepted the "pure Whig" variant of their literary model and another 44 per cent, other variants of the literary model. *Ibid.*, pp. 69–73.

[45] *Congress: Its Contemporary Role* (3rd ed.; New York: New York University Press, 1961), p. 7.

instead, adaptable to new definitions of constitutional roles which maintain the sharing of powers among separated institutions that characterizes our governmental system.

Where the responsible party model achieves coherence in the federal system through program and the pluralist model through bargaining, the constitutional model assigns greater importance to rational-legal procedure, free discussion and debate, and compromise or consensual decision. Congress functions as a deliberative body that makes important decisions by freely forming, rather than partisan, majorities; and the President respects this deliberative role assigned to Congress.

In summary, the constitutional model is basically a *rational-legal* model. Congress has important institutional roles to play, complementary with the roles of the President, but to do so it must maintain its position as an independent critic and coequal to the President. The underlying assumption is that Congress can *balance* the enhanced power of the modern Presidency through innovating new roles for itself.

The Whig or congressional supremacy model.[46] The last of the four perspectives on legislative-executive relations that we shall outline differs in an important way from the previous perspectives. Each of the three perspectives discussed has to some degree assumed presidential leadership or initiative. The President has been viewed as the leader of a disciplined national party system that extends into the Congress, or as the most powerful center of interest-based power which may intervene in bargaining, or as a constitutional coequal of Congress who has developed a variety of leadership roles in legislation as well as administration. While the constitutional model requires strong, complementary congressional roles — at the cost of increasing executive-legislative tension (especially in performing the task of administrative oversight) — it still assumes the President will in most instances provide the focus of leadership. He will continue to control

[46] Binkley notes that the term "Whig" historically carried the connotation of "opposition to executive prerogative, particularly the king, and on the other hand an attachment to parliamentary or, in this case, Congressional superiority to the Executive." *Op. cit.*, p. 99. Alfred de Grazia, who has articulated the most recent version of the congressional supremacy model, calls it a "New" or "Republican Force" model of Congress. Some of de Grazia's highly imaginative proposals imply merely an enhanced role and functions for the Congress (the constitutional model), but his clear opposition to executive force including numerous proposals to check executive initiative place him among the spokesmen for congressional supremacy.

the formulation of the budget, present Congress with his legislative program, and administer the executive departments.

The Whig or congressional supremacy model rejects the concept of the strong President and executive-centered government. Congress is the locus of decision making and policy leadership. Historical precedents date back to the Presidencies of Madison and Monroe, when the House caucus of Jeffersonian Republicans dominated the Executive. Full expression of the model came in the Radical Republican "directorate" of the post-Civil War Congresses. Historians have since noted a recurring pattern of strong Presidents followed by aggressive Congresses seeking to re-establish prerogatives yielded earlier to the President.[47]

Thus the Whig model reverses the contemporary roles of President and Congress. Congress as *the* representative of the people normally provides leadership in the political system. The President is weak; his powers, "strictly constructed"; his discretion in administering the law, limited. Congress controls policy and program through a congressional budget. (Many of the coordinating functions now performed by the Bureau of the Budget are transferred to a Congressional counterpart.) It maintains detailed oversight of administration through congressional staff arms and participates extensively in executive agency decision making.[48] The statutory relationship of the Joint Committee on Atomic Energy to the Atomic Energy Commission is perhaps the closest approximation to this aspect of the model.

Historically, the Whig model has assumed leadership of the federal government by a congressional oligarchy. The exponents of the Whig perspective today still think that Congress should direct the executive bureaucracy but on a much reduced scale of government. They see less need for federal intervention in the economy and society, less need for legislation and governmental programs in general. The model is adaptable, however, to legislative initiative and vigorous legislative programs as determined by the congressional leadership. Henry Clay's national program of public works and Radical Republican legislation passed over President Andrew Johnson's vetoes are examples.

In summary, the Whig or congressional supremacy model is *repub-*

---

[47] Binkley's analysis is representative. Clinton Rossiter suggests, however, that this alternation has ceased with the advent of the "modern Presidency." *The American Presidency* (New York: Harcourt, Brace & World, 1956).

[48] See de Grazia's proposal that "Congressional tribunes" be assigned to each executive agency, to report to the appropriate committee of Congress each year "in the role of a devil's advocate." Schlesinger and de Grazia, *op. cit.*, p. 67.

lican in its emphasis on Congress as *the* representative of the people, *oligarchic* in its requirement that Congress provide leadership in the federal system. Its best approximations have been found in periods of weak Presidencies. It is not a programmatic model in that most of its exponents do not favor a coordinated legislative attack on the status quo. The contemporary Congress, from this perspective, has permitted a dangerous erosion of its prerogatives to the President and the courts.[49] It has yielded control of the federal budget to the President and the Bureau of the Budget. It has delegated much of its legislative function to the Executive. It has granted the President broad authority to reorganize departments and agencies.

The Whig perspective assumes that this trend can be reversed, that Congress can regain what it has lost. Rather than develop stronger complementary roles to the modern Presidency (the constitutional perspective), it argues that Congress must wrest back traditional roles that have been assumed by the Executive.

FOUR MODELS OF INTERNAL LEGISLATIVE ORGANIZATION

Each of the four perspectives we have just considered defines a different posture for Congress and the President in the American system in terms of the roles that each should properly perform. How should Congress organize itself to assume these various postures? In answering this question, we shall first discuss four alternative models of internal organization, each based on a different model of decision making. Finally, in relating the two sets of models, we shall examine some of the dilemmas of congressional power.

Control by presidential party. This model of congressional organization clearly complements the presidential-responsible party model of legislative-executive relations. From this perspective, the President has, or should have, the resources and means to control his party's congressional leadership. Effective control of Congress resides in a presidentially dominated national party *external* to the Congress.

The model, with its idealized definition of the national party system, assumes a coincidence of direction, based on the national party

---

[49] See Congressman F. Edward Hebert, "Keynote Address: The Challenge to American Democracy," *Final Report of the Seventh Air Force Academy Assembly: The Congress and America's Future* (Colorado Springs: U.S.A.F. Academy, 1965). Congressman Hebert's speech is a classic statement of the congressional supremacy perspective.

platform, for President, majority leadership in Congress, and the majority of the party caucus. (It also ignores the problems of divided party control and bicameralism or assumes that truly national parties will receive general mandates that will, in effect, eliminate these problems.) The committee structure is to be responsive to this direction, generally to the Speaker or Majority Leader who is charged with execution of the President's legislative program. Responsiveness is facilitated by strong committee chairmen functioning as agents of the majority leadership. Committees are clearly under the control of the majority party. Such a reformer as Woodrow Wilson even urged that the minority be given *no* representation on the standing committees in order to strengthen party accountability. In the House, the Rules Committee is an extension of the majority party leadership.

Two variants of the model can be distinguished, depending on the relative emphasis accorded presidential leadership and party caucus operation. In the first instance, the party leadership in Congress follows presidential direction with the party caucus playing a minimal role. In the second, effective decisions on legislation are reached within the caucus of the majority party. In caucus rule, assuming complete party discipline on votes in the Congress, a simple majority in the majority party caucus can control the legislative process, including rules and procedure and the selection of party and committee leaders.[50]

The individual representative is linked to his constituency through party. He functions as a delegate responsible to his party, rather than to his local constituency. He is generally removed from the centralized power of the leadership and participates in party decisions only as a member of the party caucus. His votes are dictated by party and program, not by personal deliberation and independent decision.

Control by presidential party ultimately rests on the theory of majoritarian party democracy. Majority rule, in the model, concentrates power in the hands of the party leadership, for a concentration of power is required for effective decision or action. The translation of the popular will into governmental action requires leadership and organizational power. Hence the responsible party model leads to some sacrifice or restriction of the majority principle. The legislature

[50] Congressman Richard Bolling states: "There is every reason to justify the right of the majority of the majority to have its major proposals voted on by the whole House without undue delay, much less without deliberate dilatory tactics that prevent a vote on a major issue from ever occurring." Bolling's principal reform proposals, accordingly, deal with strengthening the caucus. See *House Out of Order* (New York: E. P. Dutton & Co., 1965), esp. pp. 236–44.

is organized to facilitate party majorities (that can be controlled), not freely forming majorities. Discharge and other "democratic" devices that limit the discretionary power or force the hand of the leadership are opposed. Party policy is decided by the party hierarchy in the Executive and Congress, supported by a powerful professional bureaucracy.

Control by congressional party. A second means for controlling the Congress and the legislative process is through strong centralized parties *within* Congress. At first glance, this model for organizing power appears to parallel control by presidential party in its emphasis on party government.[51] However, there are important normative distinctions between the two.

This perspective rejects unified national parties under presidential control. *Congress* is the focus of the party system and the representational system. Rather than operate under the aegis of party national committees, the congressional party maintains itself as a cohesive independent force within a loose national party structure. It sustains congressional party committees for legislative policy, fund raising, and campaigning. It places less emphasis on strong national party organization and more on party simply as a conglomerate of strong state organizations. Party organization in Congress at the turn of the century, the time of the centralized speakership under Reed and Cannon, affords the best example. With its emphasis on congressional control, this model for organizing Congress shares some of the normative assumptions of the Whig theory of legislative-executive relations.

Control by congressional party differs from control by presidential party in other ways. The President must bargain with the congressional leadership rather than lead it. The national party platform provides less of a frame of reference for party policy within Congress; the preferences of senior party members, usually from securely held con-

---

[51] Note, for example, former Speaker Reed's emphasis on party government after the rules reforms of 1890. "Party responsibility has begun, and with it also the responsibility of the people, for they can no longer elect a Democratic House and hope the minority will neutralize their action or a Republican House without being sure that it will keep its pledges." William A. Robinson, *Thomas B. Reed: Parliamentarian* (New York: Dodd, Mead & Co., 1930), p. 232. For other views of party government at this time, see Kenneth W. Hechler, *Insurgency: Politics and Personalities of the Taft Era* (New York: Columbia University Press, 1940); and William R. Gwinn, *Uncle Joe Cannon: Archfoe of Insurgency* (New York: Bookman Associates, 1957). Davidson, Kovenock, and O'Leary note a preference among some congressmen today for a stronger Congress *and* stronger parties. *Op. cit.*, p. 72.

gressional districts, more. Accordingly, there is likely to be greater friction between the party leadership in Congress and other elements in the party.

Party leadership committees, including the more powerful committee chairmen, are the center of the congressional party "directorate." The power and prerogative of the congressional party leadership rather than loyalty to the program of the President dominate the control of the committee system.[52] The biases of seniority and safely held districts imply that the directorate will be more "conservative" than the President and the Congress as a whole.

Control by congressional majority. The third model for organizing Congress differs from both previous models in its rejection of party discipline. Power in Congress and the committees must remain responsive to the majority in Congress, not to the President or to an entrenched congressional party leadership. Decisions are made by deliberation and freely forming, or ad hoc, majorities. The model incorporates elements from both Jeffersonian and Progressive theory.[53]

From the Jeffersonians it takes the view of Congress as a deliberative body. During the first few sessions of Congress, the focus for decision making (the determination of "principles") was the Committee of the Whole. Select, rather than standing, committees were commonly used for handling the details of legislation. Jeffersonian theory held that committees were clearly subordinate to the whole House. They received specific instructions as to their authorities and duties. It was understood that committees would report back to the House whether their findings were favorable or unfavorable and that they could not change the principles that the House as a whole had decided. The ad hoc nature of committees was underlined by the practice of dissolving select committees when their assigned work was done. Discharge, accordingly, was no problem.

Jeffersonian theory also assumed the rational legislator, a man capable of informing himself of the basic facts of an issue, and, through discussion with his colleagues in Committee of the Whole,

---

[52] Cannon used the Speaker's power of appointment effectively in this regard. Senator Joseph Clark has commented upon a contemporary form of committee control by the congressional party leadership. See Joseph S. Clark and other senators, *The Senate Establishment* (American Century Series; New York: Hill & Wang, 1963).

[53] Joseph Cooper's analysis of Jeffersonian and Progressive attitudes toward the proper role of committees in the House of Representatives (*op. cit.*, Chaps. II, III) has been an invaluable resource for the following summary.

arriving at a general decision on principles. Select committees would then settle details within this framework. Committee members and the chairman were appointed from the majority on the particular issue. The general understanding was that committee business would be governed by democratic procedure; the chairman would function as the agent of the committee.

The model draws its basic rationale against party government and in support of majority rule by ad hoc majorities from the Progressive era. Congress, ideally, should act by spontaneous agreement of a majority of its members, each member's position being determined by his own constituency and conscience. While paying obeisance to party, the Progressives who overthrew Speaker Joe Cannon in 1910 and stripped the speakership of most of its formal powers were unwilling to subordinate the dignity of the individual legislator and his personal relationship with his constituency to the requirements of party government. They valued the opportunities (and potential for achieving progressive legislation) afforded by free and spontaneous (bipartisan) majorities, i.e., letting the Congress work its will. The progressives feared the concentration of unresponsive power that had been necessary under rule by an inflexible party majority. These values are still widely held within the Congress.

Whether the leaders of the Progressive reforms of 1909–11 relating to the powers of the speakership, the House Rules Committee, Calendar Wednesday, discharge, and the Committee on Committees accomplished their ideal is another issue we cannot examine here. Their intent, clearly, was to make the flow of legislation through the standing committees responsive to a majority of the House, not an entrenched minority such as the majority party leadership or a powerful committee chairman.

Bargaining and decentralized control. The three previous models organize power and define rules and procedures to *facilitate control* of the legislature either by the President, congressional party leaders, or congressional majorities. The last model we shall consider assumes that power is so dispersed within Congress that, at best, "decentralized control" is possible through mutual adjustment among legislative leaders, the President included.

The decentralized control model complements the presidential-pluralist model of legislative-executive relations. As in the pluralist model, decisions are made at various levels of the system by bargaining and constructing coalitions. The speed at which effective or win-

ning coalitions may be built varies with the structural constraints of
the system, such as the apportionment system, the number of steps
involved in the passage of legislation, requirements for extraordinary
majorities for certain types of decisions.[54]

As in the pluralist model, decentralized control values decision making or rule by "interests" rather than by majorities. The decentralization of Congress into the "miniature legislatures" of the standing
committees allows all of the basic interests concerned some weight in
the development of a particular policy or bill. Such a mechanism facilitates compromise at an early stage in the legislative process and
helps to avoid problems such as a large number of legislative defeats
for the leadership and the development of ideological disputes that
would polarize the Congress.[55] Similarly, Ralph Huitt observes that
dispersion of power in the system of standing committees provides
"the ultimate check on party government in the United States." [56]

The model of decentralized control implies, therefore, that congressional party leadership should have limited means for imposing solutions on the membership. The standing committees remain the basic
units of power, and the leadership must still negotiate with the independently powerful committee chairmen to advance the President's
legislative program.[57] Like the model of control by congressional
majority, the bargaining model works against the hierarchical organization of power in Congress. It is also a positive argument in
behalf of interest negotiation within congressional committees rather
than decision making by deliberation and majority vote of the full
Congress.

[54] For a comprehensive discussion of bargaining in Congress, see Lewis A.
Froman, Jr., *The Congressional Process: Strategies, Rules, and Procedures* (The
Study of Congress Series; Boston: Little, Brown & Co., 1967). See also Richard
F. Fenno, Jr., "The Internal Distribution of Influence: The House," in Tru-
man, *The Congress and America's Future*, pp. 60, 70–76.

[55] Froman, *op. cit.*, p. 201.

[56] "The Internal Distribution of Influence: The Senate," in Truman, *The
Congress and America's Future*, p. 89.

[57] David Truman states that the absence of integrated and continuing leadership in Congress enhances interest group activity in legislative decision making.
"Under such circumstances, logrolling and alliances between groups — inevitable elements in a process that relies upon the device of majority rule to settle
differences — becomes a means for compensating for the diffusion of power."
The Governmental Process, p. 392. For a different evaluation of this process and
its susceptibility to "control" by an "economic elite" see Daniel M. Friedenberg,
"A Fabian Program for America," in Irving Howe (ed.), *The Radical Papers*
(Garden City, N.Y.: Doubleday Anchor Books, 1966), pp. 101–24.

THE DILEMMAS OF CONGRESSIONAL POWER

We have examined alternative structural arrangements for organizing power at two levels while emphasizing some of the values underlying them. What can we now say about the relative probabilities of their occurrence or survival in the American political system? And what relationships can we observe in the real world between the two sets of models we have abstracted? Some major problems are soon evident.

Bicameralism and the problem of divided control. All the models of legislative-executive relations are greatly complicated by the several possibilities of divided control afforded by the separate elections for the Presidency, House of Representatives, and Senate. The problem of bicameralism was solved in the British Parliament by the subordination of the House of Lords to the House of Commons. Presidential party control in the United States requires the unification of both the county-organization base of congressmen *and* the state coalitions of powerful senators into a national, presidentially dominated party.[58] The Whig model faces even greater problems in building a republican force, so long as the President can play one House of Congress against the other. Both of these models, when they have occurred historically, have had difficulty sustaining themselves because of the self-correcting dynamics of the constitutional system which work against unified control.

The control of congressional committees: the parts versus the whole. Those models which assume that Congress will play a vigorous and independent, if not dominant, role in legislation and administrative review, face the added problem of controlling powerful standing committees. How is the intent of Congress to be defined? Through the decisions and actions of its committees? Or through the deliberation of the full membership? The Progressives, having weakened the powers of central party leadership, found they had, in turn, to check

---

[58] Presidential party control would require, in James MacGregor Burns' estimate, extensive intervention in Congress. "Not only would the minority devices of the congressional parties be swept away, but the President would have to throw himself into the legislative battle to fashion party machinery for the more effective debating and handling of legislation. . . . The President's job is to strengthen the presidential party machinery in Congress." Burns, *Deadlock of Democracy*, pp. 338–39. Burns has no answer for bicameralism, however, conceding the virtual impossibility of shortening the Senate's tenure to coincide with a four-year House term.

the new discretionary power of committees, by giving instruments of control back to the leadership. Devices such as Calendar Wednesday and the discharge petition, designed to curb an arbitrary Speaker, were now used by the leadership *and* the majority to check the arbitrary power of Rules and other House committees.

Congress has developed a number of techniques for controlling its committees, for keeping its parts in some type of harmonious relation with the whole. Such techniques, used with varying effectiveness, include the appointment of new members, the elaboration of full House and committee rules, caucus discipline, the enlargement and packing of committees, checks on committee funds and staff, alteration of committee jurisdictions, modifications in the strict seniority principle, utilization of alternative procedures (alternative routes to the floor, authorization vs. appropriations), floor review of legislation, and amendment.[59] The adequacy of these controls again depends in part on the normative assumptions of the observer, especially the degree to which he values centralized direction and coordination in the legislative process and the nature of the oversight role he defines for Congress.

The costs of centralizing leadership in Congress. In addition to an effective committee system, the Whig (and for some purposes the constitutional) model requires the concentration of power under strong congressional leadership. The Whig perspective assumes that Congress will assume policy planning, coordination, and leadership roles previously exercised by the Executive. The dispersion of power to the standing committee system prevents a coordinated congressional voice and offers the President, executive agencies, and interest groups important points of leverage in the legislative process.

But in centralizing power the Whig model encounters two of the fundamental dilemmas of congressional power. First, can Congress impose central leadership mechanisms on the semi-oligarchy of the decentralized standing committee system in a bicameral legislature? Samuel Huntington states: "The only effective alternative to oligarchy is centralized authority. Oligarchies, however, are unlikely to reform themselves." [60] The experience of Congress with the Joint Committee

---

[59] See Richard Fenno's analysis of full House and Senate sanctions on the appropriations committees in *The Power of the Purse: Appropriations Politics in Congress* (Boston: Little, Brown & Co., 1966), pp. 42–78, 517–29.

[60] "At present the central leaders of Congress are, with rare exceptions, products of and closely identified with the committee oligarchy. Reform of Congress would depend upon the central leaders' breaking with the oligarchy, mobilizing

on the Legislative Budget in the late 1940's appears to support his contention. After several unsuccessful attempts to impose a congressional budget ceiling, the two-House super committee comprising the four major fiscal committees ceased any effort to implement its mandate of budgetary control under the Legislative Reorganization Act of 1946.[61] Simply stated, the dilemma is: How can Congress *both* decentralize power to maintain specialization in legislation and oversight *and* centralize power to develop a coordinated congressional posture?

Second, if Congress *can* centralize power within itself, can it do so without losing its autonomy to the President? Alfred de Grazia thinks not.

> American history shows that the political party has been from the beginning intended by its organizers either to control the country by means of the presidency. . . . The party has to remain decentralized or it falls into the hands of the presidential faction.[62]

Another observer still feels that a centralized congressional party could maintain its independence, "restore to Congress a more positive role in the legislative process and strengthen it vis-a-vis the executive branch." [63]

For the advocate of a constitutional balance model of legislative-executive relations, the centralization of leadership power — hierarchy and control — is antithetical to its rational-legal emphasis, to free deliberation. The same tension exists between majority rule (control

---

majorities from younger and less influential congressmen, and employing these majorities to expand and to institutionalize their own power." In Truman, *Congress and America's Future*, p. 27. Just such an alliance appears to have emerged within the Democratic party of the 89th Congress. See Davidson, Kovenock, and O'Leary, *op. cit.*, Chap. V, "The 89th Congress and Reform."

[61] Saloma, *op. cit.*, pp. 54–58.

[62] *Republic in Crisis*, pp. 45–67, and *Congress and the Presidency*, p. 63. De Grazia already perceives "a growing centralization, bureaucratization, strengthening, and integration of the party" supported by "a rationale of responsible and efficient government supplied by intellectuals on the one hand, and shifts in the nature of the constituencies on the other hand." Stephen K. Bailey agrees that in the last analysis the centrifugal influences against party in the legislature may represent "the precondition of maintaining in Congress a healthy independence from executive domination. In the last analysis Congress can have no power if congressmen and committees have no power." *The New Congress* (St. Martin's Series in American Politics; New York: St. Martin's Press, 1966), p. 64.

[63] Huntington, in Truman, *Congress and America's Future*, p. 28.

by congressional majority) and the need for organizational leadership (control through party mechanisms).

As we said in the beginning of this chapter, the problem of power in the American system has no determinate solution. Our purpose in defining various perspectives of Congress has been to provide some initial guidelines for assessing Congress in the American system. Although we shall find some interpretations more prevalent than others in historical experience and the preference of observers, we shall exclude none from the analysis of congressional performance. A personal preference for the constitutional balance model is developed in the concluding chapter of the book.

PART TWO

The Contemporary Congress

CHAPTER THREE

The Capacity for Representation

> Congress is the mirror of the people, and it reflects the ag-
> gregate strengths and weaknesses of the electorate. Its mem-
> bership might include just about the same percentage of
> saints and sinners, fools and geniuses, rogues and heroes as
> does the general populace. Congress is a highly concentrated
> *essence* of the virtues and faults of the nation as a whole.[1]

Congress is explicitly a representative assembly of the people. All its
activities are shaped by regular election. The only other full-time participant in the political process at the national level who stands for
election is the President, and even he stands only twice, at most. How
well has Congress performed its function of representation, articulated
the opinions and interests of the American people, and integrated the
diversity of demands and support for popular public policies?

The critics of Congress reply that it has lost stature as a representative institution by frustrating the public will. Former Senator Joseph
Clark (D-Pa.) sees in the legislatures of America — local, state, and
national — "the greatest menace in our country to the successful operation of the democratic process." "In my judgment," Clark states,
"there is no other legislative body in the free world as incapable of
action, when action is desired by a large majority but strongly resisted
by a minority, as the Senate of the United States." [2] Congressman
Richard Bolling (D-Mo.) argues that the Congress, and particularly
the House, "labors under the disadvantages of being unrepresentative,
parochial in its outlook on national policy, and inherently in conflict

---

[1] Congressman Jim Wright, *You and Your Congressman* (New York:
Coward-McCann, 1965), p. 15.

[2] *Congress: The Sapless Branch* (New York: Harper & Row, 1964), pp. 23,
15.

with the Executive." [3] These views find support among journalists and academics. Walter Lippmann holds that Congress is "using a procedure of smothering and strangling, rather than of debating and voting, which violates the basic principles of representative government." [4] In a recent critique of congressional adjustments to the twentieth century, Professor Samuel P. Huntington concludes that perhaps the most important trend in congressional evolution has been "the growing isolation of Congress from other social groups and political institutions." During this century, the Executive branch has become more powerful principally because it has become more representative. "One key to the 'decline' of Congress," Huntington observes, "lies in the defects of Congress as a representative body." [5]

The reform-oriented literature on Congress discusses to a great extent "defects" that prevent Congress from exercising its "proper" representational function: the filibuster, the House Rules Committee, seniority, antiquated congressional rules and procedure in general, a fragmented party system, and coalition politics. Most of the party-reform literature as well directly and explicitly discusses the function of representation in the American political system and the Congressional subsystem.

Defenders of Congress reply that Congress is "the center of a ring of institutions that compose the republic." [6] In the words of Senator Gordon Allott (R-Col.), "Because Congress is closest to the people and more clearly reflects the judgment of the people, it must be a source of guidance and surveillance over the other two branches." [7]

Given these diametrically opposed views of the contemporary Congress, how can we objectively assess the capacity and performance of Congress as a representative institution? We can begin with as clear a *description* of representation in the American system as we can derive from our understanding of American politics. Second, we can define general *criteria* or *values* that are thought desirable for a good system of representation and examine the alternative models of Congress developed in Chapter Two in terms of these criteria. Third, we

[3] *House Out of Order* (New York: E. P. Dutton & Co., 1965), p. 30.

[4] "A Critique of Congress," *Newsweek*, January 20, 1964, pp. 18–19.

[5] Huntington, "Congressional Responses to the Twentieth Century," in David B. Truman (ed.), *The Congress and America's Future* (Englewood Cliffs, N.J.: Prentice-Hall, 1965), pp. 8, 16.

[6] Alfred de Grazia, *Republic in Crisis: Congress Against the Executive Force* (New York: Federal Legal Publications, 1965), p. 7.

[7] Joint Committee on the Organization of Congress, *Hearings: Organization of Congress*, 89th Congress, 1st Session, 1965, p. 201.

can examine specific cases that illustrate more generally some of the problems of representation. (Congressional apportionment and the reform proposal of a four-year term for members of the House have been selected for the purpose.) Finally, on the basis of these partial analyses we can draw some general conclusions about Congress and representation.

REPRESENTATION IN THE AMERICAN SYSTEM: THE TWO MAJORITIES

Representation involves the expression of individual and group opinions and interests in the political process. A representational system structures, through formal and informal constraints, the political inputs of the system. It defines how public officials are selected and elected; it comprehends the requirements and term of office, the size and shape of constituency, nomination and election procedures, and campaign regulation.[8]

The American political system has been based formally on dual systems of representation — the presidential and the congressional. These are supplemented by an informal system of representation, notably through the executive bureaucracy.[9] Here we shall limit ourselves to the two representational systems defined by constitutionally specified elections.

How do presidential and congressional representation differ? Is the President or the Congress more representative of the people and in what areas? A useful point for initial contrast is the nature of the two majorities they represent — a contrast suggested by Willmoore Kendall.[10]

The congressional system of representation antedates presidential representation. Madison and the founders expected the popular ma-

[8] See Alfred de Grazia, *Essay on Apportionment and Representative Government* (Washington, D.C.: American Enterprise Institute, 1963), pp. 12–18.

[9] Samuel Huntington suggests that we actually are moving toward three basic systems of representation. "Particular territorial interests are represented in Congress; particular functional interests are represented in the administration; and the national interest is represented territorially and functionally in the Presidency." *Op. cit.,* p. 17. Group theorists, such as David B. Truman, are more impressed by the multiplicity of points of access for organized interest groups. See *The Governmental Process: Political Interests and Public Opinion* (New York: Alfred A. Knopf, 1951), Chaps. XIII–XV.

[10] Kendall, "The Two Majorities," *Midwest Journal of Political Science,* November 1960, pp. 317–45.

jority to be "articulated through and counted within the constituencies of Congress." [11] They expected that the President would normally be elected by the House of Representatives, the electoral college having failed to provide a clear majority. With the advent of the Jacksonian party system and the popularly nominated and elected President, a second popular majority was "engrafted" on our political system.[12] Both systems assume the majority principle — they differ in its application.

The congressional majority is heterogeneous; the presidential majority homogeneous. By definition Congress is plural, the President, singular. This means that Congress is in fact many Congresses and that it often speaks in several, sometimes contradictory, voices. The President, even with the development of the institutionalized Presidency, speaks through the authority of one man. The distinction is fundamental.

The congressional majority is continuous; the presidential majority discontinuous. The congressional majority is expressed in two stages: congressional elections and the formation of legislative majorities within Congress. The presidential majority is expressed once every four years through the count of the Electoral College. While this single vote does not constitute a comprehensive mandate, it can have the effect of setting broad new directions for government. Given this distinction, Kendall observes that the congressional majority is capable of expressing itself simultaneously with individual policy decisions as it evaluates them.[13]

While these structural differences between the two majorities operating in American politics are fairly obvious, their consequences are

[11] *Ibid.*, p. 335. The initial constituencies of Congress were in many instances the states. Congressional *districts* were not formally required until 1842. For an analysis of the electoral consequences of districts (as opposed to at-large elections) see Milton C. Cummings, Jr., *Congressmen and the Electorate: Elections for the U.S. House and the President, 1920–1964* (New York: The Free Press, 1966), Chap. VI, "The Impact of the Electoral System on the Presidency and Congress."

[12] Walter Dean Burnham makes the point in his analysis of American party systems that "the development of mass parties in the 1830's destroyed the basis of consolidated party leadership which had existed during the time of the first party system [the "experimental system" of 1789–1820], permanently activated the cleavage between executive and legislature, and gave enormous impetus to the decentralizing influence of federalism." "Party Systems and the Political Process," William Nisbet Chambers and Walter Dean Burnham (eds.), *The American Party Systems: Stages of Development* (New York: Oxford University Press, 1967), pp. 279–80.

[13] *Op. cit.*, p. 337.

not so clear. Easy generalizations, often unfavorable to the Congress, abound. It is commonly held, as we have noted, that presidential representation is "liberal" and congressional representation "conservative" in bias. While the Presidency has national breadth, the legislative branch is supposedly subject to "the dispersive influences of the local basis of representation" and has "peculiar vulnerability to domination by special interests." [14] The President is the great unifier — the centripetal force of American government; the Congress seeks "to fragmentize the executive by means of individual or committee influence over administrative units." [15] Willmoore Kendall makes the further generalization that the electoral process of the congressional system is essentially "aristocratic" in character; the electoral process of the presidential system, essentially "democratic." The "discussion processes" leading to the election of the President and members of Congress are fundamentally different — one goes forward in "the national forum," the other in the constituencies.[16] Samuel Huntington makes a parallel comparison. Congressional leaders "come up through a 'local politics' line while [political] executives move up through a 'national organization' line." [17] Congressmen, Huntington argues, are part of a "local consensus of local politicians, local businessmen, local bankers, local trade union leaders, and local newspaper editors who constitute the opinion-making elite of their districts." This means that congressmen are "segmentally" or "provincially" oriented; members of the President's administration, "nationally" oriented.

These generalizations about the presidential and congressional systems of representation are translated into specific public policy "tensions"; i.e., the two majorities are seen as having different policy emphases. Table 3.1 summarizes Kendall's frequently cited contrast of presidential versus congressional policy emphases.

Without developing the contrast further, it should be clear to the reader that stereotypes about both President and Congress underlie much of the discussion about representation in the American system. While there is undoubtedly an element of truth in the interpretation,

[14] Rowland A. Egger and Joseph P. Harris, *The President and Congress* (Foundations of American Government Series; New York: McGraw-Hill Book Co., 1963), p. 7.

[15] James MacGregor Burns, *Deadlock of Democracy: Four Party Politics in America* (Englewood Cliffs, N.J.: Prentice-Hall, 1963), p. 262.

[16] *Op. cit.*, pp. 339–41.

[17] *Op. cit.*, pp. 14–16.

TABLE 3.1
RELATIVE EMPHASES OF PRESIDENTIAL
VS. CONGRESSIONAL REPRESENTATION

Public Policy Area	Congressional Emphasis	Presidential Emphasis
1. Internal Security	Strong legislation supplemented by permanent congressional investigatory staff.	Becomes active only under insistent pressure from Congress
2. Public Works	Unabashedly for the "pork-barrel"	Appeals to national rather than local constituency interest
3. Foreign Trade	Protectionist	Free trade
4. Foreign Aid	Drags its feet unless a demonstrable military payoff	Deeply committed to foreign aid programs
5. Integration	Withholds authority that would ease executive action	Ready to act, even without public mandate
6. Immigration	Perpetuates restrictive quotas	Applies egalitarian standard
7. Economic Policy	Watches the national debt; traditional sound government finance	Accepts Keynesian position on debt and government spending
8. Defense; Welfare	Increases size of air force; military expenditures take precedence over welfare expenditures	Resists congressional pressure to increase military; cuts welfare spending
9. Foreign Policy	Nationalistic; no quarrels with right-wing dictatorships	Internationally minded; committed to democratic forms of government

SOURCE: Suggested in Willmoore Kendall, *op. cit.*, pp. 318–20.

it has been overdone to the point where it has clearly contributed to public misinformation and misunderstanding of the role of Congress. For every assertion one could cite important examples that contradict it; particularly as representation relates to specific policy areas. For example, Congress, under the major civil rights acts of the 1960's, has given the President broader authority than he has subsequently been willing to use.

There is a need for a more balanced interpretation of dual representation in the American system. Several less recognized aspects of representation may serve this purpose.

Congress is a forum for deliberation and decision on national policy. The emphasis on parochialism and localism in Congress is overdrawn. As Roger Davidson has pointed out, congressmen are not limited merely to representing geographic constituencies. "Subject matter specialization through the standing committee system has been effectively used to supplement geographic representation; and the efficiency and vitality of the committees is a primary instrument of congressional survival." [18] Each congressional committee trains its members in an area of national policy. Attentive members may gain competence in national policy making that is broader in perspective and more extensive in program experience than that of their executive agency counterparts. Moreover, every member must vote on a staggering range of legislative proposals. Simply by following the broad contours of debate on the floor, a congressman is exposed to an education in public policy that few members of the Executive branch ever experience. Congressmen are by definition part of a national political elite. The fact that Congress has provided a clear majority of presidential and vice-presidential nominees in the past decade underlines the point.

Congressmen enjoy considerable independence from their constituencies on most policy matters. What we might describe as the "rustic" interpretation of Congress emphasizes the dependence of congressmen on their local constituencies. They campaign on local issues, are part of a local community power structure, advance through a local politics line, and feel that they *should* act as representatives of local distinct interests. However, there is mounting empirical evidence that challenges this interpretation. First, what V. O. Key, Jr., describes as the classical model of constituency pressure and sanction on the representative appears to hold in only a limited range of cases.[19] As we have noted, according to one national survey, 57 per cent of all Americans did not know the name of their congressman and less than 20 per cent could identify their congressman's vote on *any* major item of legislation. The Bauer, Pool, and Dexter analysis found that, at least in the area of American trade policy, the congressman enjoys considerable

---

[18] Davidson, "Congress and the Executive: The Race for Representation," in Alfred de Grazia (ed.), *Congress: The First Branch of Government* (Washington, D.C.: American Enterprise Institute, 1966), p. 411. See also "Representational Roles of Congressmen," paper prepared for 64th annual meeting of the American Political Science Association, Washington, D.C., September 3–7, 1968, and a forthcoming book, *The Role of a Congressman.*

[19] *Public Opinion and American Democracy* (New York: Alfred A. Knopf, 1961), Chap. XIX, "Representation."

freedom from his constituents.[20] Each congressional district is usually a complex, permitting the congressman choice in what groups he will represent in his coalition. His supporters will normally defer to his leadership. The voters in his district seldom know exactly what they want or how to communicate their preferences in a timely or effective manner. Finally, the legislative process is so complicated, and the actions of the congressman frequently so hidden, that the average voter has no idea what his congressman has actually done on a matter of specific interest to him. The Miller and Stokes study of constituency influence on Congress found one policy area, however, where constituents did exercise an effective sanction on the member — civil rights.[21] Even where clear sanctions are not applied, the study suggested that congressmen, as "dealers in increments and margins," were sensitive to incremental changes of opinions and votes and to the more subtle general evaluations constituents made of them based on fragmentary information and cues.

In sum, the evidence points increasingly toward a view of *weak* formal sanctions from the constituency on the congressman's behavior. What "control" the local constituency exerts is more likely to be the congressman's view of the "anticipated reaction" of his constituents to his overall performance.[22]

Congressmen have become professional national politicians well removed from the image of the "instructed delegate" from the local district. In the past few decades, the job of a congressman has become a full-time professional position. As Harvey Mansfield notes, the ability of congressmen to secure their place in national politics on a "career basis" is an essential reason for their maintaining a significant and powerful position for the American Congress.[23] Not surprisingly,

20 Raymond A. Bauer, Ithiel de Sola Pool, and Lewis Anthony Dexter, *American Business and Public Policy: The Politics of Foreign Trade* (New York: Atherton Press, 1963), esp. pp. 403–24.

21 Warren E. Miller and Donald E. Stokes, "Constituency Influence in Congress," *American Political Science Review* (APSR), March 1963, pp. 45–56. A comprehensive report of the Miller and Stokes research, *Representation in Congress*, will be published by Prentice-Hall.

22 For a further refinement of the Miller and Stokes model, see Charles F. Cnudde and Donald J. McCrone, "The Linkage between Constituency Attitudes and Congressional Voting Behavior: A Causal Model," *APSR*, March 1966, pp. 66–72. The study concludes that the congressman's perception of constituency attitudes rather than elite recruitment is the basis of constituency control.

23 "Introductory Address: Criteria for Congressional Reform," *Final Report of the Seventh Air Force Academy Assembly: The Congress and America's Future* (Colorado Springs: U.S.A.F. Academy, 1965), p. 2. Mansfield and Huntington give opposite evaluations of the increasing tenure of office and importance

congressmen view their jobs in much broader terms than the stereo-type of congressional representation implies. A recent survey of 116 members of the House of Representatives, based on the typology of representative roles developed by Wahlke and Eulau, found that about 20 per cent of the sample described themselves as "delegates" bound by instructions either actual or implied, from their constituencies. Almost 30 per cent viewed themselves as "trustees" acting independently on the basis of their knowledge and convictions.[24] Half of the sample, referred to as "politicos," alternated these roles on a rather sophisticated basis. The focus of their representational roles was equally revealing. Roughly 16 per cent were concerned with their district only; another 19 per cent, with their district first and the nation second; *over* 60 per cent gave equal or stronger weighting to national concerns.

We might well anticipate a further strengthening of trustee, politico, and national roles with a corresponding decline in delegate and district roles. The delegate role becomes increasingly difficult to hold as issues become more complex.[25] The educational level of congressmen will most likely continue to rise with the general level of education in the public. (It is already well in advance of the general population.) While the residency requirement may keep congressmen based in their local constituencies, reapportionment has introduced a new element of fluidity. Jet transportation between constituency and Washington, to speaking engagements and political functions around the country, and for overseas fact-finding tours has made the congressional life increasingly cosmopolitan. And the sheer size of the congressional constituency, which will increase some 26 per cent from 450,000 people today to about 564,000 by 1980, will further compel the congressman to think and act in broader terms.

Emerging changes in our political parties, congressional recruit-

---

of seniority in Congress. For additional data see Nelson W. Polsby, "The Institutionalization of the U.S. House of Representatives," APSR, March 1968, pp. 144–68.

[24] Roger Davidson, "Congress and the Executive," p. 394. The study found that pure "trustees" were concentrated among southerners, members from rural constituencies, and members with seniority. "Delegates," conversely, were found disproportionately from competitive or marginal districts. Other observers have noted an important strain of southerners, like Albert Rains of Alabama and Wilbur Mills of Arkansas, who "have concentrated their principal attention on natural issues and largely ignored the South's often parochial concern over the Negro." Neil MacNeil, *Force of Democracy: The House of Representatives* (New York: David McKay Co., 1963), p. 278.

[25] See John C. Wahlke et al., *The Legislative System: Explorations in Legislative Behavior* (New York: John Wiley & Sons, 1962), pp. 282–86.

ment, and congressional campaigning give added weight to a revised interpretation of congressional representation. First, the regional bases of party strength, sharply defined in the presidential election of 1896, have within the past decade given way to the steady nationalization of the major parties.[26] Frank J. Sorauf sees this as one of the major "new directions" in the American party system:

> Increasingly it is difficult to isolate and quarantine a local party system from the influences of national politics. Both the third-party and the one-party subsystem in the United States reflect a localism that is passing from American life. Radio, television, the magazines, and newspaper chains and syndicates bring the same political figures, debates, and opinions to all parts of the country, just as they bring the same comic strip or weekly drama. In the nationalization of American culture, local ways of life, local identifications and pride, even local folkways, yield their place. Increasingly, the same political symbols, the same political issues and appeals, the same political personages dominate American politics.[27]

Second, a strengthening of the national parties has accompanied the trend to nationally competitive two-party politics. Previously congressional nominations and campaigns functioned on a completely decentralized basis. Each congressional district or state (in the case of the Senate) was virtually autonomous. The fact that congressional district boundaries in all but one or two states bore no statutory relationship to the component layers of *state* party organization left the congressional nomination and election in the interstices of American party politics — decentralized with respect to the presidential and national congressional party but not articulated through the state parties. Increasingly, however, national party organs and national interest groups and related political organizations have invested in congressional races.[28] The term "target seats" has become part of the

---

[26] See E. E. Schattschneider, "United States: The Functional Approach to Party Government," in Sigmund Neumann (ed.), *Modern Political Parties: Approaches to Comparative Politics* (Chicago: The University of Chicago Press, 1956), pp. 194–215; and Samuel Lubell, *The Future of American Politics* (3rd ed., rev.; New York: Harper & Row, 1965), esp. pp. 1–25.

[27] Sorauf, *Political Parties in the American System* (Basic Studies in Politics; Boston: Little, Brown & Co., 1964), pp. 36–37.

[28] For a discussion of the evolving National Committee role in congressional elections see Cornelius P. Cotter and Bernard C. Hennessy, *Politics Without Power: The National Party Committees* (New York: Atherton Press, 1964), pp. 61–105. The announced Republican party national budget for 1967 alone

political lexicon. And the off-year congressional elections are now widely regarded as national plebiscites on the program and performance of the President.[29]

How these trends will effect legislative behavior is difficult to predict. They may mean more cohesive, program-oriented legislative parties. They do suggest, in any event, that the congressional majority, while an aggregate of majorities in decentralized constituencies, will take an increasingly national perspective and posture.

Dual representation offers both the Congress and the President the positions of initiative and opposition. In comparing presidential and congressional majorities, Willmoore Kendall notes that the congressional majority does not need to be "positive" in the sense that the presidential majority (with an assumed mandate) is. "It is as likely to express itself in prohibitions and 'vetoes' as in imperatives." [30] The statement should be extended to the Presidency as well. E. E. Schattschneider has shown how the Republican party from 1896 to 1932 worked through the *Presidency* to minimize the role of the national government in the economy.[31] Alfred de Grazia supplements the argument with the observation that "historically, the Congress has been more often the advocate of social change than the President." [32]

A tally should not be necessary to prove the point. When the public is able to express itself through two majorities, simultaneously and at staged intervals, it can give differentiated and subtle signals to both President and Congress. During the 1950's, for instance, the same electorate endorsed Eisenhower's foreign policy and Democratic party domestic policy. Congress in the late 1950's frequently forced President Eisenhower to veto legislation. The American system, in its very complexity, increases the capacity for representation. The existence of

---

was a record for a non-election year — $6.7 million (including $2.8 million for the Republican Congressional Campaign Committee, $500,000 for the Republican Boosters Club, and $400,000 for the Republican Senatorial Campaign Committee). *Congressional Quarterly*, Weekly Report No. 4, January 27, 1967, p. 120.

[29] Cummings concludes, "To a considerable extent the general tenor of executive-legislative relations depends on the electorate's most recent expression of sentiment." Milton C. Cummings, Jr., *op. cit.*, p. 4.

[30] *Op. cit.*, p. 338.

[31] *Op. cit.*, pp. 198–201.

[32] Arthur M. Schlesinger, Jr., and Alfred de Grazia, *Congress and the Presidency: Their Role in Modern Times* (Rational Debate Seminars; Washington, D.C.: American Enterprise Institute, 1967), pp. 79–81.

Congress helps to open up the system and provide greater opportunities for access and for accommodation among interests.

CRITERIA FOR EVALUATING
CONGRESSIONAL REPRESENTATION

A system of representation cannot be value free.[33] Representation affords numerous points of entry for preferred social values. Every representational system institutionalizes the values of some groups in the system at the expense of others. And any reform proposals that would restructure or modify the representational system would, whether intended or not, reallocate values in the system.

With this proviso, what criteria might we use to assess congressional representation? What values are generally thought to be desirable in a representative system? We can ask: Does the system of representation contribute to the overall *integration* and *maintenance* of the political system? Does it work? Is it widely accepted as "legitimate"? What changes in the functioning of the system would be likely if an alternative representational system were adopted? In addition we may evaluate a representative system in terms of specific criteria, four of which are discussed below.

The capacity for governmental action. Authority should be delegated in the representational system so as to enhance the capacity of government to act. How this is to be accomplished in the American system is complicated by the fact that authority is delegated through separate electoral systems to two agents — President and Congress — who share constitutional authority. Most commonly discretion for executive action is emphasized.

Representativeness. The representative assembly, according to this criterion, must represent a cross-section of opinions and interests in the polity. It is a microcosm of the community and a mirror of public opinion. A wide variety of interests should be represented, and there should usually be some safeguard to minority rights.

Control or responsibility. Basic to all democratic theories of government is the tenet that rulers are to be held responsible to or controlled by the ruled. There may be individual or group (i.e., party) responsibility. In the first instance control is exercised through the personal relationship of the representative to his constituency; in the second,

---

[33] See Alfred de Grazia, *Essay on Apportionment and Representative Government*, p. 20.

through party government and the voter's evaluation of party performance. Responsibility, as a goal of representation, implies (a) accountability of individuals or groups for given decisions and actions with a corresponding requirement that decision makers be identifiable, and (b) the capacity and tendency of representatives to act on the basis of rational consideration of the pertinent facts and values.[34]

Responsiveness. This criterion, implicit in democratic theory, may be defined in two senses: responsiveness to popular demands or pressures, or responsiveness to some conception of "the public interest." [35] Responsiveness in the first sense implies degree. Under democratic theory, the principle of majority rule (the numerical or absolute majority) is assumed as the standard for responsiveness. The majority principle, however, does not provide a measure of the intensity of feeling, either of the majority or of interests in the minority. A representational system that requires delay of majority decisions or extraordinary majorities is less responsive to a numerical majority but offers more incentive and opportunity both for considered, rational action and for accommodation, through bargaining, with non-majority interests (representativeness). Responsiveness to "the public interest" assumes that some values should be introduced into policy making by the representative or the governmental official (i.e., that certain values will not generate adequate popular support through the majority principle).

We could extend the list of possible criteria; for example, representation should be on an equal population basis; or the representational system should maximize opportunities for participation. The four general criteria selected are sufficient, however, to illustrate many important potential value conflicts in evaluating Congress. Increased representativeness, for example, reduces the speed of decision making and administrative efficiency. The conditions for deliberation and independent judgment and action may conflict with the need for accountability. Accountability usually assumes party government and precludes individual responsibility. Responsibility in the sense of rationally considered action may conflict with responsiveness defined

---

[34] See J. Roland Pennock, "Responsiveness, Responsibility, and Majority Rule," *APSR*, September 1952, pp. 790–807.

[35] For a summary of some alternative theories of the public interest see Glendon Schubert, *The Public Interest: A Critique of the Theory of a Political Concept* (Glencoe, Ill.: The Free Press, 1960), pp. 198–224.

by the majority principle. Responsiveness to pressure may be inconsistent with the need for opinion leadership.

Different systems of representation will emphasize different values. Political philosophers and theorists have developed a variety of ideal systems of representation and conceptions of the public interest with radically different prescriptions as to what should be represented and how.[36] It should be clear that much of the disagreement about the contemporary role of Congress stems from different theories of representation.

APPLYING THE CRITERIA TO ALTERNATIVE MODELS OF LEGISLATIVE-EXECUTIVE RELATIONS

The presidential-responsible party model places highest value on control or responsibility in the sense of accountability (i.e., party responsibility). The electorate can hold the President and his party accountable for the program on which they campaigned. High value is also placed on capacity for action. The President must have the means for implementing his program. Decision makers are responsive to the presidential majority through enactment of the party platform rather than to changing popular demands and pressures (the majority principle). The model accords no role to the congressional majority, thereby rejecting (or, more usually, reforming) the system of dual representation.

The presidential-pluralist model assigns highest value to representation of different interests. Bargaining and compromise yield decisions that are broadly representative of interests in the political community and accordingly have broad acceptability. Responsiveness is defined as "open access to interests." Since the presidential-pluralist model relies on strong presidential leadership, it values highly the capacity for action. Majority rule limits the possibilities for bargaining (Calhoun's classic contrast of the functioning of concurrent versus numerical majorities). Finally, the bargaining process, by its very nature, precludes the identification of decision makers required for accountability.

The constitutional balance model contrasts with the previous two models in its emphasis on control or responsibility by means of rational-legal procedure, free discussion, and consensual decision in

---

[36] See Charles E. Gilbert, "Operative Doctrines of Representation," *APSR*, September 1963, pp. 604–18; and Carl J. Friedrich (ed.), *Nomos V: The Public Interest* (New York: Atherton Press, 1967).

the representational process. The model assumes representativeness and responsiveness to *both* presidential and congressional majorities as well as a rational-legal conception of the public interest. It values cooperative presidential-congressional capacity for action.

The Whig or congressional supremacy model values the republican notion of Congress as *the* representative of the people. It reverses the representational emphasis of the presidential-responsible party model, assumes responsiveness in terms of the congressional majority, and accords no role to the presidential majority. The model values positively a capacity for congressional action — again, a reversal of the presidential-responsible party model.

These brief observations may help to focus the public debate over Congress as a representative institution. When we relate this theoretical discussion to our earlier description of representation in the American system we see that at least two of the models assume a fundamental change in the representational system. Both the presidential-responsible party and the congressional supremacy models challenge the concept of dual representation. Of the two the presidential-responsible party model probably will have more relevance with the trend toward nationalization of our parties. The presidential-pluralist and constitutional balance models, however, appear to approximate most closely representation in the contemporary American political system.

REPRESENTATIONAL CRITERIA AND THE INTERNAL ORGANIZATION OF CONGRESS

Much of the criticism of Congress as a representative institution is directed at the *internal* organization of Congress and the power structure, rules, and procedures that hamper the realization of various representational goals. It may be useful to consider the alternative models for organizing power in Congress that we developed in the previous chapter and the representational goals realized in each.

Control by presidential party. This model for congressional organization parallels, as we have noted, the presidential-responsible party model of legislative-executive relations. It extends the criterion of responsibility (accountability) into the committee structure of Congress: committee leaders are expected to support the President's program. This model challenges the assumption that government can be held accountable for its policies through individual representatives;

instead it substitutes party responsibility for individual responsibility. The model values responsiveness to presidential party leadership external to Congress and denies the expression of a separate congressional party majority or ad hoc bipartisan majorities in the legislative process.

Control by congressional party. This model substitutes congressional party leadership for a President at the apex of the party structure and is by definition responsive to the congressional party majority. It invests the congressional party leadership with a capacity for action independent of the presidential party. In contrast with the previous model, control by congressional party weakens accountability by its defense of a more decentralized national party system.

Control by congressional majority. The third method for organizing power in the legislature maximizes the value of responsiveness to the congressional majority in the electorate. With its emphasis on the principle of majority rule, the model understates the need for organizational power and institutionalized leadership in the legislative process. In an effort to make the leadership of Congress more responsive to various majority opinions, the Progressives of 1909–11 greatly weakened the power of the speakership. They did not foresee that organizational power would survive in less visible forms, more difficult to identify or hold accountable than the centralized speakership. Nor did they see the necessary relationship between power and the formation of majorities. Power in the legislature could be distributed and organized so as to facilitate the formation of party majorities or bipartisan majorities, but not both (unless the party majority was large enough to permit a relaxation of party discipline). The Progressives thought they could retain party government *and* freely forming majorities, just as they saw no basic inconsistency between individual and party responsibility. The Progressive model was an overstatement of certain representational ideals. While it was probably easier for bipartisan majorities to form after the revolt, "leadership by commission" made it more difficult for certain majorities to gain leadership support.[37] Perhaps the most ironic twist of events was the emergence of the House Rules Committee during Roosevelt's second administration as

[37] An excellent illustration of the problem of "majority building" is provided by Richard F. Fenno, Jr., "The House of Representatives and Federal Aid to Education," in Robert L. Peabody and Nelson W. Polsby (eds.), *New Perspectives on the House of Representatives* (Chicago: Rand McNally & Co., 1963), pp. 195–235.

a conservative power base in Congress. The Progressives had removed the Speaker from the committee to make Rules more responsive to the Progressive majority in Congress. When a bipartisan conservative coalition gained a majority in the late thirties, the Rules Committee became its agent. The Liberals of the 1960's have moved to reintegrate the Rules Committee into a centralized leadership power structure.[38]

Bargaining and decentralized control. This model emphasizes mutual adjustment of pluralist interests rather than hierarchical control by public authority. Representativeness is its chief value. The building of coalitions within Congress restricts control or responsibility in the sense of accountability.[39] The model assumes that interests should be represented at the early stages of the legislative process and especially in the standing committees where they can have their greatest influence. The congressman's dominant constituency interests will influence his selection of congressional committees. Subgovernments of interested congressmen (at the committee or subcommittee level), executive bureaus, and pressure groups predominate, although the President (usually aided by the congressional leadership) may decide to intervene, breaking the group equilibrium in the "public interest."[40]

Representation within the Congress combines various goals from these models. Party remains the most important factor in legislative majorities, but congressmen are undecided about which party — the presidential or the congressional.[41] And they refuse to yield their independence to party discipline. The result is a hybrid of party leadership, bargaining within Congress, and rule by congressional majority. This

[38] See Milton C. Cummings, Jr., and Robert L. Peabody, "The Decision to Enlarge the Committee on Rules: An Analysis of the 1961 Vote," in Peabody and Polsby (eds.), *op. cit.*, pp. 167–94.

[39] Charles E. Lindblom describes this process as the formulation of "rational policy through mutual adjustment." See *The Intelligence of Democracy: Decision Making Through Mutual Adjustment* (New York: The Free Press, 1965). Lewis Froman also discusses "the cross-section principle" in the organization of congressional committees in *The Congressional Process: Strategies, Rules, and Procedures* (The Study of Congress Series; Boston: Little, Brown & Co., 1967), pp. 195–202.

[40] J. Leiper Freeman analyzes the semi-autonomy of subsystem leaders in *The Political Process: Executive Bureau-Legislative Committee Relations* (Studies in Political Science; New York: Random House, 1955).

[41] Roger H. Davidson, David M. Kovenock, and Michael K. O'Leary found that many congressmen favored stronger parties but rejected executive-branch domination of those parties. *Congress in Crisis: Politics and Congressional Reform* (Belmont, Cal.: Wadsworth Publishing Co., 1966), pp. 73–74.

distinctive form of American party government, according to Arthur Holcombe, means "a legislative process in which action depends upon the practical capacity of the majority-party leaders to find majorities for their measures wherever they may exist regardless of party. Unorganized numerical majorities of the House are ordinarily incapable of action to which the majority-party leaders are opposed." [42]

The rules and procedures of the Congress and the organization of power within Congress generally reflect the *majority* sentiment of the membership. The majority accepts the existing internal organization as desirable or functional, or a determined majority can effect virtually any change in organization it wills (witness the reforms of 1909–11 and the frequent rules changes in the House since 1945). Admittedly there are some qualifications to this observation. The organization of power may reflect the lack of a majority determined enough to press for a change, in view of the costs involved. An intense minority in the Senate can invoke the requirement of an extraordinary majority. Also it is difficult to sustain a determined majority position without the assistance of the leadership. And a lengthy, multi-staged bargaining process is inherently more advantageous to an intense minority against an apathetic majority. While such factors as the standing committee system, tenure, and seniority may introduce conservative biases in the congressional system, Congress still operates on the assumption of majority rule.[43]

We now examine two major reforms that bear directly on the representational function of Congress in the American political system — reapportionment and the proposal for four-year terms for members of the House. Both reforms reflect concern with attaining an ideal electoral system for Congress; both illustrate the problems of evaluating congressional representation and reforming the representational system to improve Congress' capacity for representation.

---

[42] *Our More Perfect Union: From Eighteenth-Century Principles to Twentieth-Century Practice* (Cambridge, Mass.: Harvard University Press, 1950), p. 182.

[43] Some of the inherent biases against pure majority rule in the Congress are discussed by Froman, *op. cit.*, Chap. X, "Congressional Organization and Majority Rule." The tendency for committees or subcommittees to develop particular interests that are not congruent with majority opinion within the Legislature is held in check by a subtle network of reciprocal expectations between the committees and the Legislature, backed by the sanction of the legislative majority. One recent study emphasizes the controls and sanctions available to the House of Representatives against its most powerful committee. See Richard F. Fenno, Jr., *The Power of the Purse: Appropriations Politics in Congress* (Boston: Little, Brown & Co., 1966).

CONGRESSIONAL REPRESENTATION:
THE CASE OF APPORTIONMENT

One of the most severe indictments that has been leveled against Congress by its critics is that it is *not* a representative body. By a criterion of "representativeness" defined on a population basis Congress supposedly "fails." Rural interests are heavily overrepresented at the expense of the growing populous urban areas of the nation. Congress, by this evaluation, stands as a conservative force fighting a rearguard action for sparsely populated rural America, unresponsive to the accelerating urban crisis of our metropolitan centers. The critique extends generally to American state legislatures, where prior to Supreme Court intervention in *Baker* v. *Carr*, malapportionment on a population basis far exceeded any rural bias in Congress.

How valid is this evaluation of Congress? What, more specifically, can we say about the "representativeness" of the House of Representatives on a population basis and the appropriateness of the "equal population" criterion? We shall bypass the Senate on the constitutional point that its basis of representation is not population. Ironically the Senate, which offers by far the greatest leverage for population minorities, has been the more responsive of the two bodies to new urban legislation in recent years. (The ten most populous states with over 50 per cent of the nation's population control one-fifth of the vote in the Senate; the twenty-six least populous with about 17 per cent of the population control a Senate majority. The filibuster further enhances the leverage of the smaller states, although it also affords a safeguard to the urban states.) The most obvious explanation is that senators are elected in state-wide constituencies, most of which have large urban population centers. It is the House, however, the popular branch of the legislature, that has been the subject of public attention.

Under the Constitution, Congress has exercised control over the apportionment of the House of Representatives. Article I, Section 4 specifies:

> The Times, Places and Manner of holding Elections for Senators and Representatives, shall be prescribed in each State by the Legislature thereof; but the Congress may at any time by *Law* make or alter such Regulations, except as to the Places of Choosing Senators. [Emphasis added.]

The Constitution (Article I, Section 2) provides for congressional apportionment *among* the states on the basis of population and extends the franchise to all those qualified to vote for the lower house of the state legislature. Neither the Constitution nor the debates of the constitutional convention spelled out how congressional representatives should be distributed *within* the states, although Andrew Hacker concludes that there is a good deal of evidence that the framers "intended that the House of Representatives have as its constituency a public in which the votes of all citizens were of equal weight." [44]

Until the Apportionment Act of 1842, Congress' first action in regard to apportionment within states, many states elected their representatives on an at-large or, in effect "winner-take-all" basis. The Act of 1842 required distinct, single-member, geographic *districts* of "contiguous territory" but did *not* require population equality. In 1872 Congress added an equal population requirement; in 1901, a requirement that districts be "compact territory" (i.e., not only contiguous but geographically concentrated). The permanent Apportionment Act of 1929, however, which empowers the President automatically to allot congressional seats among the states after each census according to a specified formula, dropped all three requirements; i.e., contiguous, compact districts of equal population. Prior to the 1964 Supreme Court decision of *Wesberry v. Sanders*, which invalidated Georgia's congressional districts for not being substantially equal in population, congressional attempts to reinstate the requirements, with presidential support, had failed. The usual recommended criterion for equitable districts was within a maximum deviation of 15 per cent from the state's average district population (i.e., from 85 per cent to 115 per cent of the state norm). [45]

How well-apportioned were congressional districts at the time of *Wesberry v. Sanders* after 35 years of congressional deference to the states? Table 3.2 compares the largest and smallest districts in each of the 43 states with more than one congressional district. Five states had a three or greater "value of vote" in their smallest district: Texas, Arizona, Colorado, Ohio, and Georgia. (The smallest district in these

44 Hacker, *Congressional Districting: The Issue of Equal Representation* (rev. ed.; Washington: The Brookings Institution, 1964), p. 14. For an opposite interpretation see L. Brent Bozell, *The Warren Revolution: Reflections on the Consensus Society* (New Rochelle, N.Y.: Arlington House, 1966), pp. 80–112, "Wesberry v. Sanders."

45 This variation was suggested by both President Harry S Truman and the reapportionment committee of the American Political Science Association following the 1950 census. See "The Reapportionment of Congress," APSR, March 1951, pp. 153–57.

states was one-third or less the size of the largest district; therefore, its votes weighed or were valued three or more times as much). The greatest congressional district malapportionment (Texas) was 4.4 to 1. The number of congressional districts that exceeded the 15 per cent deviation was 158 of a possible 423. It should be noted, however, that malapportionment exhibits a time cycle as well. Hacker's study and projections from the 1950's through the 1970's suggest that it is greatest immediately following the decennial census, decreases by the mid-decade as some state legislatures redistrict their congressional seats, and then increases again as the census figures become steadily out of date.[46]

The Supreme Court's intervention has greatly accelerated the process of equalization based on 1960 census figures. By the end of 1965, for example, Texas had reapportioned so that the ratio of its largest and smallest districts was 1.2 to 1; Colorado, 1.2 to 1; Ohio, 1.3 to 1; and Georgia, 1.4 to 1.[47] Table 3.3 illustrates the impact of the *Wesberry* v. *Sanders* decision through September, 1966. These figures show some malapportionment, although, we would argue, far less than the average state legislature that provides the immediate public stereotype of the malapportioned legislature. (Comparable ratios for state legislatures before *Baker* v. *Carr* are the Texas House, 8.4 to 1; Arizona Senate, 84.8 to 1; Colorado House, 8.1 to 1; Ohio House, 14.5 to 1; and Georgia House, 99.0 to 1.[48])

What changes would result from a relatively complete equalization of congressional districts? How much representation would various population groups gain or lose? How would complete reapportionment affect policy outcomes? Answers to these questions provide additional measures of Congress' "representativeness." Two studies completed *before* the impact of *Wesberry* v. *Sanders* suggest some unexpected answers.

The first of these studies, released by *Congressional Quarterly* on February 2, 1962, classified congressional districts as urban, suburban, or rural, breaking from the usual urban-rural dichotomy.[49] An "ideal" reapportionment to give each class of districts congressional seats pro-

[46] *Op. cit.*, pp. 109–12.
[47] Gordon E. Baker, *The Reapportionment Revolution: Representation, Political Power, and the Supreme Court* (*Studies in Political Science*; New York: Random House, 1966), p. 82. See also *Congressional Quarterly*, Weekly Report No. 37, September 16, 1966, pp. 2004–2139, "Redistricting Action Reviewed State-by-State for the Years 1960–1966."
[48] Hacker, *op. cit.*, pp. 44–46.
[49] Weekly Report No. 5, pp. 153–69.

TABLE 3.2
VARIATIONS IN POPULATIONS OF CONGRESSIONAL DISTRICTS IN 43 STATES AS OF MARCH 1, 1964

State	Number of Districts	Largest District (000)	Smallest District (000)	Value Vote Smallest District (Largest = 1)	Average District Deviation	Deviating over 15 Per Cent — Number	Deviating over 15 Per Cent — Per Cent	Last Districting
Alabama	9	635	236	2.7	24.1%	5	56%	1931
Arizona	3	663	198	3.3	36.3	2	67	1961
Arkansas	4	575	333	1.7	22.4	4	100	1961
California	38	589	302	2.0	10.1	10	24	1961
Colorado	4	654	196	3.3	30.9	2	50	1921
Connecticut	5	690	319	2.2	25.9	4	80	1931
Florida	12	660	237	2.8	19.2	5	42	1961
Georgia	10	824	272	3.0	26.1	6	60	1931
Idaho	2	410	257	1.6	28.6	2	100	1911
Illinois	24	553	279	2.0	12.0	9	38	1961
Indiana	11	698	291	2.4	19.4	6	55	1941
Iowa	7	442	353	1.3	5.1		0	1961
Kansas	5	540	374	1.4	10.9	1	20	1961
Kentucky	7	611	351	1.7	28.9	4	57	1962
Louisiana	8	536	264	2.0	16.2	4	50	1912
Maine	2	505	464	1.1	4.3		0	1961
Maryland	7	711	244	2.9	44.9	6	86	1951
Massachusetts	12	479	376	1.3	6.3		0	1962
Michigan	19	490	306	1.6	9.2	3	16	1963
Minnesota	8	483	375	1.3	7.7		0	1961

Mississippi	5	608	295	2.1	19.4		60	1962
Missouri	10	507	378	1.3	8.5	1	10	1961
Montana	2	401	274	1.5	18.7		100	1917
Nebraska	3	531	405	1.3	9.3	2	0	1961
New Hampshire	2	332	275	1.2	7.0		0	1881
New Jersey	15	586	255	2.3	34.8	10	60	1961
New York	41	464	350	1.3	5.1		0	1961
North Carolina	11	491	278	1.8	12.7	4	36	1961
North Dakota	2	333	299	1.1	5.4		0	1961
Ohio	23	726	236	3.1	21.4	13	57	1951
Oklahoma	6	552	227	2.4	27.1	4	67	1951
Oregon	4	522	265	2.0	20.0	3	75	1941
Pennsylvania	27	553	303	1.8	10.4	9	33	1962
Rhode Island	2	460	400	1.2	7.0		0	1931
South Carolina	6	531	272	2.0	17.3	3	50	1932
South Dakota	2	498	183	2.7	46.3	2	100	1931
Tennessee	9	627	223	2.8	23.2	6	67	1951
Texas	22	952	216	4.4	34.0	19	86	1957
Utah	2	573	318	1.8	28.6	2	100	1931
Virginia	10	540	313	1.7	14.5	4	40	1952
Washington	7	511	343	1.5	8.6	2	29	1957
West Virginia	5	422	303	1.4	12.0	1	20	1961
Wisconsin	10	409	382	1.0	1.5	0	0	1963

SOURCE: Howard D. Hamilton and Robert M. Howard, "Congressional Districting in Indiana," *Indiana Public Affairs Notes*, March–April, 1964. Reprinted in Howard D. Hamilton (ed.), *Legislative Apportionment: Key to Power* (New York: Harper & Row, 1964), p. 131.

TABLE 3.3
MAXIMUM POPULATION VARIATIONS FROM STATE AVERAGES

State [a]	BEFORE FEBRUARY, 1964 (*Wesberry* v. *Sanders*) Maximum Variation	Total Districts	Number Outside 15% Limitation	AS OF SEPTEMBER, 1966 New Maximum Variation
Alabama [b]	+ 21.4%	8	2	+ 8.4%
Arizona [b]	− 54.3	3	2	− 7.8
Arkansas [b]	+ 28.8	4	4	+ 1.6
California	+ 42.4	38	9	—
Colorado [b]	− 55.4	4	2	+12.6
Connecticut [b]	− 37.1	6	5	+14.1
Florida [b]	+ 60.3	12	5	+13.2
Georgia [b]	+108.9	10	6	+16.4 [c]
Idaho [b]	22.9 [d]	2	2	9.4 [d]
Illinois [b]	− 33.6	24	9	+ 7.5
Indiana [b]	+ 64.6	11	6	−12.8
Iowa	+ 12.3	7	0	—
Kansas [b]	+ 23.9	5	1	− 9.6
Kentucky [b]	+ 40.8	7	4	− 3.8
Louisiana [b]	− 35.2	8	4	+13.7
Maine	4.3 [d]	2	0	—
Maryland [b]	+ 83.5	8	7	−14.9
Massachusetts	− 12.3	12	0	—
Michigan [b]	+ 84.8	19	14	− 2.1
Minnesota	− 13.2	8	0	—
Mississippi [b]	+ 39.7	5	3	+ 3.2
Missouri [b]	+ 17.3	10	1	+10.1
Montana [b]	18.7 [d]	2	2	3.1 [d]
Nebraska	− 14.0	3	0	—
New Hampshire	9.3 [d]	2	0	—
New Jersey [b]	+ 44.8	15	9	+ 8.7
New York	+ 15.1	41	1	—
North Carolina [b]	− 32.9	11	4	− 8.9
North Dakota	5.4 [d]	2	0	—
Ohio [b]	+ 72.1	24	14	−20.9 [c]
Oklahoma [b]	+ 42.5	6	4	+ 4.1
Oregon [b]	− 40.0	4	3	− 8.6
Pennsylvania [b]	+ 31.9	27	9	+15.0
Rhode Island	7.0 [d]	2	0	—
South Carolina [b]	+ 33.9	6	3	+ 6.1
South Dakota [b]	46.3 [d]	2	2	3.4 [d]
Tennessee [b]	+ 58.2	9	6	+14.4
Texas [b]	+118.5	23	20	+10.2
Utah [b]	28.6 [d]	2	2	1.5 [d]
Virginia [b]	+ 36.0	10	4	+ 5.8
Washington [b]	+ 25.2	7	2	−13.1
West Virginia	− 18.6	5	1	—
Wisconsin	+ 3.4	10	0	—

[a] *Alaska, Delaware, Hawaii, Nevada, New Mexico, Vermont,* and *Wyoming* seats are filled at large and therefore are not listed.

portionate to its share of the 1960 population, would yield, according to the analysis, the following shifts: urban seats, a net gain of 7 (with 9 in the South); suburban seats, a gain of 20 (including 8 in the East and 6 in the Midwest); and rural seats a loss of 27 (including 11 from the South and 8 from the Midwest). The second study, by Andrew Hacker, adopted a four-fold typology of districts: urban, suburban, mid-urban, and rural.[50] Hacker argued that his mid-urban districts followed a fairly standard pattern that did not easily fit the *Congressional Quarterly*'s urban-suburban-rural classification. They included all or part of a medium-sized city, ranging in population from 50,000 to 250,000; a suburban fringe; and an outlying rural area with no one section dominant. A comparison of actual and weighted (population ideal) districts by this scheme showed: urban seats, adequately represented; suburban seats, underrepresented by 10; mid-urban seats, underrepresented by 6; and rural seats overrepresented by 16. In 1963 *Congressional Quarterly* revised its analysis to include a new type approximating the "mid-urban" district of the Hacker study: the "mixed" district. Table 3.4 summarizes the revised distribution of seats in an "ideal" apportionment with this classification.

Three rather striking conclusions emerge from these studies of congressional malapportionment in 1962 and 1963, which, it should be stressed, antedate *Wesberry v. Sanders*. First, the number of new districts that would be created and, conversely, old districts abolished is quite small (18 by the *Congressional Quarterly* estimate and 19 by Hacker's estimate out of 435 in the House), although a number of powerful senior members might lose their seats in the process. Most reapportionment to effect greater population equality could be handled by marginal adjustments in the boundaries of congressional districts that would *not* substantially alter the broad demographic composition of the districts involved. Second, the image of heavy rural overrepresentation (in population terms) finds little support in the data. The revised *Congressional Quarterly* figures show, at the extremes, an overrepresentation of 12 rural seats and an underrepre-

---

[b] *Redistricted since* Wesberry v. Sanders. (*New plans in Louisiana, Washington, and Oklahoma were not scheduled to go into effect until after the 1966 general elections.*)

[c] *Even after redistricting, Georgia had two seats outside 15 per cent limitation, and Ohio one seat.*

[d] *State has only two districts; thus one district is the stated percentage above the average and the other district is the stated percentage below the average.*
SOURCE: *Congressional Quarterly*, Weekly Report No. 37, September 16, 1966, p. 2006.

[50] *Op. cit.*, pp. 88–95.

TABLE 3.4

CONGRESSIONAL SEATS IN AN "IDEAL" APPORTIONMENT

| | URBAN | | | | SUBURBAN | | |
	Actual	Ideal	Change		Actual	Ideal	Change
East	36	36	0		26	29	+ 3
South	16	21	+ 5		2	4	+ 2
Midwest	32	32	0		12	15	+ 3
West	19	20	+ 1		10	12	+ 2
Total	103	109	+ 6		50	60	+10

| | RURAL | | | | MIXED | | |
	Actual	Ideal	Change		Actual	Ideal	Change
East	32	32	0		28	25	− 3
South	85	77	− 8		16	17	+ 1
Midwest	61	57	− 4		20	21	+ 1
West	25	25	0		15	12	− 3
Total	203	191	−12		79	75	− 4

SOURCE: *Congressional Quarterly*, Weekly Report No. 8, February 21, 1964, p. 352.

sentation of 10 suburban seats. Moreover, population malapportionment tends to be spread regionally. The only region that would undergo a substantial change under ideal apportionment is the South, which would lose 8 rural seats and gain 5 urban seats.[51] These disparities with the population ideal have subsequently been reduced by Supreme Court mandate. Third, according to Andrew Hacker, "Liberals have little to gain by reforms in the direction of equitable districting or even the curtailing of gerrymandering." [52] Hacker finds that in four key roll-call votes of the 87th Congress (on the Department of Urban Affairs reorganization plan, the Emergency Educational Aid Bill, the Food and Agriculture Bill, and the enlargement of the House Rules Committee), the Kennedy administration would have received *fewer* votes if the votes of representatives had been weighted by the populations of their districts. *Congressional Quarterly* concludes:

> It seems unlikely that "ideal reapportionment" of seats . . . would substantially change Congressional voting on important liberal versus conservative issues. Party loyalty appears to be a

[51] *Congressional Quarterly Almanac*, 88th Congress, 1st Session, 1963, pp. 1170–84.
[52] *Op. cit.*, pp. 95–99.

much stronger influence. Indeed, in most areas the slightest change in the political winds, causing one party to gain a few House seats at the expense of the other, would have a far greater effect on "liberal" and "conservative" voting than any likely reapportionment.[53]

If anything, reapportionment, by benefiting the Republican party in the suburbs and southern cities, might make the House *more* conservative.

It is not unreasonable to conclude then that the House of Representatives is reasonably well apportioned on a population basis. The degree of remaining disparity between districts is likely to narrow even further through congressional action or continued Court rulings.[54] But is "representativeness" in terms of population an adequate or valid measure of congressional representation in itself? Probably not, for two quite different reasons.

First, as opponents of the Court's application of the "one-man, one-vote" principle point out, the criterion assumes a *particular* theory of democracy — "populistic" democracy — and a representational (or at least an electoral) system based upon it.[55] As we have noted, there is strong support for this egalitarian interpretation in the American political tradition. But Americans have equally long-standing traditions that complicate any extreme or simple statement of democratic practice. Justice Felix Frankfurter dissented in *Baker* v. *Carr*:

> Apportionment, by its character, is a subject of extraordinary complexity, involving — even after the fundamental theoretical issues concerning what is to be represented in a representative legislature have been fought out or compromised — considerations of geography, demography, electoral convenience, economic and social cohesions or divergencies among particular local groups, communications, the practical effects of political institutions like the lobby and the city machine, ancient traditions and ties of settled usage, respect for proven incumbents of long experience and senior status, mathe-

[53] Weekly Report No. 5, February 2, 1962, p. 155.

[54] HR2508, 90th Congress, 1st Session, as amended by the Senate, specifies a 10 per cent maximum population variation between the largest and smallest district within a state. The Supreme Court has also applied a more stringent population criterion in its 1967 actions. See "Supreme Court Orders Imperil Districts of 22 States," *Congressional Quarterly*, Weekly Report No. 3, January 20, 1967, pp. 101–2, 106.

[55] See Alfred de Grazia, *Essay on Apportionment and Representative Government*, Chap. III, "Doctrines and Ideologies."

matical mechanics, censuses compiling relevant data, and a host of others.[56]

The Supreme Court reapportionment decisions have gradually defined a *single-factor* apportionment formula. In the process the Court has become "the crusading political philosopher of populism." [57]

The congressional reaction to the Court's assertions on apportionment is another story that we cannot recount here. Intense sentiment in both Houses of Congress for a modification of the reapportionment decisions has been effectively frustrated by liberals using some of the classic techniques of filibuster and delay.[58]

Second, the equal-population criterion tends to overvalue the role of elections in the representational system. Martin Shapiro, in an incisive critique of "the excessive and mistaken preoccupation" of populistic theory with majority rule in elections, suggests that in achieving equality in the electoral process, inequality in politics *generally* might be heightened. The system of interest group representation, for instance, is oriented toward the President and the bureaucracy and generally favors the urban and industrial sectors of American society. Equalitarian reapportionment in Congress at a time when political power is rapidly shifting away from the rural and agricultural sectors might result in a serious underrepresentation of the rural populace in the broader American political system.[59] The representational system as a whole achieves some type of balance between these divergent communities and interests. In the opposite direction, even if Congress satisfies the equal-population criterion, it still does not appear to meet the expectations of some critics concerning its "responsiveness" to the legislative needs of urban America.

In summary, "equal population" provides a convenient and easily

[56] 369 U.S. 186 (1962).

[57] Martin Shapiro, *Law and Politics in the Supreme Court: New Approaches to Political Jurisprudence* (Glencoe, Ill.: The Free Press, 1964), p. 252.

[58] For an account of political strategies of both sides see Royce Hanson, *The Political Thicket: Reapportionment and Constitutional Democracy* (Englewood Cliffs, N.J.: Prentice-Hall, 1966), pp. 82–101. Conservatives tried unsuccessfully to overcome liberal opposition invoking some extraordinary devices such as discharge by the Rules Committee of the Tuck bill (stripping the federal courts of jurisdiction in apportionment cases) from the House Judiciary Committee. When Senator Strom Thurmond (R-S.C.) offered the Tuck bill in the Senate, however, it was defeated by a majority vote.

[59] See Shapiro's analysis of the Court's apportionment decisions, *op. cit.*, Chap. V, "The Supreme Court as Lawyer, Political Theorist, and Political Scientist: Baker v. Carr and After," esp. pp. 228–32.

applied standard for assessing the representative capacity of Congress. When we apply it we find that Congress *is* by and large "representative." However, we also find that the criterion avoids none of the problems of defining what is adequate representation. It solves the dilemma of competing theories of representation, only by assuming one of them to be absolute. And it measures a facet of congressional representation at the expense of a broader interpretation of Congress as a representative subsystem in the American political system.

CONGRESSIONAL REPRESENTATION: A FOUR-YEAR TERM FOR MEMBERS OF THE HOUSE?

The proposal for a four-year term for members of the House, although less frequently discussed than reapportionment with reference to Congress' function of representation, has a much greater potential for changing the American system of representation. President Johnson in his special message to Congress on January 20, 1966, proposing in part a constitutional amendment to provide four-year House terms, primarily emphasized the *legislative* function of Congress.[60] Besides the accelerating volume of legislation and the resulting longer sessions of Congress, the President stressed the increasingly complex problems upon which Congress must act.

> It is no longer sufficient to develop solutions for an agricultural nation with few foreign responsibilities; now a man or woman chosen to represent his people in the House of Representatives must understand the consequences of our spiralling population growth, of urbanization, of the scientific revolution, of our welfare and education requirements, and of our responsibilities as the world's most powerful democracy.

Proponents of the four-year term, especially members of Congress, have emphasized its potential contribution to the improved "efficiency and effectiveness" of Congress — usually in the performance of its legislative function.[61] The President did note some secondary effects the

[60] *Congressional Record*, 89th Congress, 2nd Session, January 20, 1966, pp. 702–4.

[61] See, for example, Congressman Jeffrey Cohelan's (D-Cal.) statement before the Joint Committee on the Organization of the Congress: "A 4-year term would enable Members of the House of Representatives to devote more of their time to legislative duties. It would allow them to be more responsive to national issues while not neglecting important local needs. It would, in brief,

reform would have on the *quality* of representation. By reducing "the inexorable pressures" of biennial campaigning for re-election and the "financial and political" cost of holding congressional office, the reform would serve to attract "the best men in private and public life into competition for this high public office." He cited the lesson of growing professionalism in other branches and levels of government: "That brief and uncertain periods in office contribute not to the best interests of democracy — but to harassed inefficiency and the loss of invaluable experience."

The idea of a four-year term had enjoyed growing majority public and congressional support before the President's speech.[62] By the end of the 89th Congress, however, the proposal appeared dead. Why? The arguments for improved congressional performance were convincing until the full implications of the reform — for representation in the American system — were considered.

The President recommended not only a four-year term but that each member of the House run for office during a presidential election year. Thus his recommendation paralleled that of the advocates of a presidential-responsible party model for the American political system. One of the more articulate rationales for the reform, developed by James MacGregor Burns, makes explicit this preoccupation with the *representational* base of American politics:

> The aim is to draw congressional and presidential party leaderships to each other by drawing the two party electorates more closely together — more specifically, by combining the smaller congressional party electorates in the states. As far as possible the President and his party majorities in Congress

---

be a step forward for good government." *Hearings: Organization of Congress,* 89th Congress, 1st Session, 1965, p. 1913.

62 The Gallup Poll has shown a steady increase in public approval of a four-year term from 42 per cent (43 per cent against, 15 per cent no opinion) in 1955 to 61 per cent (24 per cent against, 15 per cent no opinion) in 1964. "Four-year Term for Congressmen?" *Public Opinion News,* Gallup Political Series, No. 11, March 13, 1955, and *The Washington Post,* January 14, 1966. Congressman Frank Chelf (D-Ky.) polled the House in the Spring of 1965 and found 259 members in favor of a four-year term, 40 opposed, and 66 doubtful. The Chelf proposal is for a staggered term. See *Hearings: Organization of Congress,* pp. 694–96. *Congressional Quarterly,* however, found a change in congressional climate by the time the President made his proposal. *Congressional Quarterly,* Weekly Report No. 6, February 11, 1966, p. 364. See also the results of the Brookings survey of congressional opinion included in Charles O. Jones, *Every Second Year: Congressional Behavior and the Two-Year Term* (Washington, D.C.: The Brookings Institution, 1967).

should be elected by substantially the same electoral group-
ings, for the sake of clarity of policy, unity in government,
and responsibility to the majority.[63]

Burns recommends a four-year term for representatives, to coincide
with presidential terms. He reluctantly accepts the impossibility of a
four-year Senate term, although he would group candidates for President, senator, and congressman on the ballot in such a way that the
voters "could choose a straight national party ticket simply by mark-
ing one party circle or by pulling one party lever." [64] Burns argues that
the two-year congressman is "unduly vulnerable to sudden gusts of
public opinion" and that off-year elections "usually raise havoc with
the President's support in Congress." [65]

Proponents of the four-year term who feared that the election of
the House and President at the same time would favor the Executive
to an intolerable degree devised a proposal for staggered terms, with
half the members of the House running for four-year terms during
presidential years, half during off years. This in turn raised several new
objections, notably the danger that the House would polarize into two
classes of congressmen: those who would support and those who would
oppose the program of the President (separating and accentuating the
characteristics of the presidential and congressional systems of representation). Few entertained seriously the proposal to elect all representatives during non-presidential years.

A further compromise, aimed at lengthening congressional terms,
preserving balance between President and Congress, and avoiding the
possibility of permanent polarization within Congress, was suggested
by Congressman Donald Rumsfeld (R-Ill.). The Rumsfeld proposal
would *alternate* two- and four-year terms for each member so that over
a twelve-year period each member would run only four times — twice
with the President, twice on his own.[66]

---

[63] Burns, *op. cit.*, pp. 326–27.

[64] *Ibid.*, p. 328. Former Senator Joseph Clark has articulated the argument
for a four-year Senate term. See *Hearings: Organization of Congress*, pp. 1521–34.

[65] *Op. cit.*, p. 331. See also Pearl Olive Ponsford, *Evil Results of Mid-Term
Congressional Elections and a Suggested Remedy* (Los Angeles: The University
of Southern California Press, 1937).

[66] Summaries of the various proposals are given in Robert L. Peabody, "Rebuild the House?" *Johns Hopkins Magazine*, March 1966, pp. 8–11, 21–22,
and "Proposals for 4-Year Terms for Members of the House of Representatives"
(American Enterprise Institute Legislative Analysis Series; Washington, D.C.:
American Enterprise Institute, 1966). See also Jones, *op. cit.*

The complexity of the various alternatives and the lack of consensus in support of any single plan meant eventual failure for the reform effort. To the problems we have noted one should add the technical problems of reapportionment, limitations on seeking other office (notably the Senate), and internal organization of the House. But we are primarily concerned with what the debate tells us about congressmen's perceptions of an ideal system of congressional representation. What different representational values, for instance, did the various alternatives assume or attempt to maximize?

Each of the proposals served to reduce the responsiveness of Congress to a *separate* congressional majority in the electorate. Under the two major proposals there are either no off-year House elections or only half of the electorate is able to participate in them. While Americans are free to continue to split their ballots between presidential and congressional aspirants, the opportunity to do so (including splitting ballots over time) is reduced by virtue of the smaller number of electoral choices. A separate "congressional referendum" or national plebiscite between presidential elections is either eliminated or truncated. While the President discounted the need for separate congressional elections altogether — because of modern communications, public opinion polls, and "mountains of mail" — the fact remains that changes in public sentiment are most effectively translated into changes in congressional attitude toward legislation and party balance through the ballot box. The President and responsible party advocates would eliminate popular electoral expression during years when the President could not be part of that expression. The staggered-term proposal, on the other hand, reduces the responsiveness of the House to *both* the presidential and congressional electorates by halving the number of seats that can reflect changes in public sentiment during either election year.

The President's proposal clearly maximized the values of control and capacity for action; the staggered-term proposal ran the risk of reducing Congress' capacity for action in its attempt to preserve some degree of responsiveness to a separate congressional constituency. The value fostered by the two-year term but not by all the reform proposals was responsiveness within a system of dual representation. Senator (then Congressman) Robert P. Griffin (R-Mich.) expressed succinctly his concern as a member of the Joint Committee on the Organization of the Congress:

> I think we ought to note the obvious fact that when we are moving to a four-year term, we are giving the American

people less opportunity, if not infrequent opportunity, to register agreement or disagreement with the positions that their Congressman is taking.[67]

The arguments pro and con the four-year term also suggested congressional concern with the changing nature of representation in the American system, although again there was little consensus. The revolutionary impact of communications and transportation technology within the lifetime of senior members was cited frequently. Some members argued from this that opinions could be communicated rapidly, thereby reducing the need for the congressman to spend time campaigning among constituents. Others cited the decision of the Constitutional Convention to set congressional terms at two years instead of one to permit members sufficient time to travel and communicate with constituents (implying that two years was now more than adequate for legislative work *and* campaigning). The complexity of government as a factor also cut both ways. Some felt they should spend more time in Washington studying legislation; others felt that, as the last personal link between their constituents and an ever more impersonal bureaucracy, they were needed more at home. The mounting expense of congressional campaigns was a frequent worry, although a longer term of office was not thought to be the only solution. Similarly the enormous demands on the time of a congressman were acknowledged, but all members did not agree that a cutback in political campaigning was the answer.

Debate over lengthening the term of members of the House — a reform that one would expect congressmen readily to favor — revealed that congressmen have broader concerns about how adequately they are fulfilling their representative function. Congress' failure to accept reform will undoubtedly be interpreted by some as a sign of congressional insensitivity. Others will rate Congress more favorably, taking into account the broader implications of reform.

SOME CONCLUDING OBSERVATIONS

Representation in a political democracy is a complicated and organic phenomenon. Attitudes toward congressional representation are im-

---

[67] *Hearings: Organization of Congress*, p. 733. Robert Peabody states: "The argument [for or against a four-year term] turns on the commitment to the principle of coordinate branches of government. . . . Variation in the length of terms among our political leaders is one of the most fundamental safeguards against any single leader or institution dominating all the others to the detriment of democratic freedoms." "Rebuild the House?" p. 10.

bedded in deeper and more ambivalent American attitudes toward authority and its exercise and control.

We have concluded our examination of Congress as a representative body with a discussion of two major reforms. The first of these has largely succeeded — through the authority of the Supreme Court and a supporting factor of political irreversibility (i.e., the unlikelihood that reapportioned legislatures will support a return to previous malapportionments), in implementing one specific representational value (population equality) — but without significantly changing congressional performance. Thus reformers have looked toward more direct and penetrating means for changing congressional representation. The device they have most frequently chosen is party reform. Our second reform while requiring a constitutional amendment, is essentially part of a broader reform of American political parties.[68] But such a route is potentially frustrating as well. Frank Sorauf has warned against the "unreal hopes and illusions" of those who see American parties as the agents of broader political reform.

> The parties are, as are all social institutions, deeply conservative organizations, rooted in political cultures, conventions, and other institutions. . . . They are unplanned instruments by which democratic majorities amass and effect their political power. . . . [T]hey are means by which we promote and facilitate the systems of representation and decision-making in a democracy. They are not, however, the key to that system.[69]

A key to an understanding of congressional representation is the American tradition of dual representation. If we begin with this assumption rather than with a conception of political parties that denies much of the American historical experience, we may be in a much better position to appraise the adjustment of the contemporary Congress to new governmental problems.

[68] See Burns, *op. cit.*, pp. 323–40.
[69] Sorauf, *op. cit.*, pp. 168–69.

CHAPTER FOUR

Legislative Initiative and Response

Criticism of Congress has focused largely on congressional performance of the legislative function. While the Constitution vests in Congress "all legislative powers," the modern President has assumed the dominant role in the legislative process. Two pessimistic extremes see Congress on the one hand as a shadow of its former self, "rubberstamping" elaborate legislative drafts prepared by the President and the executive bureaucracy, and on the other as a frustrated Legislature with power but limited prerogative, blocking executive initiative to the detriment of the nation. Both evaluations, as we shall see, are much overdrawn. What they call our attention to, however, is the radical change in the problems requiring legislative action and the consequent need for both President and Congress to develop new roles in legislative decision making.

THE CHANGING LEGISLATIVE FUNCTION

Legislation in its classical definition is the making or enactment of laws or rules having the force of authority by virtue of their official promulgation. In the narrow sense legislation refers only to those governmental decisions that are embodied in the laws and enactments of the full Congress as signed by the President. Legislation in a broader sense includes rules or decisions made within the Executive branch (sometimes referred to as "executive legislation") or the Judicial branch ("judicial legislation"). The three are obviously related, although our major concern here will be with the more limited definition.

How well the legislative function is performed by the President and Congress (we shall assume that they share responsibility for performance, both constitutionally and by practical necessity) will affect the functioning of the political system as a whole. For example, the legislative function affects such general functions as conflict management, integration, and legitimation.

The legislative function of Congress overlaps most of its other major functions. Through legislation, Congress sets policy guidelines for executive agencies. The control function of Congress is in an important sense an extension of its legislative function. As Theodore Lowi observes, "the problem of legislation" has changed under executive-centered government. "[T]he major problem and major focus of Congress is no longer simply that of prescribing the behavior of citizens but more often that of *affecting the behavior of administrators*." [1] Control involves the clarification of law as well as an evaluation of its actual consequences (with feedback into the legislative process). Investigation may provide important new imputs for legislation, as may attention to problems constituents encounter with existing legislation. Finally, the informative function of Congress has a legislative dimension. The acceptability and workability of major new statutes assumes a certain level of public familiarity and understanding.

We have suggested that there is a changing power equilibrium between President and Congress in the American political system. The current equilibrium of executive-centered government implies a mutually acceptable allocation of roles between the President and Congress in the legislative process. Briefly stated they are:

1. The President, as chief legislator, will normally take the initiative in the legislative process. He will develop, through the executive budget and the central clearance of agency requests for legislation, a coordinated agenda for congressional action. He will develop legislative proposals for Congress utilizing the expertise of the executive bureaucracy. He will work through legislative leaders in Congress to enact the priority items of his program.

2. The Congress, exercising its legislative powers, reviews the requests of the Executive. It may extensively amend or reject executive drafts. It retains "secondary initiative" in the legislative process; i.e., it prefers to let the President do the preliminary work of screening and coordinating agency requests, but it retains the right to "second-guess" his determination of national priorities. Congress does not at-

---

[1] *Legislative Politics U.S.A.* (2nd ed.; Boston: Little, Brown & Co., 1965), p. xvi.

tempt to duplicate the process of policy making within the Executive
but chooses rather to exercise initiative selectively. If it feels the Executive is inattentive to a legislative need, it can and frequently does
assume initiative in that area.

3. With the increase of delegated ("executive") legislation, Congress has extended its control or review of administration. Congress
still specifies its "intent" through broad legislation. It permits the
Executive wide discretion in complicated areas of public policy, such
as tariff agreements and foreign aid programs, while increasing its own
capacity for oversight. The archetypal example of this new relationship
is the legislative veto exercised by Congress over executive legislation.

The new equilibrium of President and Congress in the legislative
process has been misunderstood or oversimplified by some observers.
First, the congressional role of "secondary initiative" has been greatly
understated. Even during periods noted for the vigor of presidential
leadership, Congress has asserted itself. Arthur Schlesinger, Jr., notes
that during "the hundred days" of the first New Deal, Congress forced
the President, who was preoccupied with banking, agriculture, and
relief, to turn to industrial recovery and a federal public works program.[2] Even more dramatic was congressional leadership in labor
legislation. The President "saw himself as holding the balance between business and labor." He took a strict hands-off attitude toward
Senator Wagner's legislation and was advised by some in his administration to veto it. Other congressional initiatives included the federal
deposit insurance system and public housing legislation. The general
pattern, however, was executive initiative. Ernest S. Griffith states:

> Gigantic research and action bureaus grew overnight and gen-
> erated still further legislation. The evidence concerning these
> first two or three years would indicate that fully 80 per cent
> of the important legislation was for practical purposes White
> House and bureau generated, rather than originating in Con-
> gress itself.[3]

The professional staffing of Congress, accomplished under the Legislative Reorganization Act of 1946 was, to a significant degree, a
direct response to the growing superior technical competence of ex-

[2] Schlesinger, *The Coming of the New Deal*, Vol. II of *The Age of Roosevelt*
(Boston: Houghton Mifflin Co., 1959), pp. 95–96, 400–406, 553–56.
[3] *Congress: Its Contemporary Role* (3rd ed.; New York: New York University Press, 1961), p. 7.

ecutive-branch staff. Congress has continued to exercise a role of secondary initiative, beyond the review and amendment of executive proposals. Some examples from the first session of the 90th Congress (1967) include: an initiative to reduce American troop commitments in Europe, efforts to define "creative federalism" and a new system of federal revenue sharing with the states, the Percy proposal for a National Home Ownership Foundation, continued congressional pressure on the Executive to fund earlier congressional initiatives in water pollution control — The Water Quality Act of 1965 — and the block-grant and National Institute of Law Enforcement and Criminal Justice provisions of the House version of the anticrime bill.[4]

Second, there has been a tendency to oversimplify the origins of legislative proposals. While some legislative ideas may be clearly identified with a President or prominent member of his administration or conversely with a member of Congress, the great majority enter the legislative process through a variety of sources. A major piece of legislation will normally combine several initiatives, frequently crossing the separation of institutions. One of the most thorough case studies of a major piece of legislation, Stephen K. Bailey's classic analysis of the Employment Act of 1946, underlines the diverse origins of public policy through "the impact of seminal ideas on strategic persons at propitious times." [5] Accordingly a simple scoreboard of executive versus congressional initiative is misleading. The format assumed in this study is that the President will normally present Congress with a legislative agenda and outline, but that both parties retain options for initiative within the legislative process.[6]

[4] See "Senators Press Study of American Troops in Europe," *Congressional Quarterly*, Weekly Report No. 11, March 17, 1967, pp. 395–99; "Steps Initiated to Implement Creative Federalism," Weekly Report No. 12, March 24, 1967, pp. 441–43, 450; "Congress Shows Increasing Interest in Tax Sharing," Weekly Report No. 14, April 7, 1967, pp. 523–25; "Republican Housing Bill Introduced in Both Chambers," Weekly Report No. 17, April 28, 1967, p. 687; "Water Pollution Control," Weekly Report No. 20, May 19, 1967, p. 840; and "House Votes Block Grants in Anticrime Bill," Weekly Report No. 32, August 11, 1967, pp. 1503–5, 1537.

[5] *Congress Makes a Law: The Story Behind the Employment Act of 1946* (New York: Columbia University Press, 1950), p. 236.

[6] Much of the current emphasis in the literature on executive initiative stems from Lawrence Chamberlain's classic, *The President, Congress, and Legislation* (New York: Columbia University Press, 1946). For example, James A. Robinson concludes, "An extension of Chamberlain's study from 1945 to 1965 would be expected to show that this collaboration has now yielded to virtually exclusive initiation by the executive. The decline in Congressional power has been especially acute with respect to its innovative or creative contributions to public

Finally, little recognition has been given to the congressional role of oversight or control of administration as an extension of congressional initiative. Congressional involvement in administration has generally been deplored, yet we have described its growth as a logical corollary of the American system of separated institutions sharing powers.

The current equilibrium of legislative roles may well be disturbed by the impact of new information and data processing systems. Congress, in its second-guessing capacity, will probably enjoy an enhanced position in the legislative process. It will have the informational capacity to review executive proposals and operating programs on a coordinated basis for the first time since the initiation of the standing committee system. A full discussion of these possibilities is deferred to the concluding section of this volume.

TWO ALTERNATIVE VIEWS AND EVALUATIONS OF THE LEGISLATIVE PROCESS

Is Congress Responsive to National Legislative Needs? The Standard of Legislative Output

One view of congressional performance places primary emphasis on legislative output. Congress is evaluated by its responsiveness to legislative needs. These needs are usually defined from a liberal policy perspective. They assume a view of the public interest that leads rather than follows democratic majorities: Congress, as a vital partner in the federal government, should deal effectively, through legislation,

---

policy." *Congress and Foreign Policy-Making: A Study in Legislative Influence and Initiative* (rev. ed.; Homewood, Ill.: The Dorsey Press, 1967), pp. 174–75, 1–15. The Chamberlain study, however, considers less than a decade of legislative history under the [Executive] Reorganization Act of 1939 (and establishment of the Executive Office of the President) and none after the Legislative Reorganization Act of 1946. Ralph K. Huitt has suggested a new interpretation emphasizing "policy systems" in which all parties involved in a particular category of issues *share* regularly in the making, alteration, and execution of policy. "There is almost continuous interchange among committee members, their staffs, the executive (that is, agency personnel, White House staff, and private persons appointed to 'task forces,' and the like) and representatives of private associations at almost every stage of the process, from the first glimmer of an idea to compromises in conference and to the administration of the act. . . . Indeed, much initiation is simply the reasonable next step in the view of those within a given policy system. . . ." "Congress, the Durable Partner," in Elke Frank (ed.), *Lawmakers in a Changing World* (Englewood Cliffs, N.J.: Prentice-Hall, 1966), p. 19.

with clearly recognized problems and develop legislative answers before these problems reach a critical point. Thus Congress is held responsible for the delay in developing effective civil rights legislation (1964, 1965) and the failure to give enough federal aid to primary and secondary education or approve medical care for the aged under Social Security until 1965. It has not developed comprehensive and effective programs for unemployment, the growth of the megalopolis, poverty, disarmament, and a staggering range of problems. "The failure of Congress to act," concludes former Senator Joseph Clark, "has resulted in grave damages to the state of the Union and the continuation of years of abuses which should have been terminated much earlier." [7] Congress is held responsible by the administration and others for the current urban crisis in America, for its "inexcusably slow action," and lack of a sense of urgency.[8]

Since this view of Congress and its legislative performance is so forcefully and effectively expressed by the critics of Congress, it deserves our careful examination. A comprehensive assessment of this standard would require an investigation into recent legislative history that is far beyond the scope of this book. Why was there no comprehensive civil rights legislation until 1964? What legislative efforts and accomplishments preceded it? What educational and medical programs has Congress supported? What prevented majority support or action in Congress for elementary and secondary schools? For Medicare? What is the nature of the urban crisis, and what solutions to it have been proposed? An evaluation of legislative performance in terms of output requires an understanding of the reasons for action or inaction. The surface answers — "The majority was not able to express itself because the bill did not come to a vote," "The Rules Committee refused to report it," "The Committee didn't even call hearings because the Chairman opposed it," — tell us very little.

Fortunately there is an ever expanding literature of case studies in the legislative process which is enhancing public understanding of legislative performance. The case study approach, however, gives only a fragmentary view of overall legislative performance. It probably overemphasizes the controversial and exceptional problems Congress faces, and pays less attention to routine yet important matters. Attempts to integrate the findings of case study literature will most likely lead to a new definition of research requirements for the legislative process.

[7] *Congress: The Sapless Branch* (New York: Harper & Row, 1964), p. 25.
[8] *The Boston Globe*, August 1, 1967, pp. 1, 4.

Factors affecting legislative output. It should be possible, on the basis of our existing understanding of the legislative process, to define some of the factors that delay or expedite legislative action. Why are some Congresses, like those of Woodrow Wilson's and Franklin D. Roosevelt's first terms and the recent 89th Congress (1965–66) so productive? Why are others lethargic or stalemated? Why does Congress act in some areas and not in others? We can suggest several critical factors that affect legislative output. While some of these may appear obvious to the reader, they are frequently glossed over in evaluating Congress's legislative record.[9]

Party or electoral balance. If party is the most important factor in the roll-call behavior of the individual legislator, it obviously follows that the relative strength or balance of the two parties in the Legislature is critical for many policy outcomes. Each of the highly productive Congresses noted above was heavily imbalanced in favor of the President's party (Democratic) by margins of better than 2-to-1 in four of the five.[10] Three of these Congresses were coincident with the election of reform Presidents. These presidential party victories by overwhelming margins in the electoral college, against a divided or dispirited opposition, were interpreted as mandates for new eras of social reform. "Effective majorities" of this kind are unusual in American politics.[11]

Party balance without disciplined parties is, however, a crude predictor of outcomes in the legislative system. Party leadership must often work with ad hoc bipartisan majorities to accomplish its ends. In building some coalitions, for example, the leadership may find the Congress divided into "hard-core liberals," "hard-core conservatives,"

---

[9] A similar but narrower list of "conditions" favoring the House leadership in its legislative strategy is developed by Lewis A. Froman, Jr., and Randall B. Ripley, "Conditions for Party Leadership: The Case of the House Democrats," *American Political Science Review* (APSR), March 1965, pp. 52–63. Also see Ripley's discussion of the conditions for legislative success in *Majority Party Leadership in Congress* (The Study of Congress Series; Boston: Little, Brown & Co., 1969), pp. 184–87. For another interpretation of factors influencing legislative outcomes see Michael J. Shapiro, "The House and the Federal Role: A Computer Simulation of Roll-Call Voting," APSR, June 1968, pp. 494–517.

[10] The five Congresses were the 63rd (1913–14), 290D–127R–18Misc; the 64th (1915–16), 231D–193R–8Misc; the 73rd (1933–34), 313D–117R–5Misc; the 74th (1935–56), 322D–103R–10Misc; and the 89th (1965–66), 295D–140R. The 67th Congress (1921–22), elected with Warren G. Harding as part of "the return to normalcy," was the most lopsided Republican Congress of this century, 300R–132D–1Misc.

[11] See Samuel Lubell's conclusion to *The Future of American Politics* (3rd ed.; New York: Harper & Row, 1965), Chap. XII.

and "negotiables," as is frequently the case on major partisan issues. Neil MacNeil observes that during the Kennedy Congresses "about fifty to sixty of the seventy-odd negotiable Representatives could be classified as doubtful on any given major issue that drew taut the lines of political controversy." [12] The defection of southern Democrats has been an additional problem for Democratic Presidents since Franklin Roosevelt, although the "administration support" scores of most southern Democrats is higher than suggested by the public's image of a southern Democratic–rural Republican conservative coalition. Northern and southern Democrats have split on about three out of every ten roll calls over the past decade and have united against the Republicans on the remaining seven.[13]

The wider the party margin in favor of a reform President, the easier it should be for him to gain legislative action on his program. As the party margin narrows, a swing group in the Legislature including members of both parties can determine the fate of the President's program. On occasion he may have a minority position in the Legislature.

Public opinion or mood. The general distribution of party identification in the electorate tends to remain stable, with occasional upheavals like the Depression producing fundamental party realignment. Shifts in public opinion or mood are much more frequent. They may be reflected in off-presidential-year congressional elections or within a given Congress. Public opinion may be galvanized by dramatic events as it was in the case of the civil rights revolution during 1964 and 1965. The President and Congress both responded in legislative action that broke through decades of inaction and the most intractable congressional obstruction — the southern filibuster.[14] Public opinion may move in directions the President, his advisors, and some members of Congress oppose — as in the reaction to urban violence and the demand for repressive anti-riot control measures. Shifts in public

---

[12] *Forge of Democracy: The House of Representatives* (New York: David McKay Co., 1963), p. 280. The spectrum of congressional support and opposition on any given issue usually reflects more gradations with corresponding opportunities for a range of legislative and bargaining strategies.

[13] See *Congressional Quarterly*, Weekly Report No. 5, February 3, 1967, pp. 176–79. However, southern Democrats faced with Republican opposition have been under increasing pressure to withhold support of Democratic social welfare legislation.

[14] See *Revolution in Civil Rights* (3rd ed.; Washington, D.C.: Congressional Quarterly Service, 1967).

moods for economizing or spending will be felt within Congress.[15] Some deeply held cultural attitudes may dictate or prevent certain legislative action. Efforts to control "subversive" or "un-American" activities, for example, have received a much more favorable response within Congress than have proposals for a negative income tax or guaranteed annual income. (The decision of the leadership of the House Un-American Activities Committee to change the committee's name to the House Internal Security Committee in the 91st Congress suggests a longer-term change in such attitudes, however.)

Congress, we have argued, is more sensitive to shifts in public opinion because half of the time the electorate has passed judgment on it more recently than the President. Advocates of more disciplined presidentially oriented parties discount the value and deplore the impact of public opinion on Congress. They would prefer both President and Congress to operate on less frequent party electoral verdicts. However, the American system of dual representation affords a greater play for public opinion. Economizing moods translated through Congress, in particular, may require the President to set new legislative priorities. The contrast between the 89th (1965–66) and 90th (1967–68) Johnson Congresses is instructive. The former enacted major new Great Society legislation; the latter, under the mounting costs of the war in Vietnam, refused to fund or extend several of these.

Even if the President has a clear party majority, he may not have the necessary public opinion to support everything he wants to do or everything the critics of Congress feel needs to be done. Limiting or impulsively moving our government by public opinion is one of the continuing tensions of our form of democracy. Relief of this tension lies in the direction of political leadership and a more informed electorate, not in denying the validity of opinion às the basis of democratic government.

The complexity of legislative problems. The standard of legislative output judges legislative performance or action against the *total* range of problems government faces. Conversely it ignores many practical limits on legislative initiative by either the President *or* Congress. Obviously resources, such as the time of political executives, are limited, and priorities must be defined. New problems may not be readily understood or legislative remedies easily stated. Some problems may

[15] See Richard F. Fenno's discussion of the shift of public mood in the politics of appropriation in *The Power of the Purse: Appropriations Politics in Congress* (Boston: Little, Brown & Co., 1966), pp. 471 ff.

not be easily solved at a given level of understanding or technique. Compare, for example, the level of sophistication in basic data and tools of economic analysis available to top policy makers in the 1930's with today. Arthur Schlesinger, Jr., attributes the confusion of the lopsided Roosevelt Congress of 1935–36 in part to the exhaustion of the policy initiatives of the Hundred Days. The basic reason for inaction was that Roosevelt "could not lead until he knew where he wanted to go." [16] The response of both President and Congress to the urban crisis and racial unrest of the 1960's exhibited some of this uncertainty.

The failure of Congress to legislate, therefore, may be rooted in part in the nature of the problems themselves. At issue is not the performance of Congress *in vacuo* but the capacity of our entire governmental system. It is not realistic to expect Congress to have legislative solutions to every question. It *is* fair to ask whether the President *and* Congress have made explicit the agenda of national priorities, whether the public understands and supports these, and whether the President *and* Congress are investigating, developing, and enacting appropriate legislation.

The intensity and extent of opposition. Another critical factor in determining the success of a particular item of legislation is the presence of an intense minority opposed to the legislation. An intense minority, at important risks and costs, may exercise the option of the filibuster.[17] It may delay a legislative process that assumes comity and operation by unanimous consent at innumerable points. It can usually frustrate an apathetic majority. The opposition of the solid Democratic South to all forms of civil rights legislation is the classic example. In the face of intense southern opposition, liberal civil rights advocates in the 1950's frequently could not muster a majority on key test votes, let alone the necessary two-thirds to break a fili-

[16] *The Politics of Upheaval,* Vol III of *The Age of Roosevelt* (Boston: Houghton Mifflin Co., 1960), p. 11. James L. Sundquist, in an analysis of major domestic legislation from 1953 through 1966, defines a *dual* legislative process. Problems are first identified and solutions generated before legislation can be successfully guided through the executive hierarchy and Congress. *Politics and Policy: The Eisenhower, Kennedy and Johnson Years* (Washington, D.C.: The Brookings Institution, 1968).

[17] The southern forces in the civil rights debate of 1964, led by Senator Richard Russell (D-Ga.), misjudged their ability to block cloture. The result of total resistance was a much stronger bill than they might have obtained through compromise with the Senate majority. See *Revolution in Civil Rights,* pp. 58 ff.

buster.[18] Not until 1964 was there a determined majority capable of decisive action. Another classic case is the combined opposition of racial and religious interests to federal aid to education. Although President Kennedy may have had a nominal majority in the House in favor of federal school aid, his 1961 education bill was defeated by a majority coalition of the reconstructed Committee on Rules *and* a majority of the House (on a Calendar Wednesday vote).[19]

Certain rules and procedures in the Congress — notably the cloture requirement of an extraordinary majority in the Senate — make it possible for an intense minority, liberal or conservative, to delay or obstruct legislation. There are effective limits, however, to how far a minority will push its point against a determined majority. Informal norms and expectations place important constraints on minority obstruction. Lewis Froman, Jr., states that it would be possible for a single congressman to tie up the House of Representatives for "many hours on any day," if he were so disposed. "The fact that members employ delaying tactics infrequently, and normally only when many other members support them," he concludes, "is illustrative of the importance of informal as well as formal rules and procedures." [20]

In summary, effective minority obstruction in the legislative process usually indicates the presence of an intense and widely based minority. Our system permits this exception to majority rule. In fact much of the debate about the cloture rule in the Senate since it was first instituted in 1917 has centered on what constitutes an acceptable extraordinary majority (i.e., two-thirds of the Senate, two-thirds present and voting, three-fourths, etc.) rather than the total elimination of such a requirement.

Leadership commitment — presidential and congressional. Without leadership commitment, the prospects for a given item of legislation are dim, a point that is often overlooked. To maximize chances for

---

[18] On most of these votes, Senate liberals did not have leadership support. See Howard Shuman, "Senate Rules and the Civil Rights Bill," *APSR*, December 1957, pp. 955–75.

[19] See H. D. Price, "Race, Religion, and the Rules Committee: The Kennedy Aid to Education Bills," in Alan F. Westin (ed.), *The Uses of Power: 7 Cases in American Politics* (New York: Harcourt, Brace & World, 1962), pp. 1–71.

[20] Froman, *The Congressional Process: Strategies, Rules and Procedures* (The Study of Congress Series; Boston: Little, Brown & Co., 1967), p. 63. For an example of the breakdown of informal procedures, see the account in the *Congressional Record*, October 8 and 9, 1968, of Republicans' holding the House in continuous session for more than 27 hours.

favorable action a legislative request as a general rule should be clearly stated and presented to Congress early in the session. The President and his spokesmen should carefully follow the legislation through Congress, continually giving congressional leaders both advice on administration priorities at each turn of the legislative process and support as requested. Congressional leaders who will manage the legislative strategy within Congress must in turn know that they have the President's support and must be willing to commit leadership resources and prestige to a bill.

A bill may fail to get such full leadership support for a variety of reasons, some of which we have already mentioned. The President may have a narrow margin in Congress and as a result may have to choose which bills he will actively support. He may make requests, give them nominal support, and let them die. This was, in part, the fate of Kennedy's education legislation.[21] Or he may, like Harry Truman, know in advance that he cannot get congressional action and submit a legislative program that he can use as a campaign issue. Or the President may sense an economizing mood in Congress but be unwilling to cut legislative and funding requests, thereby limiting his effectiveness with Congress.[22]

The President may delay legislative requests because of division within his own administration or uncertainty about how to proceed with legislation. Delays in introduction mean delays in legislative action. Uncertainty in administration strategy almost surely means trouble for congressional leaders. The congressional leadership itself may be unwilling to make a full commitment. The leaders in Congress most likely have a better reading than does the President of the intensity and extent of opposition to a given bill. And since it is *their* institutional leadership that is at stake, they are understandably less enthusiastic than the President about risking defeat against a hostile House or Senate.

21 H. D. Price concludes that the lack of presidential leadership was evident. "The President was simply not prepared to jeopardize his whole legislative program — and perhaps his chances for re-election — by a bitter fight to the death for aid to education. Lacking a popular ground swell in support of the program, the President's chief alternative was to press for some acceptable compromise to aid for non-public schools. And this was a move involving the very greatest risks for a Catholic President." *Op. cit.*, p. 68.

22 This was an obvious problem of President Johnson's relations with the 90th Congress. See also Richard Neustadt on Eisenhower and budgetary politics, *Presidential Power: The Politics of Leadership* (New York: John Wiley & Sons, 1960), pp. 64–80.

One way in which the party leadership in the House or an opposing majority in the House avoid embarrassing floor defeats of the President's program is to use the Rules Committee either to delay a vote on a bill until a favorable majority can be built or to prevent the bill from coming to a vote at all. Thus while serving as a public "whipping-boy," the committee may actually function to enhance leadership control over scheduling and timing and the chances for successful legislative outcomes.[23]

Leadership commitment, then, is a critical factor in certain marginal votes. But if one or more of the factors previously noted sharply reduces the prospects for legislative success, presidential or congressional leadership may well be a matter of form.

Biases introduced through congressional representation. Another factor that has marginal yet potentially decisive influence in certain legislative outcomes is bias introduced into the congressional system of representation. In the previous chapter we examined the popular conception of rural overrepresentation and found that by the mid-1960's, under the impact of court-ordered reapportionment, the House was rapidly approaching districts of roughly equal population. Other factors in the electoral system, however, when combined with internal rules and procedures, have effectively overrepresented certain interests. The major historical example has been the one-party Democratic South. One-party hegemony in national politics was designed to protect the South's regional interests, notably opposition to federal civil rights legislation.[24] In this case representational bias coincided with an intense minority. Noncompetitive congressional districts meant congressional seniority and power on committees. Southern influence in the Democratic party in the immediate postwar period was further enhanced by a northern Republican sweep in 1946. However, today northern urban Democrats account for an increasing share of safe seats within the House, and continued Republican party growth has broken up much of the solid South.[25]

[23] For an interpretation of the less recognized functions of the Rules Committee in the congressional system see Robert L. Peabody, "The Enlarged Rules Committee," in Robert L. Peabody and Nelson B. Polsby (eds.), *New Perspectives on the House of Representatives* (Chicago: Rand McNally & Co., 1963), pp. 129–64.

[24] See V. O. Key, Jr., *Southern Politics in State and Nation* (New York: Alfred A. Knopf, 1949), Part II: "Political Leadership — The One-Party System in the Nation," pp. 315–82.

[25] See Raymond E. Wolfinger and Joan Heifetz, "Safe Seats, Seniority, and Power in Congress," APSR, June 1965, pp. 337–49.

Committee specialization and seniority confer legislative advantage on members from noncompetitive districts. The characteristics of these districts have become much more varied and complex over the past two decades. Compared with other factors such as party balance and the presence of intense minorities, representational bias appears to have declined to the point where it is much less critical to legislative outcomes.

Biases introduced through rules and procedures. Like the previous factor, rules and procedures appear to be of marginal or secondary consequence in determining legislative outcomes. We have noted that rules tend to reflect majority strength in Congress. (The one exception is the Senate cloture rule.) The recent history of the 21-day rule is a good illustration of the "see-saw" effect of alternating liberal or conservative majorities in organizing the House. Liberal majorities were sufficiently large to enact the 21-day rule during the 81st (1949–51) and 89th (1965–67) Congresses. The rule gave the House Democratic leadership, with the backing of the liberal majority, additional leverage on the Rules Committee to report legislation. In its most recent form, the rule authorized the Speaker, at his discretion, to recognize the chairman or any member of the committee so authorized to call up any resolution which had been pending before the Committee on Rules for 21 days.[26] When a more conservative majority was elected to the 82nd and 90th Congresses, the rule was dropped. The fact that the leadership could institute such a rules change in the first place indicates that it enjoyed a favorable enough party balance to pass other critical legislation as well.

This suggests a basic dilemma of congressional reform. One study on the subject concludes: "When majorities are able to work their will in Congress, they see little need for procedural change. When majorities are slender or unstable, the need for attaining high-priority legislative goals diverts attention from reform efforts." [27] Another way of stating the problem is that a majority determined enough to reorganize power in the Congress is probably powerful enough to achieve its legislative objectives without reorganizing power and, conversely, a reorganization of power to favor certain legislative outcomes can survive only so long as it and the desired legislative outcomes enjoy majority support.

[26] See Froman, *op. cit.*, pp. 97–99, for a discussion of the two forms of the 21-day rule and the extent of their use.

[27] Roger H. Davidson, David M. Kovenock, and Michael K. O'Leary, *Congress in Crisis: Politics and Congressional Reform* (Belmont, Cal.: Wadsworth Publishing Co., 1966), p. 110.

Thus the controversy over congressional rules — at least insofar as it is concerned with the specific question of legislative output — is directed at somewhat of a straw man.

In discussing factors affecting legislative outcomes, we have attempted to qualify the emphasis on legislative output as a standard of congressional performance. The most important factors impeding legislative output originate outside of the legislature and are not readily or directly susceptible to change by the legislature: party strength, public opinion, the complexity of legislative problems, intense minorities, and presidential leadership. The standard of high legislative output thus assigns to Congress greater expectations than it can reasonably fulfill within the American political system. The standard assumes major reforms in both Congress and the political system as a whole.

Of the various models we have considered, the presidential-responsible party model, with its programmatic emphasis and organization of Congress under control of the presidential party, would maximize legislative output. In the absence of effective national parties, the presidential-pluralist model would probably be the next most favorable for enhancing the President's chances for legislative successes. Any of the models that permits a strong and independent congressional role reduce the responsiveness of the system to programmatic presidential leadership.

THE STANDARD APPLIED: CONGRESSIONAL RESPONSE TO URBAN PROBLEMS. How well has Congress functioned as a legislative body to meet the needs of the nation's cities? Its critics point to the urgent need for massive federal funds in the form of a "Marshall Plan" for urban America. They score the long record of congressional delays in enacting housing legislation, in establishing a cabinet-level Department for Urban Affairs, and in endorsing and funding a variety of executive-initiated programs for urban transportation, education, metropolitan planning, ghetto rehabilitation, etc. From a liberal policy perspective, congressional legislative output has clearly been inadequate. And the prospects for significant improvement in time to contain the nation's urban crisis do not appear bright.

The congressional response to urban problems illustrates the tension between its representative and legislative functions. A brief review of the record since 1932 reveals this tension.

Roosevelt's New Deal Congresses enacted a range of legislation that had a direct impact on urban development: The Federal Home Loan Bank Act of 1932, The National Housing Act of 1934 and the Housing Act of 1937, The Civil Aeronautics Act of 1938, support of municipal airport facilities, and the cash grant-in-aid system.[28] Roscoe C. Martin dates 1932 as "a sort of geologic fault line in the development of the federal system." The cash grant-in-aid and depression-spurred recovery programs established the cities as a third tier in the American federal system with direct channels to the federal government. Congress shared in the definition of this new direct public commitment to urban America, and it has since been reluctant to relinquish its role as a partner.[29] The rapid emergence of a "metro-urban" society following World War II and the limitations on an active state role in urban problems accelerated the trend during the past two decades.

Scarcely had the Roosevelt administration begun to define its urban program, when it encountered the resistance of a conservative coalition in Congress. In 1937, the Rules Committee in the House of Representatives fell under the control of a bipartisan majority of Republicans and southern Democrats. The powerful committee, which had backed F.D.R.'s earlier legislation, reporting ten closed rules alone during the first session of the 73rd Congress (1933), could no longer be counted upon as a reliable instrument of the majority party and its legislative program. The shift in the control of the Rules Committee was only symptomatic of Roosevelt's basic problem — he no longer had an effective majority in Congress.

Why? The answer lies in the changing emphasis of Roosevelt's legislative program and in the corresponding difficulties of mobilizing

[28] For a summary of federal programs in metropolitan areas see Robert H. Connery and Richard H. Leach, *The Federal Government and Metropolitan Areas* (Government Affairs Institute Series: Government in Metropolitan Areas, Luther Gulick (ed.); Cambridge, Mass.: Harvard University Press, 1960), Chap. I; and Roscoe C. Martin, *The Cities and the Federal System* (New York: Atherton Press, 1965), Chaps. IV–V.

[29] Martin, in an incisive analysis of the Federal-Aid Airport Program, concludes that in passing the Federal Airport Act of 1946 "Congress heard the states' rights argument, which was presented forcefully and at length, then turned to the cities as a basic partner of the national government" in the new program. "Congressional insistence on maintaining and systematizing these relations" stemmed from Congress' desire to maintain "close control over the federal-aid airport program, particularly as it involved the larger cities. . . . In recognizing the cities as partners with the federal government, Congress thus incidentally but effectively maximized its own role." *Op. cit.*, pp. 106–9.

congressional majorities to enact it. Although Roosevelt ran up record presidential pluralities, he was unable to translate these into congressional pluralities. The two majorities in the American system had begun to diverge sharply.

Roosevelt's New Deal began to assume a distinctive urban hue with the 1936 campaign. The new Democratic coalition was based on a politics of ideology rather than on the older Democratic politics of organization.[30] The 1932 campaign had blended the two. The stunning election and the sense of national crisis solidified the Democratic party behind the new President. Roosevelt staffed the new emergency apparatus of the Executive branch not from the "organization" but from the "coalition." "The executive branch, under his direct control," Schlesinger observes, "became more and more the instrument of the politics of coalition and ideology. As this happened, the legislative branch became increasingly the stronghold of the professional politician. So the normal tension between the Congress and the President was aggravated by the rising tension between the old and the new politics." [31] By 1936 Roosevelt was moving consciously beyond the traditional party base to build a predominantly northern and urban Democratic party.

The conservative upsurge after 1936 coincides with the increasingly northern urban character of the New Deal.[32] Several factors appear to have contributed to the emergence of an anti-Roosevelt coalition. The most obvious was the urban-rural split within the Democratic party. After 1937, few rural areas were exposed to an economic crisis comparable to that of 1933–35. Rural interests continued to support government programs of direct benefit to themselves, but many former New Deal supporters from rural districts balked at the increasing demands of the urban Democrats. Conservative Democratic defections were as common among newcomers (elected in 1932 or after) as veterans, although they ran higher in the South and in rural areas.[33]

With the 1938 elections the Republican party almost doubled its

[30] See Schlesinger, *The Politics of Upheaval*, Chap. XXII, "The Politics of the Second New Deal," pp. 409–23.

[31] *Ibid.*, pp. 412–13.

[32] See James T. Patterson, *Congressional Conservatism and the New Deal: The Growth of the Conservative Coalition in Congress, 1933–1939* (Lexington, Ky.: University of Lexington Press, 1967).

[33] A statistical analysis of conservative Democrats in Congress between 1933 and 1939 is included as an Appendix in Patterson, *op. cit.*, pp. 339–52.

strength (from 89 in 1936 to 169) denying Roosevelt thereafter the sizable party majorities he had enjoyed during his first six years. Much of the country sensed that the emergency was over. Business and moderate elements regained strength with economic recovery, and the House quickly reflected a new sense of self-confidence and independence from the President. The economic setback of 1938–39 served further to discredit New Deal policies in the eyes of the conservatives.

Fundamental to Roosevelt's problems was the lack of cohesion of Democratic liberals in the Congress. James T. Patterson, in his study of congressional coalitions of this period concludes:

> To liberals it is a distressing thought, but the voting behavior of nonconservatives in Congress from 1937 through 1939 exhibited little more breadth of vision — and a good deal less unity of purpose — than the behavior of conservatives. The conservative coalition was less than monolithic, but liberals, more disparate as a group and faced with the more difficult problem of agreeing upon a positive program, were hardly a coalition at all.[34]

The conclusion is fairly obvious: The political balance of support of domestic programs for urban areas was shifting against Roosevelt, and Congress reflected the balance. Roosevelt could not develop support for a general legislative program from the parochial demands of the components of his coalition, and the urban interests by themselves were, regardless of malapportionment, a minority in the Congress. (The real expansion of the suburbs and resulting population inequalities in congressional districts was a postwar phenomenon.) Roosevelt's program suffered simply because Congress was *too* representative of the political climate of the country.

The postwar period preserved the tension. The Republican congressional victories of 1946 and 1952 brought the party balance full cycle from the mid-1930's. Truman made a frontal assault on the congressional majority in the 1948 presidential campaign and succeeded in reviving the Roosevelt coalition for one more term. He used his urban and welfare programs — notably the Taft-Ellender-Wagner Housing bill which had died in the 80th Congress — in a brilliant political campaign strategy that hopelessly split the Republican party. The Democratic margin in the 81st Congress (1949–50) was sufficient to give Truman the Housing Act of 1949 but little else of the Fair

[34] *Ibid.*, p. 335.

Deal.[35] By 1952, the Democratic coalition had become, according to Samuel Lubell's description, "so furiously divided that it had lost all capacity for decisive political action." [36] The Democratic party, "deadlocked in self-conceit by its own successes" had lost the dynamism of reform.

Despite the division of the Democratic coalition, the national investment in the states and cities, through grant-in-aid programs, continued to expand during the postwar years.[37] Title I of the Housing Act of 1949 instituted a federal program of slum clearance and community development and redevelopment. The urban renewal concept was expanded and refined in amending acts of 1954, 1956, 1959, 1961, and 1964. The major Housing Act of 1965, with the exception of the controversial "rent supplement" program, enjoyed wide bipartisan support within Congress. Major new federal programs were begun or expanded in water pollution control (1948 and 1950), interstate highways (1956), airport development (1946), and mass transportation (1964). Total federal grants-in-aid to state and local governments have mounted steadily from about $1 billion in 1945 to almost $11 billion in 1965.[38] Without going into detail in any one of these areas, especially the extensive legislative innovation of the 89th Congress, we can conclude that Congress, regardless of which party has controlled the White House or Congress, has steadily expanded federal legislation and funds for urban America. How appropriate these legislative actions have been to the problems they were designed to solve and how adequate the funding of them has been remain legitimate issues for debate. The fact of extensive congressional involvement, however, is not.

The tension between President and Congress on the rate of urban investment has nonetheless continued into the 1960's. President Kennedy's failure to get congressional approval of a Department of Urban Affairs in February, 1962 was strangely reminiscent of Roosevelt's problems with Congress. The Senate by a 42–58 roll-call vote refused

[35] For a case study of the politics of housing legislation during this period see Richard O. Davies, *Housing Reform During the Truman Administration* (Columbia, Mo.: University of Missouri Press, 1966). Few pieces of legislation before Congress have been as pivotal in the electoral strategy of a presidential campaign.

[36] *Op. cit.*, Chap. II, "The Man Who Bought Time."

[37] See Connery and Leach, *op. cit.*, and Martin, *op. cit.*; also *Housing a Nation* (Washington, D.C.: Congressional Quarterly Service, 1966).

[38] See "Federal Grants-in-Aid to State, Local Governments," *Congress and the Nation: 1945–1964, A Review of Government and Politics in the Postwar Years* (Washington, D.C.: Congressional Quarterly Service, 1965), pp. 1384–91; and *Congressional Quarterly*, Weekly Report No. 12, March 24, 1967, pp. 445–50.

to discharge the Senate Committee on Government Operations from further consideration of the Kennedy Reorganization Plan, and the House disapproved the plan by an overwhelming 264–150 roll-call vote. Kennedy had similar difficulties in mobilizing a liberal coalition, winning only 137 Democratic votes and losing 18 northern Democrats on the roll call.[39] In 1965, Congress enacted President Johnson's legislative request for a Department of Housing and Urban Development (HUD).

Has Congress been responsive to the urban needs of America? It probably has, to the extent that the American people have sensed these needs. Mayor John Lindsay's testimony to the Joint Committee on the Organization of Congress in May, 1965, while he was still a congressman, is a particularly timely interpretation of congressional performance:

> One reason it works is that the people make it work. Congress as a whole is never really ahead of the people. If anything, it is a little behind and it struggles to stay even. It has stayed even enough so that we have adjusted ourselves without having any real eruptions in the country. If it doesn't stay close enough you will have eruptions.[40]

The eruptions in civil disorders since then, in spite of congressional approval of such major new programs as rent supplements, model cities, and the Office of Economic Opportunity, suggest that Congress and the Executive must carefully evaluate the present legislative and program response to the urban crisis.

How Well Does Congress Legislate?
Qualitative Standards for the Legislative Process

A second view of how Congress performs its legislative function places primary emphasis on qualitative standards of the legislative process.[41]

[39] For a summary analysis of the vote see "House Kills Urban Affairs Reorganization Plan," *Congressional Quarterly*, Weekly Report No. 8, February 23, 1962, pp. 275–77, 309–11. An extensive case study on the subject, by Judith Heimlich, will be published shortly in a Brookings Institution volume of case studies on Congress and urban affairs.

[40] *Hearings: Organization of Congress*, 89th Congress, 1st Session, 1965, p. 456. Lindsay also sees biennial congressional elections as "one of the reasons the Congress moves along. . . . [T]hat is the trigger that makes the thing work."

[41] See, for example, Ernst Freund, *Standards of American Legislation* (2nd ed.; Chicago: The University of Chicago Press, 1965), pp. 215–73. Freund cites the following principles that should guide legislation: the correlation of provisions; standardization (to advance the other main objects of law: certainty, objectivity,

For example, does legislative decision making enhance the legitimacy of presidential and congressional action? Does it embody a desired set of representational values? Does it follow agreed-upon rules of procedure? Does it lead to legislation that is coherent, clear, and operable? We have already suggested tensions that exist between various representational values. Our discussion here will focus on proper procedures in the legislative process.

In contrast, the standard of legislative output views rules and procedures as means to legislative ends. It emphasizes the obstacles that must be maneuvered about or negotiated in the legislative process before a bill becomes law. Strategy and tactics dominate every stage. In Bertram Gross's words, every important bill is "a fighting document designed for combat almost as literally and carefully as any tank or artillery piece intended for a battlefield." [42] Committee hearings merely amplify the relative strengths of the contestants. Rules and procedure are manipulated by liberals and conservatives alike to achieve desired legislative outcomes.

Qualitative standards generally assume a rational-legal model of the legislative process similar to what we have previously described as the constitutional balance model of legislative-executive relations. Congress and its committees constitute a deliberative system in which decision making is both representative and rational. Congress actively seeks balanced solutions that take into consideration both the legitimate interests of its constituency and national policy requirements. According to this view Congress is more than an arena of interest-group conflict but less than a council of wise elders presiding over the destinies of the nation.

PROCEDURAL NORMS OF THE LEGISLATIVE PROCESS. We can use the following procedural norms as standards in evaluating the legislative process.[43]

---

stability, and uniformity); and, constitutional principles (the protection of vested rights and equality).

[42] *The Legislative Struggle: A Study in Social Combat* (McGraw-Hill Series in Political Science; New York: McGraw-Hill Book Co., 1953), p. 211. See also Robert Bendiner's recent commentary on Congress, *Obstacle Course on Capitol Hill* (New York: McGraw-Hill Book Co., 1964).

[43] Studies using this approach to evaluate Congress include Donald G. Morgan, *Congress and the Constitution: A Study of Responsibility* (Cambridge, Mass.: The Belknap Press, 1966), pp. 344–60; and Ernest S. Griffith, *Congress: Its Contemporary Role* (3rd ed.; New York: New York University Press, 1961), pp. 33–37. The following discussion, in part, combines criteria from these two studies.

Advance agreement on procedure. Rules of procedure are explicit and have been formally agreed upon by the Legislature. Committees follow the rules of the House and Senate. Internal committee procedure is specified in a supplementary body of committee rules. Subcommittee procedure is similarly regulated.[44] Rules are of particular importance in the House of Representatives because of the size of that body and the necessity for strict control of access to and time on the floor. The Senate, by contrast, operates mostly by unanimous consent and by informally agreed-upon procedure. Rules are more often invoked to delay rather than expedite business. In any event, all participants should know the rules of procedure, and legislators should have had an opportunity to ratify them.

Adequate preparation. The subject of legislation has been clearly stated in advance. Full and open notice has been given to all interested parties. Representative and informed testimony has been solicited. Members of Congress and committee staff have prepared themselves for committee hearings.

Fair, open, and recorded hearings. The method for selecting witnesses is public and subject to appeal. Minority points of view are fairly represented. Hearings are well attended and marked by a meaningful two-way interchange between witnesses and congressmen. Hearings are open to the public and adequately reported by the press. Committee hearings are published and indexed. Hearings are a major part of the "public record" on a given piece of legislation. How well they are constructed, managed, and reported is therefore an important qualitative standard in judging the legislative process.

Adequate, pertinent information. Adequate, timely, and relevant information is developed for legislative decisions. Committee staff process and screen information to keep subcommittee members, committee members, and congressmen in general informed at various stages of decision. Committees do not hoard information as a form of power. The legislative process serves to inform members of Congress and the public.

Committee (and subcommittee) deliberation. Since the committees are the basic units in a decentralized system of decision making, *how* decisions are reached within committee is a central qualitative

[44] A provocative discussion of majority abuse of rules (and abuse in the *absence* of rules) is provided by Senator Robert P. Griffin (R-Mich.), "Rules and Procedures of the Standing Committees," in Mary McInnis (ed.), *We Propose: A Modern Congress* (New York: McGraw-Hill Book Co., 1966), pp. 37–53.

concern. A high level of performance at this stage assumes that preparation, hearings, and the gathering of information have been adequate at previous stages. Discussion within committee is encouraged. The chairman or a few members do not dominate proceedings. Committee members are able to express their views and propose amendments. Rules are fairly applied. Decisions are put to a vote of the entire committee.

Informative committee reports. Committee reports serve to inform members on legislation to be debated on the floor. They reflect adequately the deliberations and decisions of the entire committee. They include a summary and an index, minority reports, and separate views. They are approved by the full committee before they are released.

Full public debate. The most visible and authoritative stages of the legislative process are those that place an entire house of the Congress in full public view, i.e., floor debate and voting. Adequate time must be afforded for public debate. Opposing points of view are given time for expression. Votes are recorded.

Full public debate of legislation assumes sufficient time to permit the public to grasp the significance of an issue and register preferences with elected representatives. The American legislative system with its bicameral structure and double process of authorization and appropriations (i.e., the passage of substantive legislation *prior* to any funding) affords "staged consideration" at multiple decision points. This means *both* greater opportunity to register public sentiment and represent various interests in the legislative process *and*, of course, more points for delay or obstruction. The particular and complicated form of our legislative process enhances its "representativeness" while reducing its efficiency (in legislative output). One illustration of staged consideration resulting in improved legislation is the Atomic Energy Act of 1946. The May–Johnson bill, which sanctioned military control of atomic energy, was hastily passed by the House but detained in the Senate until scientific leaders could advise a Senate Special Committee on the preparation of alternative legislation with much broader public support (the McMahon bill).[45] We would normally expect

[45] See Byron S. Miller, "A Law Is Passed: The Atomic Energy Act of 1946," *University of Chicago Law Review*, 1948, pp. 799–821. Miller concludes that the Senate Committee version, an "active group project," was "a superior piece of legislation, a testimonial to the latent capacities of free discussion. . . . [R]arely has a legislative body making its own decisions emerged with a bill reflecting as high a calibre of statesmanship . . ." (p. 809).

more controversial legislation to require more extended public and congressional debate. The option of the filibuster in the Senate enables any intense minority to demand just such a debate.

Three additional values, or criteria, may be applied to congressional debate, although they apply generally to all stages of the legislative process:

Proportionate attention. The most important provisions of the bill being considered receive the most attention. Discussion and debate are focused. At a more general level, the agenda of Congress gives proportionate time to major items of legislation in the priority defined by the President and the congressional leadership.

Opportunities for detailed amendment.[46] Assuming a dual system of presidential and congressional representation, the legislative process should afford sufficient opportunity for the amendment of legislation by Congress. This value acquires increased importance with the trend toward executive submission of draft legislation to Congress; i.e., amendment has become a central form of congressional initiative in the legislative process. Normally amendment will occur in committee, although both the full House (especially in Committee of the Whole) and Senate retain the power to amend the work of their respective committees.

Respect for opposition and minorities. As a rule, a determined majority can get what it wants in the legislative process (the one exception being that an intense minority can force the requirement of an extraordinary majority in the Senate). Majority action, however, especially partisan-majority action, may sacrifice many of the process values implied in a rational-legal or consensual view of the legislative process. A style of decision making by concurrent rather than numerical majority is more conducive to the procedural values we have enumerated.

To summarize, a second way of evaluating the congressional function of legislation stresses proper procedure in the legislative process. Proper procedure, in turn, assumes that Congress is a deliberative

46 This criterion is distinctively American. European parliamentary governments have generally professionalized the function of legislative drafting within the Executive. Ernst Freund considers American legislation qualitatively inferior to European legislation as a result. *Op. cit.*, pp. 287–94. In a similar vein Froman states that the amending process is used in Congress for the most part by those who wish to *weaken* legislation. *Op. cit.*, p. 77.

body, that it acts independently in the legislative process, and that it is capable of reaching rational, representative decisions based on a broad consensus.

THE STANDARD APPLIED: CONGRESS AND THE AID-TO-EDUCATION IM-PASSE. Two decades (1945–65) of debate on federal aid to elementary education present one of the most tortuous histories of legislation before Congress.[47] This legislative history affords a wealth of illustrative examples of how improper procedure can affect legislative performance.

More basic factors than improper procedure probably determined the legislative fate of the range of education bills that failed to win congressional approval during this period. Party balance was frequently close, thereby barring partisan legislation. Increased partisanship during the 86th Congress (1959–60) "cost the federal aid proponents critical increments of Republican and Southern Democratic support." [48] Although public opinion registered growing support for federal aid and congressional majorities were found in both Houses of Congress on more than one occasion, majorities came unhinged for a variety of reasons. Intense minorities associated with the church-state issue and the perennial Powell civil rights amendment presented the legislative leadership with an almost impossible strategic and tactical situation. Neither President Eisenhower nor President Kennedy chose to assume command of, or maintain sustained support for, his legislative proposals. At crucial junctures there was no telephone call, no public statement, from the White House. Eisenhower did not check the coalition maneuvers of House Republican leaders Joseph Martin (R-Mass.) or Charles Halleck (R-Ind.). Kennedy tried to dismiss the parochial school issue, and when it came to the fore in Congress he never squarely faced it. Nor was the congressional leadership coordinated or particularly imaginative in its approaches to the admit-

[47] See Richard F. Fenno, Jr., "The House of Representatives and Federal Aid to Education" in Peabody and Polsby (eds.), *op. cit.*, pp. 195–235; Frank J. Munger and Richard F. Fenno, Jr., *National Politics in Federal Aid to Education* (Economics and Politics and Public Education Series, No. 3; Syracuse, N.Y.: Syracuse University Press, 1962); H. D. Price, *op. cit.*; Bendiner, *op. cit.*; and Philip Meranto, *The Politics of Federal Aid to Education in 1965: A Study in Political Innovation* (Education in Large Cities Series; Syracuse, N.Y.: Syracuse University Press, 1967).

[48] Fenno, "The House of Representatives and Federal Aid to Education," p. 225.

tedly difficult problem. The anti-school aid forces in the House, led by Judge Howard W. Smith (D-Va.), Chairman of the Committee on Rules, were clearly the masters of the legislative situation. One cannot criticize the opposition for playing the legislative game as hard and as well as it can. In what appears to be even the most arbitrary power play of Judge Smith — the Rules Committee 7-to-5 vote to deny a conference rule to the 1960 federal-aid-to-education bill on the *first* occasion that such legislation had won majorities in both the House and Senate — the wily southerner exposed the confusion and lack of resolution that characterized the majority. By not challenging the Rules Committee, Eisenhower was relieved of the choice of whether or not to veto a strong Democratic bill in an election year. The Democrats in turn preferred to keep the bill a major campaign issue. At the same time northern Democrats did not want to risk a party-splitting fight over Judge Smith's prerogatives. Major interests, such as the National Education Association, decided to wait for a full loaf after the election rather than fight for a more limited bill in 1960.[49]

Underlying all these political considerations ran the tension between the congressional functions of legislation and representation. In assessing why the House of Representatives could not act on education legislation during the 1950's, Richard Fenno concludes that two prerequisites were missing — flexibility and compromise:

> Two reasons that these attributes may be difficult to achieve are the nature of House members' constituencies and the frequency of House elections. Large numbers of representatives find that they must respond to a single dominant constituency interest — be it that of private school aid, school integration, school construction, teachers' salaries, or federal control. To the degree that his district's interests are homogeneous, a congressman may be bound tightly to one position on certain aspects of the federal aid controversy. And his legislative maneuverability may be further restricted by the necessity of standing for election every two years.[50]

[49] See Robert Bendiner's discussion of this exercise of Rules Committee power. Apparently Democratic liberals wanted Judge Smith to succeed. Congressman Richard Bolling (D-Mo.) privately admitted, "We were planning a full-scale attack on the power of the Committee and we felt that the worse it looked, the better." *Op. cit.*, pp. 169–71.

[50] "The House of Representatives and Federal Aid to Education," pp. 228–29. H. D. Price makes a parallel observation. "On the explosive parochial school

Again, we are faced with the conclusion that the House, if anything, may be *too* representative of the American people.

In 1965, the election of a heavily Democratic Congress in the wake of the Johnson plurality, changed the legislative context drastically. The President, advised by a task force headed by John W. Gardner, then President of the Carnegie Corporation, presented Congress with a new formula for federal aid. The traditional approaches of across-the-board aid for school construction and teachers' salaries were scrapped in favor of an "aid to children" approach giving special types of aid to "educationally deprived" children. By concentrating on the child, the controversy over institutional aid for private and parochial schools was evaded. Equally significant to the new legislative approach was the absence of the civil rights issue, which had been removed from the aid-to-education controversy by enactment of the Civil Rights Act of 1964. The Elementary and Secondary Education Act of 1965 passed the House and Senate in near record time and by large majorities. On April 11, 1965, President Lyndon B. Johnson signed HR2362 into law in front of the former one-room school house at Stonewall, Texas, where he began his education.

This brief review of some of the factors that frustrated and finally produced a decisive legislative majority provides a setting for our primary question: How well did Congress meet the qualitative standards we have outlined for the legislative process? Two periods of the aid-to-education bill's legislative history illustrate two quite different procedural problems.

Committee obstruction: The House Committee on Education and Labor, 1946–58. The rational-legal model of the legislative process assumes that the appropriate legislative committee and its leadership are committed to positive and fair legislative inquiry and decision. For more than a decade, however, the House Committee on Education and Labor or the subcommittee of that committee charged with aid-to-education legislation was chaired by unsympathetic or hostile chairmen. Graham Barden (D-N.C.), chairman for eight years until his retirement in 1960, while professing support for federal aid to education, consistently worked to prevent passage of such legislation.[51]

---

issue, for example, compromise was accomplished *within* most senators themselves, but would have to be negotiated *between* members in the House." *Op. cit.*, pp. 51–52.

[51] For a graphic summary of House action on Federal Aid to Education Bills, 1945–65, see Meranto, *op. cit.*, p. 112.

Some of the tactics Barden employed in committee and on the floor included:

1. Refusing to institute committee rules specifying regular committee procedure;
2. Scheduling committee meetings irregularly, sometimes with gaps of two months between sessions;
3. Terminating a committee meeting by declaring the absence of a quorum, even when a quorum of the committee was present;
4. Not recognizing committee members with whom he disagreed;
5. Keeping the committee staff small and inactive;
6. Holding extensive desultory hearings without any coordinated legislative focus;
7. Arbitrarily limiting the range of subjects to be considered in committee hearings (i.e., to legislation on public schools only);
8. Calling a "quickie" vote of the committee to kill legislation when an anti-education majority was present;
9. Giving disproportionate time to opponents of aid-to-education while serving as floor manager of an education bill;
10. Resigning as floor manager of a bill during a critical period of floor consideration.

Compounding legislative sabotage by the chairman was a tradition of partisan cleavage on the committee which has survived well beyond Barden's departure. Education and Labor is rated by most members of the House of Representatives as the most partisan of House committees. During crucial months of 1961, while the fate of the Kennedy aid-to-education bills hung in the balance, the new committee chairman, Adam Clayton Powell (D-N.Y.), and the ranking minority member, Carroll D. Kearns (R-Pa.), physically split the committee staff and office facilities in a bitter public quarrel over majority-minority staff allocation. Compared with powerful committees like House Appropriations and the Joint Committee on Atomic Energy, Education and Labor lacks traditions that promote committee integration and facilitate the building of legislative consensus.[52] The committee has a dual jurisdiction over two legislative areas with high

[52] For a discussion of factors promoting integration and legislative consensus within congressional committees, see Fenno, "The House Appropriations Committee as a Political System: The Problem of Integration," APSR, June 1962, pp. 310–24; and Harold P. Green and Alan Rosenthal, Government of the Atom: The Integration of Powers (New York: Atherton Press, 1963), pp. 44–65. The absence of most of these factors is underlined in Fenno's comparative analysis of the House Committee on Education and Labor.

ideological content and major outside lobby pressures. Moreover, members have more often been recruited to the committee on the basis of their philosophical position on labor-management relations than education. Taken together, these factors and the legislative norms they reinforce are scarcely conducive to the development of enduring legislative consensus. The additional inflexibilities introduced by constituency opinion virtually precluded effective committee action.

What counters are available to the obstruction of legislation by an arbitrary chairman? In January, 1959, liberal Democrats who enjoyed a clear majority in the House Democratic caucus prevailed upon Speaker Sam Rayburn (D-Tex.) to change the committee ratio (from 17D–13R to 20D–10R) and "pack" the committee with a liberal Democratic majority. Barden fought a rearguard action from the chair, but the Democratic majority was able in 1960 — for the first time in its history — to report and win House passage of a general aid-to-education bill.

If a committee majority supports a chairman in his opposition to a piece of legislation, the entire House or the Rules Committee has power to discharge the legislation from committee consideration. In the Senate, a single senator can place a bill on the calendar, instead of referring it to committee. This rule was used, for example, to keep the Civil Rights Act of 1964 from being referred to the Judiciary Committee, chaired by Senator James Eastland (D-Miss.). Senate committees may also be bypassed by the use of discharge, non-germane amendments, or suspension of the rules.[53]

None of these alternatives are fully compatible with the rational-legal model of the legislative process. By their very nature they violate the committee basis of the legislative system. The logic of the model points toward making the legislative committees (and their leadership) more responsive to the majority of the committee and the majority of the committee more generally representative of opinion in the Legislature.[54]

Control by partisan majority: The Elementary and Secondary Education Act of 1965. The procedural abuses of anti-aid-to-education forces undoubtedly complicated the problem of building legislative

[53] See Froman, *op. cit.*, Chaps. V, VIII.

[54] George Goodwin, Jr., distinguishes between two sets of proposals for reform. The first set would change the system of choosing chairmen; the second "would attempt to mitigate the effects of the seniority system while continuing to work within it, either by more careful initial recruitment of committee members or by limiting the power of committee chairmen." "The Seniority System in Congress," *APSR*, June 1959, pp. 412–36.

majorities. But former Secretary of Health, Education and Welfare
Abraham Ribicoff spoke for the pro-aid leadership in 1961 when he
concluded, "They expected a miracle and I couldn't produce a
miracle. It was impossible to bring together a majority for a bill when
most members didn't want one." [55] With the opening of the 89th
Congress in January, 1965, the majority was at last at hand.

The result was passage of the first general aid-for-education legislation in history — one of the legislative landmarks of the post-World
War II period. At a Democratic dinner honoring the Congress in
June, 1965, President Johnson described the Elementary and Secondary Education Act of 1965 as "the most important measure that I
shall ever sign." How well did Congress legislate in the case of this
historic bill?

From the perspective of proper procedure the answer is not well at
all. With victory at last within sight, the administration, Democratic
congressional leadership, and Democratic majority within Congress
decided upon a legislative strategy to minimize any chance that the
bill might not pass. A consensus draft, acceptable to the major interest
groups involved, was hammered out within the Executive.[56] The
House Committee on Education and Labor and its General Subcommittee on Education were given some leeway in amendment, although
the basic provisions of the bill, especially the formula for allocating
funds to local districts, were not subject to amendment for fear the
consensus might be endangered.[57] The key element of strategy was to
obtain Senate passage of the House bill *without* amendment, thereby
eliminating the conference stage. The bill was given top legislative
priority by both the President and congressional leadership and passed
as rapidly as possible, again out of fear that opponents might be able
to break away some of the support for the bill if it lagged at all in the
legislative process. The President sent Congress his proposal in mid-
January. It was signed into law on April 11, 1965. A brief review of
the legislative history of the bill during that period underscores the
procedural costs of effecting legislative output.

[55] Cited in Fenno, "The House of Representatives and Federal Aid to Education," p. 234.

[56] For a discussion of the background to this new "proponent coalition" see
Meranto, *op. cit.*, pp. 66–84.

[57] A summary entitled "Major Amendments to the Elementary and Secondary
Education Act of 1965 Adopted by the General Subcommittee on Education in
Reporting the Measure to the Full Committee, February 5, 1965" is reprinted
in the *Daily Congressional Record*, 89th Congress, 1st Session, March 24, 1965,
pp. 5562–63.

The House Committee on Education and Labor, with its record of partisan division, quickly split over the new bill. Subcommittee Chairman Carl D. Perkins (D-Ky.) held hearings on the bill from January 22 through February 2, and the subcommittee reported the bill to the full committee on February 5 by a vote of 6–0. Republican Congressman Charles Goodell (R-N.Y.), who boycotted the session with two other Republicans on the subcommittee, protested the "hasty and superficial" consideration given the bill. The full committee marked up the bill from February 25 to March 2; the Rules Committee under the shadow of the revived 21-day rule gave the bill four days of hearings and cleared it by an 8–7 vote on March 22; and on March 24 the bill came to the floor of the House for debate. The three days of debate were among the bitterest of the 89th Congress.[58]

The minority opened by presenting an alternative tax credit proposal drafted by Congressmen William H. Ayres (R-Ohio), Goodell, and Thomas B. Curtis (R-Mo.) — part of the "constructive Republican alternatives" plan of newly elected Minority Leader Gerald R. Ford (R-Mich.). Curtis had asked the Rules Committee to hold up action on the bill until the tax credit approach could be studied by the Ways and Means Committee, but his request was declined. The majority and minority then sparred on the adequacy of hearings and study, with Congressman Robert Griffin (R-Mich.) stating that the bill was "an entirely new approach" that the committee and House had never considered before. Congressman Ayres pointed out that Republican members of the committee had developed a detailed critique of the bill and would offer corrective amendments. "We must make certain that this bill receives deliberate and just evaluation," he told the House. "This can only be done if we are to consider all of the alternatives. I plead with you to give us the opportunity to give this bill that deliberation that the future of our children deserves."

The second day of House debate was occupied almost exclusively with the allocation formula of Title I. The opposition argued that the formula rewarded states with the least need. As the afternoon drew on, Chairman Adam Clayton Powell, to the consternation of the minority, unexpectedly requested that all debate and amendments to Title I be terminated by 6:15 P.M. As a result seven amendments by Congressman Goodell and two by Congressman Albert H. Quie (R-Minn.) were precluded from the House discussion.

---

[58] All subsequent citations from floor debate on the bill are from the *Congressional Record*, 89th Congress, 1st Session, March 24–26, and April 6–7, 1965.

When the House leadership announced that consideration of the entire 147-page bill would be completed and a final vote taken by four o'clock on Friday (the third day of debate), so that members and their families could attend a Speaker's reception for the Gemini astronauts, the minority protested strongly. Minority Leader Ford insisted that the journal of the previous day's activities be read — an unusual gesture expressing minority dissatisfaction with the guillotining of debate. Ford asked for "a maximum, but yet a reasonable, time for a full discussion," terming the limitation of debate on Title I "unfair and inequitable." He wanted to sit down with the leadership to "work out some reasonable opportunity for us in the minority to offer appropriate amendments in Committee of the Whole." Rather than an arbitrary limitation of 4 o'clock, the Minority Leader suggested a Saturday or a Monday session. Majority leader Carl Albert (D-Okla.) replied that ever since the new Republican image "made its appearance in the legislative firmament," he had heard a lot about cooperation from the other side. But, citing the minority record on the Appalachia bill, he asked, "When is the cooperation of the new Republican leadership going to start?" Thereupon he moved the previous question, cutting off debate by an almost straight party-line vote.

The debate on the remaining titles of the bill that afternoon was interlaced with partisan rancor. "There is no question but what you gentlemen on that side of the aisle have the power and can vote us down any time you want to," Congressman Goodell told the House. But there are serious problems in connection with this legislation "that do not divide us down the middle of the aisle." The legislative product might more appropriately be called the "Railroad Act of 1965." Congresswoman Edith Green (D-Ore.), a senior Democrat on the committee, found the leadership equally unresponsive to her amendments. "Today it seems to me we have in the House a determined effort to silence those who are in disagreement." As a last resort the opposition turned to quorum calls to dramatize what it considered unfair treatment. After the smoke had cleared, the House had accepted only one minor amendment to the committee bill, Congressman Griffin's amendment to authorize a ten-member advisory council. The bill was passed by a lopsided majority of 263–153, and the House finally adjourned at 10:30 P.M.

The legislative setting in the Senate differed from that in the House in some significant regards. The Senate had regularly given majority approval to education legislation over the previous decade. Its principal committee on the subject, the Committee on Labor and Public Welfare, had a far different record in building legislative consensus than the House Committee on Education and Labor. The Senate viewed itself as the champion of education legislation, and its members accordingly anticipated a leading role in the drafting and passage of the first general aid legislation. Such was not to be the case, however.

Senators who wished to offer amendments to the bill were quietly told by the administration to submit them to the House committee. Although none of the arbitrary limitations that had been placed on debate in the House characterized either the committee or floor stage in the Senate, it soon became clear that the majority would permit no amendments by the Senate. The bill was reported from committee without amendment on April 6. The minority voted to report "with reservation." The Minority Report eloquently developed a new issue — the legislative independence of the Senate.

> It is ironic, indeed, that while this committee speaks out in behalf of this billion-dollar-plus measure to liberate children from the shackles of ignorance at the same time it draws close about it — and to the Senate which has entrusted it this important responsibility — the strong but subtle silken threads of legislative impotence. . . .

> We are told that this embargo on amendments — even technical amendments to correct drafting ambiguities — is a "one-shot proposition" but the branch of Congress that gives up its independence to an aggrandizing Executive not only lays the basis for new and greater demands of passive compliance but also begins to lose the confidence of the people whose votes have given it life.[59]

---

[59] The minority report is reprinted in the *Daily Congressional Record*, 89th Congress, 1st Session, April 6, 1965, pp. 7064 ff. During the 90th Congress, the majority of the House of Representatives similarly voted to accept the Senate version of the Omnibus Crime Control and Safe Streets Act of 1968 without amendment. Congressman Emanuel Celler (D-N.Y.), Chairman of the House Judiciary Committee, argued unsuccessfully for a conference on the bill, which came to the floor a few hours after the shooting of Senator Robert F. Kennedy: "This bill was adopted through fear. It is a very cumbersome and very comprehensive bill. I wonder how many Members of the House have read the report of the bill, accompanying the bill? It contains 284 pages. I do not think any of you have read the report. I venture the assertion that none of you gentlemen have read the bill itself. We passed a bill with 25 pages. The Senate bill contains 109 pages." *Daily Congressional Record*, 90th Congress, 2nd Session, June 5, 1968, p. H4556.

Senator Wayne Morse (D-Ore.) stated that the President and Senate majority agreed that it was best to avoid "the possible risks that are always involved in connection with an education bill in conference sessions." Senator Clark seconded the move as "a matter of pragmatic legislative procedure."

Senator Winston Prouty (R-Vt.), speaking for the minority, pointed out that the administration had sufficient majorities in both Houses to get acceptance of "any version of its choice." The purpose of a bicameral Legislature was to permit the second body "to consider, refine, and purify" the product of the other body's deliberations. Although none of the minority's amendments had been accepted, they served "a useful purpose" through the addition of language in the report which clarified some of the ambiguities of the language in the House bill. On April 9 the Senate passed the Elementary and Secondary Education Act of 1965 by a vote of 73–18. The legislative logjam of twenty years had at last been broken.

From the perspective of good legislative procedure, the aid-to-education impasse shows Congress at its worst. Both conservatives and liberals abused accepted procedure to suit their ends. The final result was legislation drafted by the Executive with virtually no opportunity for amendment by Congress after introduction. Admittedly Congress soon amended the bill, in its next session, to correct the formula that the minority had argued would discriminate against smaller states. Congress will most likely continue to exercise a significant amending role — a safeguard the American legislative system retains. But this in itself will not satisfy the qualitative standards of legislative performance.[60]

MULTIPLE PERSPECTIVES ON
THE LEGISLATIVE PROCESS

We have examined two alternative views and standards for evaluating legislative performance. Each view suggests a distinctive style of legislative decision making; each makes normative assumptions about the

[60] Legislative amendment by subsequent Congresses may serve as a useful empirical measure of the technical quality of legislation enacted by a given Congress. Many effects of low quality legislation, however, may be concentrated in the administrative process. Stephen K. Bailey observes: "One glaring deficiency emerged in the recent legislative output [of the 89th Congress]: lack of adequate attention to the *administrative* implications of 'great society' legislation. Laws were passed and money provided without appropriate questions being asked and answered about the availability of trained manpower to carry out the programs; about optimum relationships between federal, state, local, and private juris-

organization and use of power in the legislative system. The parallels to our initial discussion of the problem of organizing power in the American political system are obvious. But can we go beyond the basic conclusion that performance depends on one's perspective?

A promising line of inquiry may lie in the direction of a multiple-phase interpretation of the legislative process. Why does Congress behave in a partisan manner in one legislative situation and in a non-partisan one in another? Why are some committee hearings and debates models of congressional study and legislative innovation while others merely serve to reinforce fixed positions and prejudices? Under what conditions does the full legislative body simply ratify decisions of the subordinate committee and under what conditions are effective decisions imposed on the committee? In what cases are decisions imposed on the Legislature itself by the President and the electorate?

Congress legislates in several styles or manners. These may vary over time with changing party balance, public mood, presidential leadership, and interest group demands. They may vary by issue as well. To complicate the analytical problem even more, different portions of Congress may legislate on the same issue at different times. For example, those members that constitute the effective congressional voice on a particular issue may be the committee hierarchy or majority in one legislative situation, the congressional leadership in another, an intense minority in a third, and a House or Senate majority in a fourth. Finally, because Congress has this capacity to reach multiple decisions simultaneously, it can also speak in multiple, and at times contradictory, voices.

One effort to systematize these various modes of how Congress legislates has been attempted by Theodore Lowi.[61] Lowi suggests that different types of public policy are decided in different "arenas of power"; i.e., "for each type of policy there is likely to be a distinctive

---

dictions; or about the effective interdepartmental coordination of old and new activities. Often it is too late to handle such a gesture by *post hoc* accounting and surveillance procedures." *The New Congress* (St. Martin's Series in American Politics; New York: St. Martin's Press, 1966), p. 103.

[61] "American Business, Public Policy, Case Studies, and Political Theory: Review article of Raymond A. Bauer, Ithiel de Sola Pool, and Lewis A. Dexter, *American Business and Public Policy: The Politics of Foreign Trade*," *World Politics*, July 1964, pp. 677–715. Randall Ripley extends Lowi's classification to three broad categories of government control: techniques of subsidy, regulation, and manipulation. See Ripley (ed.), *Public Policies and Their Politics: An Introduction to the Techniques of Government Control* (New York: W. W. Norton & Co., 1966), pp. vii–xviii.

type of political relationship." He defines three policy categories and their associated political relationships.

Distributive policies are decided *within* the congressional committee or executive agency through a process of log-rolling or "mutual non-interference" of uncommon interests. The decisional structure comprises a non-conflicting elite with supporting groups. Patronage and the rivers and harbors "pork-barrel" are classic examples. Policies in this arena can be "disaggregated" and dispensed unit by unit.

Regulatory policies cannot be resolved within the congressional committee but rather in Congress as a whole. Decisions are reached through bargaining; coalitions which share interest in the subject-matter are formed. The decisional structure is pluralistic, assumes a "theory of balance," and tends to be unstable. In the regulatory arena policies cannot be disaggregated to the individual or single firm (as was the case with distributive policies) but must be made by application of a general rule. Communications and transportation are classic examples.

Redistributive policies are made outside of Congress between the Executive and "peak associations." Decision making is ideological and class oriented. The decisional structure is stable and assumes conflicting elites; i.e., an elite and counter-elite. The congressional role seems largely to be one of "ratifying agreements that [arise] out of bureaucracies and the class agents represented there." Redistributive policies require "complex balancing on a very large scale" that is beyond the capability of Congress. Welfare state programs provide the primary examples.

Lowi would probably consider urban programs and general aid-to-education in the third category. The locus of decision has shifted to the President because a decentralized and bargaining Congress cannot handle problems of this complexity.

Lowi's classification is a useful beginning but should be expanded to include national economic policy and foreign policy, which are not easily fitted to the threefold typology. Viewing Congress as part of several different arenas of power suggests that *different* levels of expectation and standards of legislative performance may be appropriate in different situations. Congress may have a greater capacity and hence a greater responsibility for legislative performance in some policy areas than others.

To return to our initial theme, any evaluation of congressional performance must take into account the changing dimensions of the legislative function. As Congress perfects techniques for evaluating the impact of legislation (part of the control and investigative functions of Congress discussed in the next chapter) and gains a new information capacity in general, we may anticipate improved performance of the legislative function of Congress.

CHAPTER FIVE

Legislative Effectiveness:
Control and Investigation

While public attention has been directed to the decline of Congress as a legislative body (i.e., to increased executive initiative in the legislative process), few observers have noted the significance of related developments in the control and investigative functions of Congress.[1] Congressional participation in, and "oversight" or review of, the administrative process in government is one of the least understood functions that Congress performs. In this chapter we examine the control and investigative functions of Congress in the broader context of legislative performance.

THE RELATIONSHIP OF CONTROL AND
INVESTIGATION TO LEGISLATIVE EFFECTIVENESS

Congressional control over administration has been an issue in American government since Congress attempted to specify the duties of the Secretary of the Treasury in the first Washington administration. The controversy over the investigative powers of Congress dates back to 1791 when Congress created a committee to investigate the disastrous expedition of Major General Arthur St. Clair to control Indians in the Ohio territory. The very exercise of these two related functions rests on certain assumptions about the role of Congress in the American political system. The British Parliament enjoys no comparable autonomy or authority in control of the Executive. At best, it provides broad review and general debate of cabinet policy. The bureaucracy is

---

[1] Two notable exceptions are Charles S. Hyneman, *Bureaucracy in a Democracy* (New York: Harper & Bros., 1950); and Roland Young, *The American Congress* (New York: Harper & Bros., 1958).

screened from the Legislature by the instruments of ministerial and cabinet responsibility. Parliament has virtually no capacity to initiate investigations of the Executive, let alone of broad problem areas requiring legislation.[2]

We have already suggested basic structural features of the American system that precluded the development of a parliamentary form of government and the tradition of a neutral civil service controlled by a cabinet ministry. The American solution of separated institutions sharing powers guaranteed the development of an open, politicized, executive bureaucracy subject to the competing directives of presidential and congressional executives.[3] The rationalization of the executive bureaucracy has taken place within this framework of dual executives. While executive-centered government has meant great presidential *initiative* in the legislative process and enhanced control of the bureaucracy through the executive budget, it has implied a corresponding new emphasis on congressional *control* and *review* of both legislation and administration. It is understandable that the administrative mind should balk at this complex form of a rationalization with its inherent bar to unity of control. We merely note that dualism in administration is an inherited assumption of our contemporary political system. Once this assumption has been granted, Congress may adopt a number of legitimate aims in the exercise of its control and investigative functions.[4] Broadly defined, they include:

Control of unacceptable forms of bureaucratic behavior. In sharing with the Presidency the objective of insuring a responsible bureaucracy, Congress must control bureaucratic growth and independent action, cases of administrative abuse or arbitrary actions affecting citizens, and malfeasance.

Effecting the legislative intent of Congress in the administrative process. Under the American system of representation, both the President and Congress (acting through separate majorities) have a respon-

[2] Bernard Crick concludes, "Scrutiny of the vastly increased scope of modern administration is badly underdeveloped." See *The Reform of Parliament* (Garden City, N.Y.: Doubleday Anchor Books, 1965), p. 178. Also Andrew Hill and Anthony Whichelow, *What's Wrong with Parliament?* (Baltimore, Md.: Penguin Books, 1964), esp. Chap. V, "Committees to Advise and Recommend."

[3] See David B. Truman, *The Governmental Process: Political Interests and Public Opinion* (New York: Alfred A. Knopf, 1951), pp. 404–10.

[4] For another discussion of the purposes of legislative control of administration, see Joseph P. Harris, *Congressional Control of Administration* (Washington, D.C.: The Brookings Institution, 1964), pp. 1–3.

sibility to maintain popular control over the bureaucracy by ensuring that the bureaucracy implements the policy objectives specified in the legislative process.

Efficiency and economy in governmental operations. This goal assumes that policy objectives have been specified and enjoy congressional support. Congress controls and reviews the administrative process to ensure a balance between spending and revenues and the establishment of spending priorities. Occasionally, "economy drives" in Congress reverse policy decisions previously reached in the legislative process.

Achieving a balance between control and discretion or flexibility in the administrative system. In the exercise of control, Congress must also provide sufficient discretion or flexibility in the administrative system to permit the administrator room for initiative and efficient operation. Over-control may impede the very objectives Congress is attempting to realize.

Determining the effectiveness of legislative policies. Ultimately, Congress exercises its control and investigative functions to determine the general effectiveness of legislation in meeting needs defined in the legislative process. If Congress is to share in guiding the direction of government, it must understand the impact of legislation on society. To be effective it must evaluate the consequences — actual and anticipated — of governmental action, utilizing the most advanced techniques of program analysis and evaluation that are available to top policy makers.

All these objectives are consistent with the assumption that Congress has a legitimate role in the administrative process. As we shall see, some critics of Congress are not willing to grant the assumption. Others would qualify the degree or forms of congressional participation. Before considering some of these arguments, we will clarify some of the terminology as it will be used in this analysis.

We shall define legislative "control" of administration to include *both* legislative *participation before* administrative action and legislative *review* or *oversight after* the fact. The terms "review" or "oversight" are sometimes used in the literature and within Congress itself in the broader sense of "control." Within this chapter, unless otherwise specified, "control" will be used in the broader sense and "review" or "oversight" in the more limited sense.[5]

[5] *Ibid.*, p. 9.

Investigation is clearly a form or instrument of legislative control. In this chapter we shall define it as congressional study and research of specific problems that may require legislation. The focus of the control and investigative functions — the administrative bureaucracy on the one hand and the actual policy problems confronting government on the other — is distinct enough to justify separate consideration. In the first instance, Congress is concerned with the capacity of the executive bureaucracy to implement legislative policy; in the second, it seeks a clearer understanding of the problems for which it and the President legislate policy for the bureaucracy.

Finally, it should be noted that "legislative effectiveness," which we listed as one of several possible standards for evaluating congressional performance, is closely related to the functions of legislative control and investigation. The efficiency-effectiveness criterion implies that Congress should be organized and should function so as to realize its will in the governmental process. If Congress is to be effective, then, it must exercise extensively its powers of administrative control and social inquiry.

THE CHANGING CONTROL AND INVESTIGATIVE FUNCTIONS

The control of bureaucracy is a relatively new problem for American government. While Congress developed detailed legislative and appropriations specifications for the new executive departments early in the legislative history of the republic, the federal civil service numbered less than 50,000 at the start of the Civil War.[6] The real period of growth began in the 1930's when the number of federal employees rose from 572,000 in 1933 to 1,014,000 in 1940. A dramatic indication of the growth of the executive bureaucracy is the fact that some three-quarters of the over 2½ million federal civil service positions today were established in the last thirty years.

This rapid growth, accompanied by the proliferation of new emergency agencies during the Depression and war years, provided a major

[6] See Lucius Wilmerding, Jr., *The Spending Power: A History of the Efforts of Congress to Control Expenditures* (New Haven: Yale University Press, 1943). For a general discussion of the history of patronage in legislative-executive relations and the development of the civil service, see Herbert Kaufman, "The Growth of the Federal Personnel System," in Wallace S. Sayre (ed.), *The Federal Government Service* (2nd ed.; The American Assembly; Englewood Cliffs, N.J.: Prentice-Hall, 1965), pp. 7–69.

impetus toward the development of the modern institutionalized Presidency and toward the rationalization of executive branch organization. Congress yielded its historic legislative power to organize the executive agencies in the Reorganization Act of 1939, giving the President the authority to draft reorganization plans subject only to a new "legislative veto." [7] The first such plan submitted to the Congress in April, 1939 established the Executive Office of the President, including the White House Office, Bureau of the Budget, and the National Resources Planning Board.

The new equilibrium of roles under executive-centered government was confirmed by a rationalization of congressional organization in the Legislative Reorganization Act of 1946.[8] This landmark legislation incorporated three basic provisions intended to strengthen congressional control of administration.

Rationalization of the standing committee system. Modernization of the standing committee system of Congress was, according to George B. Galloway, "the first aim of the act and the keystone in the arch of congressional 'reform.' " [9] In the House, the number of standing committees was reduced from 48 to 19; in the Senate, from 33 to 15. Although a prohibition against special or select committees was struck from the bill, Congress was against this alternative to the recognized jurisdictions of the standing committees. The new standing committee structure was designed roughly to parallel the reorganized executive departments on a one-to-one basis.

This organizational formula has been closely adhered to by Con-

---

[7] The "legislative veto" was used experimentally in earlier reorganization legislation such as the Economy Act of 1932. For a full discussion of the origins of the 1939 legislation see Richard Polenberg, *Reorganizing Roosevelt's Government: The Controversy Over Executive Reorganization, 1936–1939* (Cambridge, Mass.: Harvard University Press, 1966).

[8] Just as one can describe a rationalization of power within the Executive, one can identify rationalizations in the organization of congressional power. Major historical examples preceding the Legislative Reorganization Act of 1946 were the establishment of the standing committee system by 1825, periodic reform of House and Senate rules to expedite legislative business (for example, the Reed Rules of 1890 and the cloture rule in the Senate, 1917), and the fiscal reforms following World War I that unified the Appropriations Committees and established the General Accounting Office. The most important rationalization in congressional organization and procedure since 1921 has been the *indirect* discipline in the legislative and administrative processes introduced by executive reform such as the executive budget and legislative clearance. Again, the modern Presidency and the modern Congress have developed in a symbiotic relationship.

[9] *History of the House of Representatives* (New York: Thomas Y. Crowell Co., 1962), p. 54.

gress since 1946. The only new standing committees have been the House Committee on Science and Astronautics and the Senate Committee on Aeronautical and Space Sciences, both established in 1958 with the initiation of the multi-billion dollar space program. Two new joint committees, the Joint Economic Committee and the Joint Committee on Atomic Energy, were established to meet special needs that arose almost coincidentally with the reorganization legislation. Some observers hold that the rapid growth of subcommittees has negated the reform. By 1955 the number of congressional committees and subcommittees of all types (exclusive of special subcommittees) had risen to 235 compared with 230 in 1945.[10] However, the two situations are clearly not equivalent. The standing committees remain as coordinators and channels of legislative activity, and most of the parent committees retain considerable control over their subcommittees.[11] While Congress may make marginal adjustments in the standing committee structure, to reflect new federal responsibilities in education and urban affairs and consequent realignments of executive departments, the 1946 Act appears to have given Congress a stable internal organization for the exercise of its control and investigative functions.[12]

The requirement of legislative oversight by standing committees. Section 136 of the 1946 Act stated that "each standing committee of the Senate and the House of Representatives shall exercise continuous watchfulness of the execution by the administrative agencies concerned of any laws, the subject matter of which is within the jurisdiction of such committee. . . ." While this authority was granted "to

[10] George B. Galloway, *Congressional Reorganization Revisited* (College Park, Md.: University of Maryland, 1956), p. 2.

[11] George Goodwin, Jr., concludes, "The most effective controls over subcommittees lie clearly in the hands of the individual committees." In the tug of war between the chairman and the subcommittees, the chairman "deals from a stacked deck." "He should be able to maintain control even against rank-and-file rebellion unless he is politically inept. He can, in most cases, establish subcommittees, determine their size, establish party ratios, appoint the members, maintain *ex officio* membership, control the referral of bills and either assign or hold back staff and money for subcommittee operations." "Subcommittees: The Miniature Legislatures of Congress," *The American Political Science Review* (APSR), September 1962, pp. 600–601.

[12] Dr. Joseph C. Pray, in testimony before the Joint Committee on the Organization of the Congress, assessed the existing standing committee-subcommittee structure as "a valid response to the ambivalence of specialization and coordination. To force the complex stream of proposals through the choke of few standing committees aids the integration function of the parent House." *Hearings: Organization of Congress,* 89th Congress, 1st Session, 1965, p. 1205.

assist the Congress in appraising the administration of the laws and in developing such amendments or related legislation as it may deem necessary," the newly defined standing committees were to be the agents of the oversight function. The intention of the authors of the act was to achieve a three-stage performance of the oversight function: exercise of financial control before expenditure, by the Appropriations Committees; review of administrative structure and procedures, by the Expenditure (Government Operations) Committees; and review of the operation of substantive legislation by the legislative committees.[13] Just how much "continuous watchfulness" has been achieved is a subject to which we shall return.

The provision of professional staffs for standing committees. Before the reforms of the Legislative Reorganization Act of 1946, only the two appropriations committees and the Joint Committee on Internal Revenue Taxation, a staff arm of the two revenue committees, employed professional staff on a tenure basis. Section 202 of the act authorized each standing committee to appoint not more than four professional staff members and six clerks, although no ceiling was set for the appropriations committees and there was no great difficulty later in obtaining authorization for additional staff if the committee so requested.

While the development and utilization of professional staffs has been uneven, the 1946 legislation recognized the priority need to create congressional staff resources at the committee level if Congress were to perform its legislative and oversight functions.[14] Additional staff and information resources were provided by establishing a Legislative Reference Service in the Library of Congress and by authorizing studies and expenditure analyses by the Comptroller General. Separate reforms in fiscal control, notably the attempt to establish a legislative budget, were never effectively implemented by Congress because, unlike the oversight requirement, they were not integrated with the standing committee structure.[15]

[13] Galloway, "Operation of Legislative Reorganization Act of 1946," article reprinted in U.S. Senate, Committee on Expenditures in the Executive Departments, *Hearings: Organization and Operation of Congress*, 82nd Congress, 1st Session, 1951, p. 637.

[14] For an evaluation of staffing under the Legislative Reorganization Act, see Kenneth Kofmehl, *Professional Staffs of Congress* (Purdue University Studies in Humanities Series; West Lafayette, Ind.: Purdue University, 1962).

[15] See John S. Saloma III, "Congressional Attempts to Establish a Legislative Budget," *The Responsible Use of Power: A Critical Analysis of the Congressional Budget Process* (Washington, D.C.: American Enterprise Institute, 1964), pp. 54–58.

These three basic provisions of the 1946 Act organized, directed, and staffed Congress for expansion of its control and investigative functions. A number of techniques of oversight were already available to Congress. Still others were rapidly developed.[16] The basic *formal* means of control has remained the passage of legislation, through both the appropriations and the authorization processes. Through legislation, Congress has controlled the organization, programs, personnel systems, and funding of the executive departments. Although the President may now take the initiative in suggesting reorganization plans, the legislative committees have extended their control by replacing open-ended authorizations with annual or other forms of limited authorization. The two Post Office and Civil Service committees have closely watched over the federal personnel services and have consistently resisted (with congressional support) the centralization of personnel management under the President. The appropriations process is still generally considered the most important form of congressional control. Other formal controls include audit by the General Accounting Office (with review of audits by the Government Operations, Appropriations, and relevant subject-matter committees), senatorial confirmation of executive appointments, and authorized congressional investigations. One technique of control that has been rapidly extended is the "legislative veto" in several forms, including the committee veto.

Informal techniques of control do not enjoy the status of legislation or similar authoritative actions by the Congress. They are usually exercised by committees or individual members of Congress in their contacts with executive officials. They may be written into committee reports as "nonstatutory" directions or advice to the relevant agency, or they may enter the public record during committee hearings and floor debate. They may arise apart from the legislative process in a variety of contacts that a member of a congressional staff may have with an agency.

Both formal and informal techniques of control have expanded significantly since the Legislative Reorganization Act of 1946. Annual authorizations are now required in program areas such as space, foreign aid, atomic energy, and defense weapons systems, accounting for more than 35 per cent of the annual budget. The number of congres-

[16] For a comprehensive discussion of the range of control and oversight techniques utilized by Congress, see Harris, *op. cit.* The testimony of Arthur Maass before the Joint Committee on the Organization of the Congress concentrates on selected oversight techniques that have been most fully developed since 1946. *Hearings: Organization of Congress*, pp. 940–57.

sional investigations, which averaged slightly over thirty per Congress during the interwar years rose to over two hundred per Congress by the early 1950's, and funds authorized for congressional investigations almost doubled from $8.2 million in the 83rd Congress (1953–54) to $15.5 million in the 86th Congress (1959–60).[17] The legislative veto has been utilized in more than twenty authorization acts since 1950.[18]

Congressional control of administration is *pervasive* at least in the points and directions of access to the administrative process that Congress, its committees, and its members enjoy. How well has Congress exercised its functions of control and investigation since the reforms of 1946? While a variety of criticisms have been raised, only the most fragmentary empirical research on which intelligent evaluations can be based has been completed to date.[19] The more than 2,000 pages of testimony and supporting documents received by the Joint Committee on the Organization of the Congress do not contain any comprehensive statement of experience under the oversight provisions of the 1946 legislation.[20]

With the qualification that most public and congressional comment on the 1946 Act lacks adequate empirical information, we can summarize the main criticisms and concerns. As we might expect, evaluations of congressional performance in such a situation reflect the value assumptions of the observer.

[17] Harris, *op. cit.*, pp. 264–66. See also M. Nelson McGeary, "Congressional Investigations: Historical Development," *University of Chicago Law Review*, 1951, pp. 425–39.

[18] *Hearings: Organization of Congress*, p. 444.

[19] Ira Sharkansky develops six measures of subcommittee supervision and control from a content analysis of published materials on four agencies within H.E.W. See "An Appropriations Subcommittee and Its Client Agencies: A Comparative Study of Supervision and Control," *APSR*, September 1965, pp. 622–28. Also see Seymour Scher's findings on congressional oversight of selected regulatory agencies, "Conditions for Legislative Control," *Journal of Politics*, August 1963, pp. 526–51. For the past several years the Seminar on Congressional Supervision of Public Policy and Administration at Harvard University has been developing data on techniques of oversight under the direction of Arthur Maass. A major study from this series on the growth of non-statutory techniques of control by Dr. Michael Kirst will be published shortly by the University of North Carolina. Morris Ogul and Alan Fiellin are working on empirical studies of oversight as part of the Study of Congress project.

[20] Senator A. S. "Mike" Monroney, a co-sponsor of the 1946 legislation, described the performance of the oversight program as "still one of the great gaps in government" during the 1965 Hearings on the Organization of Congress. "[W]e find ourselves bogged down in an impossible situation where this regular committee oversight of the bureaus and departments under its jurisdiction is not carried out to any degree whatever." *Hearings: Organization of Congress*, p. 594.

EVALUATIONS OF CONGRESSIONAL PERFORMANCE: CONTROL OF ADMINISTRATION

We shall consider three standards for evaluating congressional performance of its control function. First, we shall examine the general criterion of constitutionality, in regard to the controversial committee veto power. Second, we shall consider the general criterion of rationality in both the legislative and administrative processes in evaluating the technique of annual authorization. Finally, we shall view the exercise of the control function in terms of congressional effectiveness and a number of reform proposals designed to enhance it.

The Criterion of Constitutionality: Lyndon Johnson Declares War on the Committee Veto

No other technique of control has received more presidential and public criticism than the committee veto, more commonly referred to as "coming-into-agreement." [21] The committee veto, usually incorporated as a provision in broadly worded authorizing legislation, normally requires the executive agency concerned, before acting on certain decisions either (1) to submit such a decision to the appropriate House and Senate committees for their consideration during a specified interval (30, 45, 60 days, etc.); or (2) to consult with and obtain the approval of, or "come into agreement" with, such committees, again sometimes within a specified time.[22]

---

[21] The American Assembly on The Congress and America's Future singled out this technique of control and urged its abandonment. " 'Coming into agreement . . .' exceeds the proper bounds of congressional oversight of administration and subverts presidential responsibility. It grants arbitrary power to chairmen of committees or subcommittees that is not subject to account." Final Report of the *Twenty-Sixth American Assembly: The Congress and America's Future* (New York: The American Assembly, Columbia University, 1964), p. 7.

[22] For a background on the history of the committee veto and legislative-executive relations, see U.S. Senate Subcommittee on Separation of Powers (the Ervin Committee), Committee on the Judiciary, *Hearings: Separation of Powers*, 90th Congress, 1st Session, 1967. Selected statements are also reprinted in *The Daily Congressional Record*, 90th Congress, 1st Session, October 11, 1967, pp. S 14671–81. The position of the Presidents on various forms of committee veto provisions is summarized in an Appendix to the statement of Assistant Attorney General Frank M. Wozencraft, *Hearings: Separation of Powers*, pp. 215–28. Pertinent also is the research of Norman J. Small, of the American Law Division of the Library of Congress Legislative Reference Service, on current use of the committee veto and appraisals of its validity, reprinted in part in the same hearings, pp. 274–82.

While wide use of the committee veto dates from the Legislative Reorganization Act of 1946, as early as 1920 President Woodrow Wilson vetoed an appropriation bill providing that no government publication could be "printed, issued, or discontinued by any branch or officer of the Government service unless the same shall have been authorized under such regulations as shall be prescribed by the Joint Committee on Printing." Wilson's veto message included the following objection:

> The Congress has the right to confer upon its committees full authority for purposes of investigation and the accumulation of information for its guidance, but I do not concede the right, and certainly not the wisdom, of the Congress of endowing a committee of either House or a joint Committee of both Houses with Power to prescribe regulations under which executive departments may operate.[23]

Subsequent Presidents and Attorneys General objected to the extension of the committee veto, intermittently, sometimes with a veto, but by the end of the 89th Congress (1966) 19 permanent statutory provisions for the veto were public law.[24] The committee veto had been adopted for control of real property transactions of military departments, public buildings, stockpiling, water resources and flood control projects, a variety of activities of the Atomic Energy Commission, mining of naval oil shale reserves, etc. The congressional committees authorized to exercise such veto power most frequently were the Armed Services Committees (six separate provisions), the Joint Committee on Atomic Energy (six), the Public Works Committees (three), the Interior Committees (two), and the Agriculture Committees (two).

President Lyndon Johnson was the most insistent objector to the committee veto and actively sought to limit and reduce the use of this form of congressional control. As early as December, 1963, Johnson objected to a provision in the Public Works Act of 1964 requiring specific committee approval of real property transfers by the Panama Canal Company on the grounds that such a provision was "either an unconstitutional delegation to Congressional committees of powers which reside only in the Congress as a whole, or an attempt to confer executive powers on the committees in violation of the principle of

23 *House Document 764*, 66th Congress, 2nd Session, p. 2.
24 *Hearings: Separation of Powers*, pp. 277–81.

separation of powers set forth in the Constitution." [25] These two arguments against the constitutionality of the committee veto were reiterated by Johnson in a series of moves against committee veto provisions.

In July, 1964, the President objected to a provision in the Water Resources Research Act of 1964 which gave the two Interior Committees the right to disapprove specific grants, contracts, or other arrangements prior to appropriations for the same. The act was amended in 1966 to require only a 60-day notice. Two committee veto provisions in the 1964 Agricultural Trade Development and Assistance legislation were held unconstitutional by the President but were interpreted and executed as a requirement to keep Congress informed and consulted.

During 1965, the President vetoed two bills, the Pacific Northwest Disaster Relief Bill and the Military Construction Authorization Bill, both containing forms of the committee veto. Congress complied with the President's suggested wording and the bills were later approved. In the first of his veto messages, the President described the "coming-into-agreement" requirement as conducive to "inefficient administration" and as "an undesirable and improper encroachment by the Congress and its committees into the area of executive responsibilities."

> The executive branch is given, by the Constitution, the responsibility to implement all laws — *a specific and exclusive responsibility which cannot properly be shared with a committee of Congress.*
>
> The proper separation of powers and division of responsibilities between Congress and the executive branch is a matter of continuing concern to me. *I must oppose the tendency to use any device to involve Congressional committees in the administration of programs and the implementation of laws.* (Emphasis added.) [26]

[25] *Public Papers of the Presidents: Lyndon B. Johnson, 1963–1964*, Vol. I (Washington, D.C.: U.S. Government Printing Office, 1965), p. 104. President Eisenhower was the first President to contest the constitutionality of the committee veto as "an unlawful delegation by the Congress to its committees of a legislative function which the Constitution contemplates the Congress itself, as an entity, should exercise." See his statement on the Small Reclamation Projects Act of 1956, *Public Papers of the Presidents: Dwight D. Eisenhower, 1956* (Washington, D.C.: U.S. Government Printing Office, 1958), pp. 648–50.

[26] *Senate Document 34*, 89th Congress, 1st Session.

The final stroke in the President's strategy against the committee veto came when he signed the Omnibus Rivers and Harbors Act of 1965 and instructed the Secretary of the Army to refrain from exercising any authority under that section of the bill which included the veto provision. The President subsequently objected on constitutional grounds to committee veto provisions in the Watershed Protection and Flood Prevention Act of 1954, the Small Reclamation Projects Act of 1956, and the Public Buildings Act of 1959, and ordered that the programs under the relevant sections of these statutes be halted until the committee veto provisions were removed by amendment.

Congress responded with the creation of a Subcommittee on the Separation of Powers, under the Senate Judiciary Committee and chaired by Senator Sam J. Ervin (D-N.C.), which began taking testimony on the committee veto in July, 1967. Open debate between President and Congress is just now coming to a head. We review here some of the arguments pro and con the "constitutionality" of the committee veto.[27] In a broader sense these are arguments about the validity of the control-oversight function of Congress itself.

ARGUMENTS AGAINST CONSTITUTIONALITY. Leaving aside arguments based on administrative theory and a criterion of administrative rationality, two major arguments have been advanced against the constitutionality of the committee veto: [28]

The principle of the separation of powers precludes a congressional share or participation in the actual execution or administration of the laws. Under this interpretation, Congress may exercise limited oversight or review but *no* before-the-fact control of administration. The President specifically is charged with seeing to the faithful execution of the laws. Congress may not encroach on this prerogative or arrogate such responsibility to itself. Congressional interference with the administration of the law, especially when responsibility is divided between a cabinet officer and committee of Congress, prevents the

---

[27] For a full discussion of the constitutional issues see Joseph Cooper and Ann Cooper, "The Legislative Veto and the Constitution," *The George Washington Law Review*, March 1962, pp. 467–516; and Joseph Cooper, "The Legislative Veto: Its Promise and Its Perils," in Carl J. Friedrich and Seymour E. Harris (eds.), *Public Policy 1956* (Cambridge, Mass.: Graduate School of Public Administration, Harvard University, 1956), pp. 128–74.

[28] Arguments against the constitutionality of the committee veto based on administrative theory and administrative rationality are discussed in Harris, *op. cit.*, pp. 213–48, 295–97.

President from efficiently discharging his accountability for the performance of the executive function.

The committee veto constitutes a delegation of legislative authority to individual committees of Congress to amend existing legislation by a procedure not sanctioned by the Constitution. Article I, Section 7 of the Constitution specifies the authorized method for legislation, including passage by the House of Representatives and Senate and presentation to the President for approval or disapproval. Congress has the option of drafting detailed or broadly worded legislation. It cannot constitutionally reserve part of its legislative authority for its committees to amend broadly worded legislation after it has been enacted. Committees cannot legislate; they do not have the legal capacity to enact legislation. Furthermore, decisions reached under the committee veto procedure are not subject to presidential surveillance or signature.

ARGUMENTS FOR CONSTITUTIONALITY. The principle arguments for the committee veto as for the extension of other forms of control and oversight are related to the redefinition of constitutional roles and functions under "executive-centered" government.

A rigid interpretation of the separation of powers principle cannot be justified in view of the difficulty of defining "legislative" and "executive" responsibilities. There is no sharp borderline between policy formulation and policy execution. Presidential and congressional responsibilities cannot be neatly compartmentalized within executive and legislative spheres. The distinction between "broad standards or policies" and "narrow, specific, detailed decision" is not an adequate guide, since Congress has throughout its history enjoyed the option of detailed legislation. The mere transfer of such decisions to the Executive through delegated legislation does not in itself change the character of the decision from "legislative" to "executive," nor does the distinction between "before-the-fact" and "after-the-fact" control offer a definitive guide to executive versus legislative responsibility.[29] The

---

[29] Joseph and Ann Cooper observe, "Legislative oversight through Congress' traditional weapons has involved and continues to involve 'before-the-fact' control . . . decision making is not static, but continuous. Thus when Congress legislates, appropriates, investigates, contacts administrators, and criticizes, it does so in the context of decision-making that has occurred or is about to occur, and it changes, affects, and determines administration decision-making that has occurred, would have occurred, and will occur. What is 'before-the-fact' and what is 'after-the-fact' is largely a relative question." *Op. cit.*, p. 495.

Supreme Court has given a liberal interpretation to the separation of powers principle concerning the delegation of legislative authority to the Executive.[30] It would be inconsistent to deny Congress a counterweight to this new discretionary authority enjoyed by the Executive by now invoking a strict interpretation of the principle.

The Supreme Court has upheld the right of Congress to attach conditions and requirements to legislation before authority so legislated can be used. The committee veto device falls within this class of conditional delegated legislation. The Court has interpreted such delegations of discretion to the President, to executive officials, and in some cases (such as the farmer referendum in agricultural stabilization legislation) to private citizens *not* to be "legislative" in character.[31] Recipients of delegated discretion, in the Court's view, have *not* been vested with a share in the legislative process to fill in an incomplete statement of congressional intent but rather have been vested with the authority to make certain findings or to fulfill certain conditions which will help to realize the basic congressional intent of the legislation. By analogy, statutory delegation of discretion to committees of Congress is not a delegation of "legislative" authority. Congressional committees merely help to effect congressional intent as stated in the basic legislation. Committee actions in themselves constitute neither legislation nor a binding veto on the Executive. Thus the objection that the committee veto is a constitutionally unauthorized manner of legislation cannot be sustained.

SOME CONCLUDING REMARKS. While we shall not develop the legal arguments further here, it should be clear that the criterion of constitutionality does not yield an easy evaluation of the committee veto. Underlying the arguments against constitutionality is a normative theory of administration and executive accountability that finds its nearest parallel in the parliamentary, responsible-party model of government. Behind the defense of constitutionality is the perceived need for Congress to develop new forms for expressing its intent if it is to maintain some semblance of balance in the face of ever greater presidential initiative. Clearly, Congress must rely on the principles of spe-

---

30 *United States* v. *Curtiss-Wright Export Corporation,* 299 U.S. 304 (1936); *Yakus* v. *United States,* 321 U.S. 414 (1944).

31 *Field* v. *Clark,* 143 U.S. 649, 690–94 (1892); *Hampton and Co.* v. *United States,* 276 U.S. 394, 404–7, 410 (1928); *Currin* v. *Wallace,* 306 U.S. 1, 15–16 (1939); *U.S.* v. *Rock Royal Co-op,* 307 U.S. 533, 577–78 (1939).

cialization and division of labor through its committee system if it is to exercise a significant control function.

The constitutional issue has not yet been and may never be resolved through litigation. It remains to be seen how strong presidential opposition to the committee veto will be. If history is any guide, presidential victories will be fragmentary. Congressional control of administration is too deeply rooted in American political history. As Joseph and Ann Cooper conclude in their analysis of the legislative veto:

> Undoubtedly the veto interferes with and controls administration decision-making. But interference in the administrative process is the price of legislative oversight and the veto is not so different in this regard, either in terms of the kind or effect of its interference, to be singled out and condemned as unconstitutional.[32]

If the committee veto survives the constitutional test as a potent technique of congressional control, its critics will have to turn to other criteria for assessing its merits and demerits.[33]

THE CRITERION OF RATIONALITY: CONGRESS MOVES TOWARD ANNUAL AUTHORIZATION

A second major controversy over congressional control — this time without the aura of a constitutional struggle — has been the trend toward annual or other forms of limited authorization. In some ways the basic issues of executive rationality versus congressional oversight are more clearly stated in this case than in the previous one.

One of the major procedural and organizational principles of Congress has been the distinction between authorization and appropriation, i.e., statements of legislative policy versus the funding of programs so defined. Appropriations are forbidden under the rules unless they have been previously authorized by law. The rules also prohibit general legislation in appropriations bills. Both Houses incorporate two parallel committee structures reflecting this distinction: the legis-

---

[32] Cooper and Cooper, *op. cit.*, p. 498.

[33] For a discussion of alternative criteria see the statement of Professor Arthur Maass, before the Ervin Special Subcommittee on Separation of Powers, *op. cit.*, pp. 185–201. Maass accepts the constitutionality of the committee veto but considers it "probably unwise for the reason that it denies to the whole Congress the opportunity to review the decisions of its committees." Instead he recommends a form of the one-House veto.

lative or authorizing committees — Agriculture, Armed Services, Banking and Currency — and the Appropriations Committee and its subcommittees. Both the authorizing and appropriations committees are divided along jurisdictional lines paralleling approximately the major executive departments. Thus a typical agency will have at least four congressional committees reporting its basic legislation and appropriations.

Annual authorization has gained significance as an expanded technique of congressional control since the end of World War II. The practice of enacting general or open-ended authorization legislation had weakened the relationships between the legislative committees and their respective agencies. The major occasions for legislative committee involvement were agency requests for new legislation or amendment of basic statutes. Conversely, the appropriations committees, working on an annual budget cycle, maintained stronger relationships with the agencies, and in some instances assumed policy roles that had been yielded by default by the corresponding legislative committees. The rapid growth of expenditures in certain program areas such as foreign operations further enhanced the power of appropriations.

One of the major purposes of the Legislative Reorganization Act of 1946, as we have noted, was to strengthen congressional control and oversight through the standing committee system, especially the legislative committees. The identification of the oversight function primarily with the legislative committees is clearly made in the testimony of Congressman Chet Holifield (D-Cal.) before the Joint Committee on the Organization of the Congress in May, 1965:

> I believe that every committee of jurisdiction has not only the legal right, the legislative right, but I think it has the responsibility of following every piece of legislation that it passes to see how it functions, because legislation is not a static thing. It is a growing, living thing and conditions change which make legislation, which has heretofore maybe been sufficient, become not sufficient.
>
> And unless the legislative committee of jurisdiction follows its legislation by continuous oversight, continuous observation, continuous calling of the agencies before the committee to find out how they are implementing it, then the Congress itself has done a futile thing in passing the legislation. . . .
>
> . . . But I think the expertise in programs lies within the committees of subject-matter jurisdiction more than in the

Appropriations Committee. I think if the committees having subject-matter jurisdiction do their job well, if they equip themselves with the kind of staff expertise that is necessary, and if they act responsibly in relation to the overall national budget, there would be less for the Appropriations Committee to do in the way of overall control.[34]

Former Senator Monroney, a co-author of the 1946 legislation, remarked later in the same hearings, "It certainly seems to me that the Appropriations Committee cannot possibly do . . . the supervisory job that we intended the legislative committee to do." [35]

A logical way for the legislative committees to enhance their oversight role was through the more systematic and frequent review of authorizing legislation. By imposing time or funding limits on previously open-ended authorizations, the legislative committees could force regular review of ongoing agency programs that might otherwise escape scrutiny. One of the more popular authorization limits, the "annual authorization," adopted initially for the postwar foreign aid programs, was extended to a wide range of programs, especially new and rapidly developing policy areas such as space and weapons systems. Annual authorization, however, meant that four congressional committees would be involved each year in the authorization-appropriations cycle for each agency.

THE FIGHT TO INSTITUTE ANNUAL AUTHORIZATION FOR THE SPACE PROGRAM. Annual authorization drew opposition from several sources, both outside Congress and within: the President, the Budget Bureau, and the Appropriations Committees in Congress. The fight to institute annual authorization for the space program is a case in point.

While the Senate was debating a Military Construction Appropriations bill in August, 1958, then Senator Lyndon B. Johnson, a leading advocate of an increased space effort, introduced an amendment stating that "no appropriation may be made to the National Aeronautics and Space Administration unless previously authorized by legislation hereafter enacted by Congress." The Johnson rider, in effect, required annual authorization prior to appropriation for the *entire* NASA budget. The Senate agreed to the amendment, and a similar provision was added to a supplemental appropriations bill in the House. The White House was quick to express its objection that the rider would

[34] *Hearings: Organization of Congress*, pp. 188–90.
[35] *Ibid.*, p. 594.

"leave real control of space development in Congress and tie up annual space programs in unnecessary legislative red tape." [36]

The Johnson rider was reported out of the conference on supplemental appropriations as an "amendment in disagreement." Majority Leader Johnson urged the Senate to further insist upon its amendment. He argued that annual authorization was a well established practice for "new, complicated and unusually large expenditure programs," that the technical complexity of the space program required the full study that only a legislative committee could give it, and that the new procedure would instruct NASA officials how "to constructively guide the appropriation bill through the Appropriations Committee." The Senate supported Johnson by an 86–0 vote.[37]

The resistance to annual authorization coalesced in the House. Republicans, who saw Johnson's move as a prod to the Eisenhower administration to raise the funding levels of the space program, solidly opposed the amendment. Congressman Gerald Ford (R-Mich.) of the Appropriations Committee stated that the rider would "hamstring" NASA and was about "95% in opposition to the basic legislation for the space agency." [38] Defending the Johnson proposal was fellow Texan, Albert Thomas, a ranking Democrat on Appropriations. In his view the legislative committees had given away the authority of Congress. "They gave it to the executive, and the only way you are going to get some of that authority back is by this language. . . . [W]hat is wrong with them coming over and letting Congress determine? After all, we do the legislating." [39] The House refused to concur with the Senate amendment, 126–236, with only two Republicans supporting the Johnson position. A second conference on the bill agreed to prior authorization for fiscal 1959 and 1960 appropriations only.

When the provision came up for House reconsideration in the following session, with the partisan overtones of the issue somewhat muted, the debate was now clearly joined between the legislative committee, Science and Astronautics, and the Appropriations Committee. During the NASA authorization hearings, Congressman James Fulton (R-Pa.) stated as a "general policy" that the committee would not hand over any of its authority to the Appropriations Committee. On

---

36 *The Washington Post*, August 19, 1958, p. 2.
37 *Congressional Record*, 85th Congress, 2nd Session, p. 18700.
38 *Ibid.*, pp. 18765–67, 18772–75.
39 *Ibid.*, p. 18773.

the floor, Congressman Ford again criticized the procedure because it would "continue to slow up the work of the Appropriations Committee." The NASA authorization bill, requiring subsequent annual authorization of the NASA budget, passed the House on a 294–128 roll-call vote (227D,67R–46D,82R) with the unanimous support of the Science and Astronautics Committee (25–0) and the opposition of Appropriations Chairman Clarence Cannon (D-Mo.), Thomas, and 34 of 48 members of the Appropriations Committee.[40]

ARGUMENTS AGAINST ANNUAL AUTHORIZATION. As annual authorizations have increased, resistance to this technique of congressional control has continued to mount. On January 21, 1964, following the record-breaking appropriations lags of the previous session (the last appropriations bill was passed on December 16), Chairman Clarence Cannon of the House Appropriations Committee announced to the House of Representatives a detailed schedule that his committee would follow in reporting appropriations bills for floor action. The last of 11 bills — foreign aid — was scheduled to be reported out of committee on Friday, June 5, and to be considered on the floor Tuesday, June 9.[41] Chairman Cannon placed the blame for previous delays squarely on the authorizing committees, although it should be noted that the major civil rights legislation introduced midway in the session, as well as a protracted test of wills between Cannon and Senate Appropriations Chairman Carl Hayden (D-Ariz.) over the prerogatives of their respective committees, both contributed to the slow pace of Congress during 1963.[42]

To hold to his schedule, even in an election year with summer

---

[40] *Congressional Record*, 86th Congress, 1st Session, pp. 8276–96, 8634. Richard F. Fenno notes that the fight over annual authorization of the NASA budget was a case of Appropriations Committee–House conflict. The result was "a sharing of influence in what had previously been the Appropriations Committee's private preserve. The House seems increasingly enthusiastic about the annual authorization technique as a device to keep themselves from becoming hostaged to the Appropriations Committee." *The Power of the Purse: Appropriations Politics in Congress* (Boston: Little, Brown & Co., 1966), pp. 72–73.

[41] Fenno, *op. cit.*, p. 420.

[42] See Cannon's remarks, "Late Enactment of the Appropriation Bills," *Congressional Record*, 88th Congress, 1st Session, December 30, 1963, pp. 24372–74, and "Senate-House Feud Stalls Appropriations," *Congressional Quarterly Almanac*, 87th Congress, 2nd Session (1962), pp. 144–46. Also see Jeffrey L. Pressman, *House vs. Senate: Conflict in the Appropriations Process* (New Haven: Yale University Press, 1966).

presidential nominating conventions, Chairman Cannon had to move some appropriations bills to the floor *before* authorization legislation had been enacted. This he accomplished by the device of a special rule from the Rules Committee, waiving all points of order challenging the validity of such action. Thus both the military construction and foreign aid appropriations were considered before the House Armed Services Committees had completed action on annual authorizations. Action on all regular appropriations bills was completed on July 1.[43] Cannon's successor as chairman, George Mahon (D-Tex.), has not seen fit to challenge the legislative committees in such a frontal manner. By the first session of the 90th Congress (1967), the appropriations schedule was back to where it was in 1963 with the added complications and impasse of an economy drive and presidential request for increased taxes.[44]

Budget Bureau support for the Appropriations Committees and against the trend toward annual authorization was made quite explicit in testimony before the Joint Committee on the Organization of the Congress during 1965. Budget Director Charles L. Schultze asked the committee whether Congress could "maintain the comity it desires among its committees without imposing upon the executive branch the burdens of the annually expiring or biannually expiring authorization system?" Observing that 95 per cent of programs in 1946 were authorized on a long-term or indefinite basis as contrasted with virtually one-third of the budget now under *annual* authorization, the Budget Director went on to underscore the costs to rational program decision and execution:

> This creates a real difficulty for the executive branch — in the late enactment of appropriations, in the indecisiveness and inability to make sound plans for the year being considered, in the requirements for executive branch witnesses to explain their program at least four different times to four different committees each year — and giving agency heads that much less time to think and manage — in the immersion of the legislative committees as well as the Appropriations Committees in the details of administration to the detriment of the longer range, broader view of missions and objectives,

[43] Fenno, *op. cit.*, p. 421.

[44] By the Labor Day recess, the 90th Congress, 1st Session had cleared only 3 of the 14 regular fiscal 1968 appropriations bills: Interior, Legislative Branch, and Treasury and Post Office.

and in prolonged congressional sessions which, in turn, hurry the executive branch beyond the economical point in reaching decisions on legislative proposals and the budget in the short time between sessions.[45]

Budget Director Schultze also scored annual authorization ceilings as limiting "the flexibility of both the Executive and Congress in allocating scarce budgetary resources to the most valuable uses" since "ceilings tend to become floors as well." In answer to a question from Congressman Ken Hechler (D-W. Va.), the Director proposed that new programs be authorized "in non-financial terms on a multiyear basis" and that "in the interest of governmental efficiency detailed budget reviews should be made only by the Appropriations Committees" and "the enactment of appropriations bills should not be contingent upon prior enactment of a series of ceilings on appropriations for individual agencies." [46]

ARGUMENTS IN DEFENSE OF ANNUAL AUTHORIZATION. While the critics of annual authorization stress the costs to rationality and efficiency in both the legislative and administrative processes, other observers note the benefits of this oversight technique for the legislative committees and for Congress as an institution.

Raymond H. Dawson, in his study of annual authorization for aircrafts, missiles, or naval vessels (Section 412[b] of the Military Construction Authorization Act for Fiscal 1960), concludes that annual authorization, properly utilized, increases congressional participation in defense policy making.[47] The regular involvement of the legislative committees strengthens congressional *access* to the processes of policy formulation in the Executive. The authorization process, unlike defense appropriations "which must roam across an immense terrain of policy decisions," also possesses the *utility of focus*. The legislative committees can give more selective attention to major policy choices implicit in the legislation. Access and focus combine to effect an additional alteration in executive-legislative dialogue. The authorization procedure creates an *expanded base of knowledge* in Congress, the prerequisite for effective, intelligent debate.

---

[45] *Hearings: Organization of Congress*, p. 1779.
[46] *Ibid.*, p. 1871.
[47] "Congressional Innovation and Intervention in Defense Policy: Legislative Authorization of Weapons Systems," APSR, March 1962, pp. 42–57.

In testimony before the Joint Committee on the Organization of the Congress, Professor Arthur Maass of Harvard University suggested the need for "relevant criteria" other than efficiency, in evaluating "this most important and recent growth in executive-legislative relations." Annual authorization may provide opportunities for policy oversight by Congress, for the education of members of Congress who are not on the Appropriations Committees, for the education of the public, and for guiding new programs in their developmental and experimental years.

> These opportunities, I suggest, would never have been available had we relied for our education on the debates relating to the annual appropriations bills.
>
> Annual authorization may provide oversight from a point of view that is significantly and perhaps constructively different from that provided by the Appropriations Committees. . . . [T]he active exercise of oversight by the legislative committees is, I believe, unexceptionable.[48]

SOME CONCLUDING REMARKS. Once again, it should be clear to the reader that different perspectives on Congress yield different evaluations of congressional performance. To those who would stress the value of administrative rationality or broad executive discretion in controlling the program structure of government, annual authorization is an unwarranted burden on executive officials. The appropriations process in Congress is a more than adequate vehicle for congressional control — potential and actual. To others, the appropriations process does not provide Congress proper understanding and control of increasingly complex processes of policy formulation. The gain in congressional knowledge and competence through the authorization process counterbalances the costs in efficiency. Different forms of authorization for different programs is a solution Congress is now beginning to accept.[49]

Finally, we should note that the controversy over annual authorization is but one aspect of the broader tension between authorization and appropriations in the legislative process. Developments in program budgeting, analysis, and information systems are likely to raise

---

[48] *Hearings: Organization of Congress*, p. 942.43.

[49] Among specific recommendations to the Joint Committee were research on trends on annual and short-term authorizations, comparative analysis of alternative techniques, and congressional guidelines on the use of short-term authorizations. *Ibid.*, p. 944.

even more acute questions about the appropriate locus of control and oversight responsibility within the Congress.

THE CRITERION OF EFFECTIVENESS:
SOME FURTHER PROPOSALS TO STRENGTHEN
CONGRESSIONAL CONTROL AND OVERSIGHT

A third evaluation holds that the oversight provisions of the Legislative Reorganization Act have been insufficiently realized; that congressional intent is still not effectively communicated to, or followed through by, executive agencies; and that a battery of new or extended oversight techniques is required. A variety of criticisms of existing performance evokes a variety of not entirely consistent proposals. The one unifying theme, however, is that Congress must increase its effective control of the executive bureaucracy.

THE NEED FOR MORE CONTINUOUS AND INTENSIVE OVERSIGHT. Frequent criticisms underline the episodic, haphazard, and incomplete exercise of oversight. How do you motivate elected politicians in such "non-glamorous, nose-grinding" work, asks Senator John Sparkman (D-Ala.).[50] One study of congressional oversight of independent regulatory agencies reported that most congressmen considered committee review of agency activity "a time expensive, low priority concern except when there was likely to be something 'big' in it." [51] The same study found that "a series of oversight bursts" or spurts of committee interest in agency activity could be explained on a kind of cost-return basis. Committee leaders were prepared to involve committee resources in studies of agency performance if and when political gains valued by congressmen were seen to outweigh prospective losses. Five such situations, meeting the "conditions for legislative control," were identified:

1. When the leadership of the majority party in Congress believes it can cause sufficient embarrassment, with accompanying profit for itself, to a past or current opposition President who is held responsible for the performance of his agency appointees, committee oversight tends to be used for this purpose.
2. When the committee leadership or powerful committee members believe that constituent or group interests impor-

[50] *Ibid.*, p. 782.
[51] Seymour Scher, *op. cit.*, p. 532.

tant to them cannot be satisfied by the routine personal inter-
cessions between Congressmen and the agency, committee
review tends to be used as a substitute.

3. When Congressmen perceive a threat, particularly from
the President, to their traditional prerogatives of primacy in
relation to regulatory agencies, committee interest in the
agencies is a likely response.

4. When, periodically, interest builds in Congress for
revising regulatory policy, committee attention to the regulatory agency tends to occur as a by-product. . . . An examination of agency conduct frequently is used . . . as a screen
behind which new legislation is built.

5. When the committee leadership becomes convinced
that interests to which it is opposed can be substantially advanced by the exposure of dramatic evidence of agency failure,
it can be expected to move first to neutralize or minimize
these gains by initiating its own inquiry.[52]

One means of strengthening control and oversight suggested by this
realpolitik interpretation of congressional-agency relations is to enhance partisan roles in Congress. This could be accomplished by
establishing separate minority staffs on congressional committees, a
proposal that has been advanced and developed by Republican members of Congress such as Congressmen Thomas B. Curtis (R-Mo.),
and Fred Schwengel (R-Iowa) and Senator Hugh Scott (R-Pa.).[53]
Another partisan reform suggested by Congressman Robert H. Michel
(R-Ill.) is minority control of the Government Operations Commit-

---

[52] *Ibid.*, pp. 541–48. Scher notes the view that "uncertainty over when a
committee will focus its attention on an agency is sufficient to keep the agency
'honest' in much the same way as would regular and frequent surveillance" (p.
540).

[53] For a comprehensive development of the arguments for minority staffing,
see speeches by Senator Scott and Congressman Schwengel, *Congressional
Record*, 87th Congress, 2nd Session, pp. 5949–54, 15326, 15327, 17067, 17372–
77, 18679–82, 19686, 20195–97; 88th Congress, 1st Session, pp. 3056, 4447,
15052; 88th Congress, 2nd Session, pp. 3184, 6314, 11449, 20794, A 4059. Also
see the bulletins of the Schwengel House Committee on Increased Minority
Staffing, the House Republican Conference, 88th Congress, 1st and 2nd Sessions,
and the Senate-House Joint Minority Staffing Committee, prepared under the
supervision of Frederick H. Sontag, Staff Director. For a more recent statement
of the case see Congressman James C. Cleveland (R-N.H.), "The Need for
Increased Minority Staffing," in Mary McInnis (ed.), *We Propose: A Modern
Congress, Selected Proposals by the House Republican Task Force on Congressional Reform and Minority Staffing* (New York: McGraw-Hill Book Co.,
1966), pp. 5–19.

tees. Under this proposal the chairmanship and majority membership of the House and Senate committees on Government Operations would comprise members of a major political party other than that of the President. Congressman Michel states:

> Perhaps the major function of Congress today is oversight of the sprawling administrative structure; this function is necessarily diminished when the party of the President and the majority party in Congress (and thus the majority on every committee) is one and the same.[54]

While a number of observers agree that "the strongest legislative control is imposed when the political opponents of the President have the upperhand in Congress," opponents of earmarked minority staff or minority control of investigatory committees contend that it will burden both the legislative and oversight functions with "phony partisanship" and create hopeless chaos in government.[55] Proposals of this nature and opposition to them usually involve a much broader set of normative assumptions about legislative-executive relations.[56]

Other proposals for effecting more continuous and intensive congressional oversight recommend facilitative, institutional, or procedural reforms. Congress should establish, fund, and staff special subcommittees on oversight on each of the legislative committees.[57] The House and Senate should establish oversight calendars giving precedence at least two days in each month to committee reports on oversight activities.[58] Another device for ensuring more effective feedback of oversight information into the legislative process would be the creation of an Office of Administrative Counsel for Congress which would screen constituent case problems from congressmen and in the

[54] "Reorganization of the Committees on Government Operations and Minority Control of Investigation," in McInnis (ed.), *op. cit.*, p. 168.

[55] See Harris, *op. cit.*, pp. 280–81; *Hearings: Organization of Congress*, pp. 954–56.

[56] See, for example, Kenneth Kofmehl's conclusions on congressional staff and the oversight of administration, *op. cit.*, pp. 126–46. "Under no circumstances should the regular staffs of the standing committees be enlarged in an attempt to maintain continuous, detailed surveillance of administration through a more or less independent staff operation. To do so could easily result in setting up a competing bureaucracy which Congress — or rather more precisely, subordinate units of Congress — could completely control and which would aggravate extant shortcomings in our system of government" (p. 146).

[57] *Hearings: Organization of Congress*, pp. 689, 727–30.

[58] Cornelius P. Cotter, "Legislative Oversight," in Alfred de Grazia (ed.), *Congress: The First Branch of Government* (Washington, D.C.: American Enterprise Institute, 1966), p. 81.

process identify patterns of administrative error or abuse. Major areas of governmental activity not currently being reviewed by the standing committees, such as foreign intelligence programs, grant-in-aid programs, and research expenditures, should be assigned either to new joint standing committees or special joint study committees.[59]

These and other similar reform proposals assume that congressional attention to oversight can be stimulated simply by filling the loopholes in the existing system. An enlarged congressional staff undoubtedly builds congressional capacity to exercise control or oversight, but such capacity is effective only insofar as members are motivated to use it. The experiences of the Joint Committee on Atomic Energy and the Joint Economic Committee suggest, however, that the institutionalization of certain policy responsibilities can significantly affect legislative behavior. With these notable exceptions, facilitative reforms, to have any significant impact, require more basic changes in congressional attitudes and motivation.

THE NEED FOR A MORE COORDINATED AND INFORMED CONGRESSIONAL OVERVIEW OF ADMINISTRATION. A second set of criticisms of inadequate congressional control stresses the fragmentation and lack of coordination of Congress itself. More important than continuous oversight is informed, coordinated oversight. The budgetary process, and especially appropriations, as the primary congressional technique for control of administration, is the major point of concern. How can Congress exercise effective control of spending when it does not monitor or control new program authorizations; when it divides and assigns the budget to separate, virtually autonomous subcommittees; when it fails to relate expenditures to revenues? A related concern is the quality of information Congress has available on which to base its decisions.

Again, a variety of reforms have been proposed. Improved information facilities range from automatic data processing to a Social and Behavioral Sciences Institute.[60] New coordinating mechanisms have frequently been suggested such as a Joint Budget Committee and a

[59] Typical proposals of this type include former Congressman John Lindsay's resolution to establish a Joint Committee on Foreign Information and Intelligence and Lucius Wilmerding's suggestion that Congress set up a Joint Committee on Public Accounts to review General Accounting audits. *Hearings: Organization of Congress*, pp. 459–70; *Hearings: Organization and Operations of Congress*, pp. 495–504. Another proposal is for a series of permanent joint study committees apart from the legislative committees. See statement of Professor Robert H. Salisbury, *Hearings: Organization of Congress*, pp. 741–42.

[60] See summary of proposals for increasing the flow of information to Congress extracted from de Grazia (ed.), *op. cit.*, pp. 484–91.

Joint Committee on National Security Affairs.[61] The relationship of these mechanisms to the existing standing committee structure remains a point of continuing tension. Are they to have jurisdiction over subordinate committees, or are they simply to be information gathering and disseminating bodies? After 1946 the attempt of Congress to impose budgetary decisions on itself through a Joint Committee on the Legislative Budget broke down because there was no hierarchical power structure sufficient to enforce such decisions. On the basis of this experiment, Aaron Wildavsky concludes that no effective joint committee determination of the budget is possible in the American system because "there is no cohesive group in Congress capable of using these devices [joint committees] to affect decision making by imposing its preferences on a majority of congressmen." [62]

Regardless of the past experience with policy coordination and budgetary reform in particular, innovations in program analysis and budgeting together with comprehensive, low-cost information systems promise to increase markedly congressional capacities for informed, coordinated control and oversight of administration. Some of the most important implications of the information revolution for Congress, explored in Chapter Seven, will be in the increased potential of Congress and its committees to oversee the Executive.

THE NEED FOR MORE RADICAL FORMS OF CONGRESSIONAL CONTROL AND OVERSIGHT. A third group of reform proposals is based on normative assumptions that accept the previous criticisms and reforms but go well beyond them. Congressional innovations, such as the committee veto and annual authorization, have been inadequate for the task. As Edward de Grazia warns:

> Respect for the constitutional doctrine of the separation of powers does not entail Congress placing undue self-restraint upon the exercise of its traditional and legitimate prerogatives concerning the administration of the laws it has helped to pass and the oversight of the agencies it has helped to create. Excessive self-restraint of this kind might work towards upsetting the balance of power and tip the scales irretrievably in favor of the executive arms.[63]

[61] *Hearings: Organization of Congress*, pp. 480–85, 1236–39.
[62] "Political Implications of Budgetary Reform," *Public Administration Review*, Autumn 1961, p. 186.
[63] "Congressional Liaison: An Inquiry into its Meaning for Congress," in Alfred de Grazia (ed.), *op. cit.*, p. 299.

The reforms advanced from this perspective would all serve to reverse or counter the model of executive-centered government. The Bureau of the Budget should be made a "joint-agency" of President and Congress, or short of this, Congress should establish its own budget office.[64] Alfred de Grazia has made the daring proposal that congressional tribunes, designated from a panel of qualified persons serving under Congress, be assigned to each agency of government. There, they would serve as a "built-in antibody" to bureaucracy, playing the role of devil's advocate, "proposing to the appropriate congressional committees that the agencies' activities, personnel, jurisdiction, and budget be eliminated, devolved to local governments or non-governmental groups, or otherwise reorganized." [65] Related to this is Edward de Grazia's suggestion that legislative liaison (now used by the Executive to influence Congress) be developed as a technique of congressional influence upon the Executive's administration of the laws, including "establishing *within the Pentagon itself* congressional offices of executive liaison whose personnel have been cleared by *Congress* for access to classified data of the most sensitive categories." [66] Other proposals of this genre are a "Resident Agent of Congress, suitably staffed and officed" to oversee federal programs at the district level and a Sub-Legislative Corps comprising all officials who have been delegated considerable legislative power and who are "certified by Congress as to their qualifications for such offices, and required to acknowledge and act in terms of the legislative capacities of their office under Congress." [67]

SOME CONCLUDING REMARKS. Those who emphasize congressional effectiveness as a criterion of performance are generally inclined to develop and extend techniques of congressional control and oversight. We can distinguish two emphases, however, based upon the

---

[64] Cotter, *op. cit.*, pp. 80–81.

[65] Alfred de Grazia, *Republic in Crisis: Congress Against the Executive Force* (New York: Federal Legal Publications, 1965), p. 238; "Toward a New Model of Congress," in *Congress: The First Branch of Government*, pp. 16–17.

[66] *Op. cit.*, pp. 316–21. G. Russell Pipe suggests that "assignment of one or more congressional staff members to each [executive department] liaison office with specific duties relating to oversight investigation is both possible and practicable. Permanent on-the-spot scrutiny is not currently practiced by any unit of Congress including the General Accounting Office." "Congressional Liaison: The Executive Branch Consolidates its Relations with Congress," *Public Administration Review*, XXVI, No. 1 (March 1966), 14–24.

[67] Alfred de Grazia, *Congress: The First Branch of Government*, pp. 13, 17.

"constitutional balance" and "congressional supremacy" perspectives of executive-legislative relations. The former, as we defined it, accepts executive initiative in legislation and administration but assumes strong independent congressional contributions to both. Balance in the constitutional system is preserved by a broad interpretation of the separation of powers in the continuing redefinition of presidential and congressional roles. The latter rejects executive-centered government for a "republican" model of government. Governmental programs are to be decentralized and phased out as soon as possible, thereby reducing the requirements for presidential leadership and enhancing possibilities for congressional control.[68] These orientations toward the oversight function are significantly different from those which would restrict it on the grounds of constitutionality or rationality and efficiency.[69]

EVALUATIONS OF CONGRESSIONAL PERFORMANCE: INVESTIGATIVE STAFF FOR CONGRESS

Few would disagree that Congress should be informed in its decisions, should understand the nature of the problems on which it legislates, and should maintain an intelligent, continuing dialogue with the Executive on matters of public policy. These are canons of responsible legislative practice which even the executive-oriented critics of Congress admit. In advancing his case for establishing an Office of Legislative Evaluation, Daniel P. Moynihan chided some of the policy liberals inside and outside government who privately fear giving Congress full information on program operation:

> The usual whispered argument, of course, is that to be candid about public policies that don't produce much progress is to

---

[68] This policy orientation is obvious in Alfred de Grazia's discussion of contemporary bureaucracy. De Grazia proposes a Zero Sum Activity policy of government. "It is quite possible to adopt a policy of requiring the cancelling of an old activity in order to begin a new activity in government. . . . The responsibility for devising a precise means of carrying out this policy should be assigned jointly to congressional leadership, to the Legislative Reference Service, to the Social and Behavioral Science Institute, to the Tribunes of Congress, and to the Sub-Legislative Corps." *Republic in Crisis,* p. 239.

[69] See, for example, Herman Somers' critique of Congress as an overseer. Somers suggests that augmented *presidential* control of the Executive branch is "one of the most realistic ways for strengthening the Congress in its overseer role." "The President, the Congress, and the Federal Government Service," Sayre (ed.), *op. cit.,* p. 75.

give a weapon to the enemies of progress. This is an unworthy
argument; there are never grounds for concealing truth about
public matters. . . . But it is also an absurd argument. The
American public supports a fantastic array of social services,
and does so in ever larger amounts. The issue, then, is not
whether, but which.[70]

It is equally clear that Congress can improve its understanding of
ever more complicated matters of public policy only if it equips itself
to do so. And this means enlarged, increasingly specialized, differentiated staff. Yet a strong argument against increasing congressional staff
has been developed and is adhered to by a surprisingly large number
of political scientists and executive officials as well as members of
Congress.

The issue of congressional staff is pertinent to all congressional
functions. Professional staff at the committee level is essential to
congressional initiation in the legislative process and to exercising the
control function. Staff attached to a congressman's office extends his
performance in constituency service. While we have chosen to discuss
congressional staff under the investigative function of Congress, the
arguments we shall develop are generally applicable to congressional
performance of all functions.

The cases for and against congressional staff, as in the debate we
have just considered on the oversight function, rest on broader normative assumptions about the role of Congress in the federal system.
Clearly, if one limits congressional control of administration to after-
the-fact review or oversight, the staffing requirements will be quite
different than if one takes an expanded view of the control function.
Much of the criticism of congressional staff, then, is, more accurately,
criticism of congressional activities with which the critic disagrees. In
such a case, the criticism should be directed at the congressional function, not at the staff which was created by Congress to perform it.

THE TREND TOWARD EXECUTIVE MONOPOLY IN PROGRAM ANALYSIS
AND EVALUATION. As the modern executive bureaucracy has grown, it
has accumulated a "monopoly of skills" in critical areas of public
policy such as space, defense weapons systems, foreign-policy intelli-

[70] U.S. Senate, Subcommittee on Executive Reorganization, Committee on
Government Operations, *Hearings: Federal Role in Urban Affairs*, 89th Congress, 2nd Session, December 1966, pp. 2645–46.

gence, and urban redevelopment.[71] Congress has been faced with the choice of how to develop its own understanding of new policy problems. It has, since the end of World War II, responded in a variety of ways. It has made adjustments in its committee structure. It has vested one committee and its staff, the Joint Committee on Atomic Energy, with extraordinary powers of access to executive information. It has developed new techniques of policy oversight like annual authorization. It has established a Science Policy Research Division in the Legislative Reference Service of the Library of Congress. In other areas the response of Congress has been limited or nonexistent. It has kept professional staffs on key committees, such as Armed Services and Space, small and generally nontechnical. It has virtually ignored the intelligence component of foreign policy. And it has just begun to reconsider committee jurisdictions and responsibilities in grasping the emerging domestic crisis of the urban ghetto.

In contrast the trend toward concentration of technical, specialized information in the Executive and the resulting dependence of Congress on the Executive for much of its policy information has been clearly discernible. Now that the Executive is moving into an important new phase of program analysis and evaluation research, symbolized by the Planning-Programming-Budgeting System (PPBS), the Executive's near-monopoly may be dramatically extended. The potential impact of the information revolution in government raises even more fundamental questions about congressional access to information and program evaluation. Daniel Moynihan concludes that "a new source of knowledge is coming into being" that is likely to raise the level of public discourse. However, the Executive branch has developed "a virtual monopoly on the product of evaluation research." Such an imbalance is dangerous because the findings of such research are not neutral. The situation should not be permitted to persist for a number of reasons:

> First, and most importantly, the Congress and other legislative bodies are put at a considerable disadvantage. A major weapon in the "arsenal of persuasion" is in effect denied them. Second, the executive is exposed to the constant temp-

71 For a perceptive interpretation of the tendencies toward monopoly of skill and monopoly of power in modern bureaucracy see Reinhard Bendix, "Bureaucracy and the Problem of Power," *Public Administration Review*, 1945, pp. 194–209.

tation to release only those findings that suit its purposes; there is no one to keep them honest. Third, universities and other private groups which often undertake such research on contract are in some measure subject to constant if subtle pressure to produce "positive" findings.[72]

The argument that Congress must equip itself to counter or check increasing executive expertise is a persuasive defense of its investigative function. It is supplemented by a more positive definition of Congress as a study and deliberative body. Former Congressman Thomas B. Curtis (R-Mo.) describes Congress, ideally and primarily, as "a mechanism for gathering together the knowledge and wisdom existing within the society to make judgments to solve the problems facing the society." [73] According to Curtis, this investigative or study function of Congress is accomplished through three primary processes: (1) the distilled wisdom (publications and other forms of stored information) contained in the Library of Congress is further refined by the Legislative Reference Staff; (2) the current wisdom of the society is collected through the standing committees of Congress with the assistance of professional staff (committee hearings provide forums in which the knowledge of experts in the Executive branch and in the private sector is brought to bear on public problems); and (3) knowledge from individual citizens — how the laws as written and administered affect them — is gathered from the letters and conversations of constituents and interest groups. These three processes suggest three levels of staff assistance: institutional staff assistance attached to Congress, the professional staffs of congressional committees, and congressional office staff servicing constituent needs. We shall limit our analysis to the first two. (Constituency service is discussed in the following chapter.)

THE DEBATE OVER ENLARGED CONGRESSIONAL STAFF. Opposition to increased congressional staff, and especially to the establishment of a legislative bureaucracy, is based on a number of negative assessments

[72] *Hearings: Federal Role in Urban Affairs*, p. 2647. Amitai Etzioni identifies another problem. "[I]ntensive and encompassing societal action requires societal backing (or 'consensus') if it is not to be alienating or prohibitively expensive. In the past, the national legislature was a major source of this consensus. Now, since legislatures are provided with insufficient information (while the scope of societal activities is steadily augmenting), their capacity to act effectively is declining. Lack of consensus is a major barrier." "How May Congress Learn," *Science*, January 1968, p. 172.
[73] McInnis (ed.), *op. cit.*, pp. vii–viii.

of congressional staff. One major concern not discussed at length here is the potential for increased competition between executive and legislative staff bureaucracies with corollary interference in the executive process by legislative actors.[74] With regard to the investigative function at least, competition in ideas and evaluation is probably a positive gain. Other concerns are discussed below.

The problem of congressional control of staff. Critics of large congressional staffs fear that they may develop into independent power centers in the legislative and administrative process. Staffs may usurp congressional roles and become "wheelers and dealers." They may develop cosy relationships with congressmen, agency personnel, and interest representatives and facilitate the growth of subgovernments that are difficult for both the President and Congress to control.

Advocates of enlarged staffs reply that staffs only exercise power that is derived from immediate political superiors. At every point, the extent of discretion staffs enjoy depends upon the working relations established with members of Congress. A staff serves as an extension of the personality of the congressman himself. It enables the member of Congress to play several roles simultaneously where he otherwise might be severely limited in his effectiveness.[75] Staffs play a variety of political roles in the legislative process. They participate extensively in the hearings and committee phase and may even do the bulk of questioning of committee witnesses.[76] Because of the political context of their employment, the temptation of a staff member to "play congressman" is great. In fact, this aspect of congressional staff work may

[74] Arthur Macmahon, for example, warns that "staffing might easily be pushed to a point where it would bring a legislative budget method into existence in rivalry with the executive budget. An ambiguous responsibility might develop in the departments. There is need for the most careful consideration, not glib endorsement of the idea of staff and more staff." "Congressional Oversight of Administration: The Power of the Purse I," *Political Science Quarterly*, June 1943, p. 187.

[75] Staffing, while extending role options, will not necessarily lighten the burden of work of members of Congress. Bertram Gross argues that "the man who tries to do a better job often turns out to be one who sees that the better job is really a bigger job. Moreover, imaginative staff aides often uncover new problems, new opportunities, and new challenges. They tend to create — or at least attract — heavier burdens." *The Legislative Struggle: A Study in Social Combat* (McGraw-Hill Series in Political Science; New York: McGraw-Hill Book Co., 1953), p. 422.

[76] See Kofmehl, *op. cit.*, Chaps. VIII–IX. The two behaviors that distinguish members of the Congress from their staff are voting and floor debate. Even here a staff may exercise influence on the actual voting behavior and stated positions of the congressman.

be one of the basic rewards provided by the system. Yet Congress could hardly function today if congressional staffs did not mimic or anticipate the behavior of their congressional superiors. Ultimately it is the responsibility of the congressman to define the acceptable range of behavior for his congressional staff. The advocates of an enlarged staff assume that congressmen individually and collectively can keep order in their own house.

Abusive or partisan behavior of congressional staff. A related concern voiced by critics of congressional staff is that an investigative staff in particular, sometimes aided by unscrupulous members of Congress, will abuse the civil rights of witnesses and pursue investigations designed to advance the personal political fortunes or limited partisan aims of their superiors. The Senator Joseph McCarthy period generated some particularly searching criticisms of the investigative powers of Congress.[77]

Advocates of investigatory staff reply that Congress has moved to adopt rules and standards of conduct that protect witnesses.[78] Moreover, the Supreme Court, notably in *Watkins* v. *U.S.*, has suggested procedural limits to the investigative powers of Congress.[79] The criticism of *particular exercises* of congressional investigation does not negate the basic value of the *general* power of Congress to act in such a capacity. As Stephen K. Bailey notes, formal investigations are "virtually the only means available to Congress for examining social and economic questions outside the framework of the federal bureaucracy." [80] A partial list of congressional investigations of national consequence includes: studies of Negro migration after the Civil War (1880), immigration of foreign contract labor (1888), strike breaking by railroads (1892), western land reclamation (1909), structural reform of banking and finance (1912), communist activities (1930), the operation of the securities market and stock exchange (1931), the

---

[77] See Telford Taylor, *Grand Inquest: The Story of Congressional Investigations* (New York: Simon & Schuster, 1955); Robert K. Carr, *The House Committee on Un-American Activities, 1945–1950* (Ithaca, N.Y.: Cornell University Press, 1952); Richard H. Rovere, *Senator Joe McCarthy* (New York: Harcourt, Brace & Co., 1959); Douglass Cater, *The Fourth Branch of Government* (Boston: Houghton Mifflin Co., 1959). For a summary of criticisms and proposed reforms predating the McCarthy era see George B. Galloway, "Proposed Reforms in Congressional Investigations," *University of Chicago Law Review*, 1951, pp. 478–502.

[78] *Hearings: Organization of Congress*, pp. 1910–11, 1915–27.

[79] 354 U.S. 178 (1957).

[80] *The New Congress* (St. Martin's Series in American Politics; New York: St. Martin's Press, 1966), p. 86.

munition industry (1934), migratory labor (1937), and monopoly (1939). More recent investigations into war production and the drug industry by former Senators Harry Truman (D-Mo.) and Estes Kefauver (D-Tenn.) have become classic examples of congressional initiative and responsible performance.[81] In sum, any instrument may be used for limited ends or abused. The proper course is to limit such abuse as far as may be practicable, not to deny the use of the instrument.

Preserving the lay element in legislative thinking. Another concern is that the growth of legislative bureaucracy will insulate the congressman from, or dilute his relationships with, either his constituents or executive officials. Arthur Macmahon believes that it is the duty of the congressman, immediately in touch with his constituents, to bring "practical public sense" to bear in the oversight of administration. The congressman interjects the criticism of a "robust, imaginative, lay mind" into highly technical operations." [82] Macmahon fears that these values might be lost if the politician-legislator dealt with administrative officials vicariously through an intermediate legislative bureaucracy.

The advocates of a technically trained staff for Congress reply that the presence of a staff does not preclude direct legislator-administrator dealings. More likely a staff may actually increase the amount and level of interchange by giving the legislator the capacity to understand what the specialist is talking about. The romanticized ideal of the lay legislator confuses the ability to deal with specialized subjects with the commitment of the specialist. As the complexity of public policy issues has increased, the job of a congressman has of necessity become a more professional occupation. Congressmen will require more staff

---

[81] See Donald H. Riddle, *The Truman Committee: A Study in Congressional Responsibility* (New Brunswick, N.J.: Rutgers University Press, 1964); and Richard Harris, *The Real Voice* (New York: The Macmillan Co., 1964).

[82] *Op. cit.* In contrast Roger Davidson concludes that the specialist and generalist orientations are both necessary. "A Congress which is estranged from the learned and scientific professions is indeed estranged from contemporary decision-making premises. In the final analysis, however, what counts is not only Congress' ability to speak for technical constituencies, but also its ability to bring these constituencies together before the bar of politics. The rhetoric of the specialist will help, but it is not sufficient. The Legislator's indispensable contribution to policy-making is his delicate feel for the political system of which he is a part. . . . His special expertise lies in his ability to interject the unique data of politics into this process, in order to render policy outcomes tolerable as well as rational." Alfred de Grazia (ed.), *Congress: The First Branch of Government*, p. 413.

assistance simply to maintain intelligent or informed dialogue with
the Executive. A case in point is the growth of a new "analyst" profession in government. With the extension of PPBS, Congress must
acquire new professional staff skills in appropriations if it is to keep
up with the dialogue that is already changing in the Executive branch.
Congressmen, if they are to serve in an effective mediating role between governmental policy and their constituents, must constantly
upgrade their understanding of government. So long as the legislator
is subject to re-election and the administrator is responsible for implementing his program, there is little likelihood that the separate value
perspectives of nonspecialized and specialized minds will be lost.[83]

The limits of staff effectiveness. Perhaps the most cogent criticism
of the opponents to increased staffing is that staffing in itself cannot
solve many problems. Whether a member of Congress or committee
will initiate an investigation, follow through on hearings and committee action, and actually vote for legislation may depend on a range
of factors completely apart from the availability of staff. Simply adding staff not only may fail to accomplish its desired objective; it may
also yield undesirable side effects such as those already noted. Many
problems are essentially intractable. Staff offers an illusory hope that
congressmen can escape the burdens of uncertainty, difficult choice,
and continuing frustration.

The advocates of increased staff reply that their definition of staff
requirements is selective and in demonstrated areas of need. They
admit that a basic problem is one of educating members of Congress
to use staff effectively.[84] (Congress has virtually unlimited power to
increase its own staff if it so desires.) While they may disagree exactly

---

[83] See Davidson's contrast of career patterns of top civil servants and members
of Congress and the differing representational roles that are developed. *Op. cit.*,
pp. 388–99.

[84] Congressman James C. Cleveland (R-N.H.), for example, concedes, "Members of the minority party have failed to prosecute actively the case for increased staffing. In an extensive survey of Republican Members' attitudes with
respect to the work and staffing of their committees, we found roughly two-
thirds dissatisfied with the performance of their committee in the exercise of
oversight of the Administration. Yet, we are able to document a grand total of
only eleven instances in which minority Members were denied requests for additional committee staff help! (One reason, undoubtedly, is that minority Members
know from painful experience that it is pointless to make such requests because
they have invariably been turned down.) This does not, of course, negate the
case for better staffing for the minority; it *does* point up the educational job we
have to do on our own side of the aisle as well as generally." McInnis (ed.),
op. cit., p. 12.

how increased staff should be allocated within the congressional system, they share an optimistic assessment that Congress could improve its functional performance significantly — in investigation and elsewhere — if it were only adequately staffed.

STAFFING FOR THE INVESTIGATIVE FUNCTION OF CONGRESS. If one grants that the advocates of increased congressional staff have the better argument, as the author is inclined to do, a number of problems remain.[85] A significant increase in congressional staff can only be accommodated outside the existing committee system. Moynihan, for example, suggests that the staff of a new Office of Legislative Evaluation be located either in a separate agency responsible to Congress, in the Library of Congress, or in the General Accounting Office. Decisions on this and other proposals, such as a RAND-type of Congressional Institute and the use of congressional commissions, will require careful attention to design, supervision, and effective utilization.[86]

The fundamental problem of allocating staff resources remains. An overall increase in the quality and quantity of congressional staff should alleviate the expressed staffing inadequacies of the minority as well as of junior members of committees. It is important to realize, however, that staff resources are an important element in the basis of congressional power and that an increase in such resources will inevitably affect the distribution of power in Congress. The allocation of staff will also have consequences for congressional performance in specific functional areas such as oversight and constituency service.

Finally, it should be noted that the debate over a professional staff for Congress since 1946 will soon be transformed by innovations in other areas. The information processing and screening functions of a staff will be radically transformed by the development and application

[85] For a previous statement, see Saloma, *op. cit.*, pp. 45–54, 79–81. Note, with reference to the particular problem of staffing the Appropriations Committees, the opposition of the House Committee on Appropriations to staff facilities not under its control and the general congressional reluctance to let institutional staff (such as the General Accounting Office) make effective political decisions on the budget.

[86] Charles R. Dechert states, "The generation of a broad spectrum of possible alternative courses of action requires increased academic study and research to supplement current investigative procedures. It also requires an aptitude for social engineering; that is, the devising of institutional structures operationally adapted to the achievement of defined goals." "Availability of Information for Congressional Operations," in Alfred de Grazia (ed.), *Congress: The First Branch of Government*, p. 205.

of computer-based information systems in government. A whole new area of social investigation will be opened by the steady improvement of budgetary analysis, coupled with a new base of social indicators and simulation techniques. As Bertram Gross depicts the passing order, executive officials and members of Congress alike have been "misled by *inadequate interpretation* of *bad information* based on *obsolete concepts* and *inadequate research* and collected by *underfed and over-lobbied statistical agencies.*" [87]

Congress has great potential for contributing to basic social and economic investigation in the coming decades. Such a function is consistent with the historical use of congressional powers. Its further development, however, will require congressional adaptation to a new era of governmental decision making. And not the least of these requirements for adaptation will be the intelligent and effective use of congressional staff.

[87] Bertram Gross and Michael Springer, "New Goals for Social Information," *The Annals of the American Academy of Political and Social Science*, September 1967, p. 209.

CHAPTER SIX

Congress and Its Constituents:
Education and Service

It is the proper duty of a representative body to look dili-
gently into every affair of government and to talk much about
what it sees. It is meant to be the eyes and the voice, and to
embody the wisdom and will of its constituents. Unless Congress have and use every means of acquainting itself with the
acts and the disposition of the administrative agents of the
government, the country must be helpless to learn how it is
being served; and unless Congress both scrutinize these things
and sift them by every form of discussion, the country must
remain in embarrassing, crippling ignorance of the very affairs
which it is most important that it should understand and direct. The informing function of Congress should be preferred
even to its legislative function.[1]

When Woodrow Wilson wrote *Congressional Government* during
1883 and 1884, he found Congress, through its standing committees,
dominant in both the legislative and administrative processes. Yet talk
on the part of Congress was more often "the profitless squabble of
words over frivolous bills or selfish party issues" than talk about the
practical concerns and processes of government which "clears the
public mind and shapes the demands of public opinion." [2]

[1] Woodrow Wilson, *Congressional Government: A Study in American Politics*
(New York: Meridian Books, 1956), p. 198.
[2] *Ibid.* A contemporary argument for the informing function of government
is suggested by Peter Bachrach. "The battle for freedom will be lost by default
if elites insulate themselves from the people and rely on countervailing forces,
institutional and social barriers, and their own colleagues to defend the system
from the demagogic leader of the mob. Democracy can best be assured of survival
by enlisting the people's support in a continual effort to make democracy meaningful in the lives of all men." *The Theory of Democratic Elitism: A Critique*
(Basic Studies in Politics; Boston: Little, Brown & Co., 1967), p. 106.

Today, the contemporary Congress enjoys resources and means to perform its "informing" and constituent service functions that Wilson could hardly have imagined: the professional staff of its committee system, the congressional office and the personal staff of each congressman, the Legislative Reference Service, radio, television, the national press corps, long distance telecommunications, jet transportation, etc. Does Congress adequately inform public discussion, or is discussion fashioned by the whims and fancies of public impulse and opinion? How much attention does Congress give to servicing the needs of its constituents, and does this attention detract from performance in other areas such as legislation and control?

THE INFORMATIVE AND CONSTITUENT SERVICE FUNCTIONS

In our initial discussion of the functions performed by Congress, we identified two that enable Congress to communicate with its constituents. In performing the *informative* function, Congress informs and educates the public on matters of public policy and communicates information to constituents. In performing its *service* function, it answers constituent requests and assists specific constituent interests, especially through casework.

Obviously both these functions are related to others we have already considered. Wilson's definition of the informing function assumes a vigorous congressional role in review of administration and investigation and a high quality of legislative debate. A congressman performing the service function intervenes extensively in the bureaucracy on behalf of constituents; i.e., he represents interests. In a limited sense, constituent service is a component of the control function of Congress. Casework may also be a direct input to the legislative work of Congress. The fact that both the informative and service functions constitute significant, identifiable portions of the congressional workload is our basic justification for defining them separately.

There is little quantitative data on congressional performance of either function. Congressmen complain that they cannot get their message reported by the media. The late Congressman Clem Miller (D-Cal.) charged, "The press seems to regard its Washington role as it does police reporting. The broader sweep of the meaningful 'why' and 'wherefore' of government is lost in the welter of what is on the police captain's blotter." [3] On the other hand, observers outside of Congress point to the "publicity powers" of the congressional investigating committee and argue that "no institution of the Executive Branch [including presumably the televised Presidential press conference] is capable of such sustained and well-manipulated publicity." [4] Estimates of congressional workload related to constituency service vary even more widely. The Arthur D. Little Management Study of Congress reported, "The volume of communications is enormous, involving hundreds of phone calls and thousands of letters to the average legislator's office each day." Others place the daily mail estimate at 50 to 100 pieces.[5] Charles Clapp reports the estimate of congressmen that many members of the House devote 90 per cent of their time to casework and that "few participants in the legislative process would deny that much time is devoted to constituent interests." [6] Other estimates which we shall review place the figure between 15 and 30 per cent.

Fortunately, we have the results of two studies undertaken as part of the Study of Congress project: a survey of 160 members of the House of Representatives on the workload of the congressional office and a content analysis of 1,500 separate printed communications from 149 representatives and 32 senators to their constituents.[7] Both of

[3] John W. Baker (ed.), *Member of the House: Letters of a Congressman by Clem Miller* (New York: Charles Scribner's Sons, 1962), p. 61.

[4] Douglass Cater, *The Fourth Branch of Government* (Boston: Houghton Mifflin Co., 1959), pp. 55–56.

[5] Commissioned by NBC News for the Special Report, "Congress Needs Help," 1965, p. 21. For an alternative estimate see Walter Gellhorn, *When Americans Complain: Governmental Grievance Procedures* (Cambridge, Mass.: Harvard University Press, 1966), pp. 57–73.

[6] Clapp, *The Congressman: His Work as He Sees It* (Washington, D.C.: The Brookings Institution, 1963), p. 54.

[7] See John S. Saloma III, "The Job of a Congressman: Some Perspectives on Time and Information," unpublished paper, February 1967, the Study of Congress project. Preliminary results of the survey are included as an appendix to Donald G. Tacheron and Morris K. Udall, *The Job of a Congressman: An Introduction to Service in the U.S. House of Representatives* (Indianapolis, Ind.: The Bobbs-Merrill Co., 1966), pp. 280–88. Also William C. Love, Jr., "The Congressman as Educator: A Study in Legislator-Constituent Relationships," M.S. thesis, M.I.T., Cambridge, Mass., August 1966. The author wishes to acknowledge the generous cooperation of the House Republican Task Force on Congressional Reform and Minority Staffing; its Chairman, Congressman James C. Cleveland; Staff Member, Miss Mary McInnis; and the congressional interns who distributed the Study of Congress questionnaire and assisted in collecting data.

these throw light on congressional performance in these largely un-examined areas of the work of Congress.

EVALUATIONS OF THE INFORMATIVE FUNCTION: INSTITUTIONAL PERFORMANCE

Congress communicates to the public through its collective activities and component parts, especially its committees. Congress also communicates through the activities of its individual members. We shall consider institutional forms of congressional communication first.

Critical evaluations of congressional performance of its informative function take at least two forms. First is the criticism that congressional committees, through publicized hearings and investigations, rarely seek to raise the level of public understanding but instead pursue limited political objectives. In Cater's estimate, "the investigating committee unhampered by the need for a clear definition of purpose, guided by the flimsiest rules of procedure and relevancy, its leadership not necessarily representative of prevailing opinion in Congress and not subject to review for its misdeeds has nearly unlimited discretion." [8] Investigations are "planned deliberately to move from a preconceived idea to a predetermined conclusion." [9] Moreover, the fragmentation of power and the independent subcommittee bases of leadership within Congress are particularly susceptible to exploitation by a politician aware of the power of publicity in the era of mass media. As we noted earlier, this criticism has been directed at other congressional functions. The basic institution for congressional communications with the public, the committee system, is seen as fundamentally deficient. The conclusion follows from the assumptions.

The second form of criticism relates to presidential versus congressional responsibilities for leading public opinion. When Wilson urged that the informing function of Congress be enhanced, he saw little possibility that the Presidency would ever regain a position of leadership in the American system. Today the modern Presidency provides the focus for publicity in government. James MacGregor Burns states, "The bulk of the Washington press does seem to be organized around, and to hold a community of attitudes and interests with, the presidential party in power and with the leaders of the out-of-power

[8] *Op. cit.*, p. 59.
[9] *Ibid.*, p. 58.

presidential party." [10] Burns and others are not concerned as much with this "seeming partiality" as with the question of whether the President can lead with sufficient vigor and imagination. Burns would oppose strengthening the publicity powers of Congress on the general grounds that "the stronger the exertion of congressional power, the more conservative and isolationist will be our national policy because of the structure of congressional forces." [11] From this perspective of legislative-executive relations, a presidentially led party, not institutional spokesmen of the Congress, perform the informing function.

Critics with alternative perspectives propose increased institutional communication for Congress. Not only has Congress failed to develop its own role in public communications, it has permitted the Executive to engage in extensive lobby activities with public funds in direct violation of the U.S. Code.[12] Congress must reform its self-image and assert itself in the public media. For this purpose the existing committee system is not adequate. Nor do current means for disseminating the massive publications of Congress meet the objective. Congress should develop new forms of expression, such as a Central Office of Congress to report congressional activities noncontroversially and in popular language to the press and public and to employ television and radio more extensively and imaginatively for the Congress.[13] The con-

[10] *Presidential Government: The Crucible of Leadership* (Boston: Houghton Mifflin Co., 1966), p. 188. See also Cater's discussion of the "publicity process," *op. cit.*; and Dan D. Nimmo's subsequent analysis of the interactions between Washington correspondents and executive-agency public information officers in *Newsgathering in Washington: A Study in Political Communication* (New York: Atherton Press, 1964). Another study of the presidential focus is provided by Elmer E. Cornwell, Jr., *Presidential Leadership of Public Opinion* (Bloomington, Ind.: Indiana University Press, 1965).

[11] *The Deadlock of Democracy: Four-Party Politics in America* (Englewood Cliffs, N.J.: Prentice-Hall, 1963), p. 264.

[12] See Ancher Nelson, M.C., "Lobbying by the Administration," in Mary McInnis (ed.), *We Propose: A Modern Congress, Selected Proposals by the House Republican Task Force on Congressional Reform and Minority Staffing* (New York: McGraw-Hill Book Co., 1966), pp. 143–59.

[13] Alfred de Grazia, "Toward a New Model of Congress," in Alfred de Grazia (ed.), *Congress: The First Branch of Government, Twelve Studies of the Organization of Congress* (Washington, D.C.: American Enterprise Institute, 1966), p. 15. Also see Robert F. Ellsworth, M.C., "The Case for Television and Radio Coverage," in McInnis (ed.), *op. cit.*, pp. 265–68. During the 89th Congress (1965) Congressman Bob Wilson (R-Cal.), Chairman of the Republican Congressional Campaign Committee, announced in a letter to House Republicans the appointment of a special Republican study group under the chairmanship of Thomas B. Curtis (R-Mo.) to review the relations of the press with Congress and to make recommendations for improving them. The project was suspended, however, when party funds were not available for it.

gressional viewpoint on principle legislative problems should be determined through the internal use of survey research instruments under a Joint Committee of Congress and publicized as an alternative to the presidential perspective.[14] Ad hoc congressional task forces empowered to commission research, hold seminars, and make field trips could supplement the agenda of the standing committees. Bipartisan teams of legislators could participate in lecture tours.[15]

These and other proposals suggest that Congress has *not* yet adequately developed its institutional voice, that Congress has been willing to let the press assume the initiative in reporting congressional activities. It is not difficult to find reasons for this. The congressional viewpoint frequently escapes definition. It is crosscut by partisan formulations and legislative strategies. The relative autonomy of each member as a spokesman unto himself and the absence of strong leadership or coordinating mechanisms do not facilitate coherent expression. Granted these limitations, there still exists, in the view of the author, slack in congressional performance. A more active public information program could at least reduce some of the misinformation about Congress that follows from executive initiative in the news.

EVALUATIONS OF THE INFORMATIVE FUNCTION: INDIVIDUAL PERFORMANCE

If the Congress has done little to develop new institutional means for public expression, how well has the individual member communicated with his constituents? The Study of Congress survey of the House of Representatives [16] revealed that members made extensive use of both radio and television as well as mass-reproduced newsletters and questionnaires and personal correspondence in communicating with constituents. Members replying to the survey averaged 8.0 radio appearances and 4.0 television appearances per month during the session. Some 56 per cent of the sample (85 out of 152 responding) gave regular radio or television reports to constituents. The most popular format was the weekly 5-minute radio report (used by 36 members) followed by the weekly 15-minute radio report (13 members).

14 Charles R. Dechert, "Availability of Information for Congressional Operations," in Alfred de Grazia (ed.), *op. cit.*, p. 204.

15 Roger H. Davidson, "Congress and the Executive: The Race for Representation," in Alfred de Grazia (ed.), *op. cit.*, pp. 409–13.

16 See Saloma, "Communications to Constituents," *op. cit.*, pp. 41–45.

The congressional newsletter was used more extensively than either radio or television — by 122 of 152 members (80 per cent) — over 30 members circulated more than one kind of newsletter. The volume of newsletter circulation was impressive. The circulation figures for 118 members, including distribution of more than one kind of newsletter, are summarized in Table 6.1. Members' newsletters often get even wider circulation through reprinting in district newspapers. Members gave high priority to their newsletter operations, compiling mailing lists cumulatively from a variety of sources. Considerable effort was devoted to the preparation of the newsletter: an average of 5.7 hours on each newsletter for the member and an average of 28.5 total staff hours for preparation and mailing.

TABLE 6.1

CIRCULATION OF NEWSLETTERS AND
QUESTIONNAIRES BY CONGRESSMEN

Circulation	Number of Members (Newsletters)	Number of Members (Questionnaires)
Less than 5,000	11	1
6,000–15,000	25	3
16,000–30,000	21	3
31,000–60,000	17	11
61,000–90,000	11	14
91,000–120,000	16	19
121,000–150,000	13	19
Over 150,000	4	7

The congressional questionnaire was found to be a surprisingly popular form of communication with constituents. Ninety-one congressmen in the sample reported using them. (See Table 6.1 for circulation figures.) An average constituent response of 16.7 per cent was recorded. Members normally reported results to their constituents through their newsletter or press release. An average questionnaire required roughly 20 hours for preparation and 118 hours for processing.

All the data point to a high quantitative level of communications. What can we say about the quality of the communication or, more generally, the educational role of the congressman?

THE EDUCATIONAL ROLE OF THE CONGRESSMAN. A separate analysis was made of printed material (newsletters, news releases, form letters, statements) circulated by individual congressmen and senators during the first six months of the first session of the 89th Congress.[17] Did members provide quality information to constituents on topics of current concern to them in a reasonably objective manner?

Four basic role types were defined and a fifth category added to include a number of members who combined the characteristics of two of these basic roles: (1) *the persuader*, the legislator principally concerned either with changing by the force of his arguments certain attitudes or values held by his constituents or with reinforcing previously held attitudes and values; (2) *the promoter*, the legislator principally concerned with enhancing his own image and advancing self-interest through the content of his written communication with constituents; (3) *the educator*, the legislator who considers the political education of his constituents a definite *responsibility* and who provides information more for its own sake than to change attitudes or advance self-interest; (4) *the reticent*, the legislator who attempts neither to lead opinion, promote his image, nor provide high quality information to his constituents on a consistent basis (i.e., a negative reflection of the three previous roles); and (5) *the promoter-persuader*, the legislator who shares most of the qualities of *both* of these basic types. The content of written communications were scored on eight indices which defined the basic role types and members classified by roles.[18] The results are summarized in Tables 6.2 and 6.3.

The educator accounted for less than 10 per cent of the sample and was the least common role in both House and Senate. The promoter

TABLE 6.2

DISTRIBUTION OF COMMUNICATION ROLES
IN HOUSE SAMPLE ANALYZED

Communication Role Category	Number in Category	Per Cent of Total
Promoter	56	38%
Persuader	33	22
Promoter-persuader	25	17
Reticent	22	15
Educator	13	9
	149	101

[17] Love, *op. cit.*

[18] *Ibid.*, Chap. III, "The Scoring System and the Basic Indices," and Chap. IV, "Discussion of Empirical Data."

TABLE 6.3

DISTRIBUTION OF COMMUNICATION ROLES
IN SENATE SAMPLE ANALYZED

Communication Role Category	Number in Category	Per Cent of Total
Promoter	14	44%
Persuader	9	28
Promoter-persuader	6	19
Reticent	2	6
Educator	1	3
	32	100

was the most common followed by the persuader. A further analysis of variables such as party and length of service yielded the findings that more Democrats in *both* the House and Senate were promoters while Republicans leaned strongly toward being persuaders.[19] The data also supported an interpretation that communication roles change with increasing seniority from a promoter orientation for freshman congressmen through a persuader orientation to a reticent posture for congressmen from safe House districts.

Without extensively digressing into the analysis, we can draw some tentative conclusions to our initial question about the quality of the individual member's informative function. Apparently only a small percentage of congressmen meet the ideal of the impartial educator. The high incidence of promoters supports the view that congressmen cultivate constituents for their own electoral ends. Yet at least as many congressmen assume the role of partisan educator (persuader and promoter-persuader) as do the pure promoter role. The results, combining quantitative and qualitative findings, suggest a mixed evaluation of individual congressional performance: intense communications activity with qualitative biases toward personal promotion and partisan education. Because of the nature of the electoral system, these findings are not surprising. A significant improvement in the informative function of Congress can probably best be achieved at the level of institutional performance.

[19] *Ibid.*, pp. 93–99. In a sample of 58 House Republicans and 57 House Democrats which excluded freshman members, Love found the following distribution of basic communication roles. For Democrats: promoter, 38%; persuader, 11%; promoter-persuader, 14%; reticent, 23%; educator, 14%. For Republicans: promoter, 19%; persuader, 38%; promoter-persuader, 22%; reticent, 12%; and educator, 9%.

EVALUATIONS OF THE CONSTITUENCY
SERVICE FUNCTION

Almost all discussion on casework and constituent services provided by congressmen has been based on the most fragmentary information and intuitive estimates of performance. Walter Kravitz of the Library of Congress Legislative Reference Service concluded in a 1965 survey of the existing literature on casework:

> The subject is seldom treated in detail or approached in any systematic fashion. Journalists, academicians, and even Members themselves (although the latter are usually more informative) tend to deal with the matter in terms of unique or vague statistics, anecdotes, polemics, and/or justifications.[20]

The lack of data has done little to deter frequent evaluations, pro and con such congressional activity. In this section we shall first summarize some of these evaluations and then examine them in light of empirical data, including the Study of Congress congressional office survey, which have been compiled since 1965.

The core of constituent service is casework. Neither "constituent service" nor "casework" has a precise, generally accepted definition, even within the Congress. A broad definition of casework would include processing constituent requests for assistance of any kind in which a personal problem is involved. A more limited definition restricts the term to the work of the congressman as a middleman between the constituent and the federal government. For our purposes we shall use this limited definition; a case requires individual attention and usually some personal follow-through by the member and his staff. We shall define constituency service in the broader sense to include answering correspondence, such as requests for information, and visiting with constituents in Washington. Correspondence, the major work activity of the congressional office, serves a mixed constituency service–information function.

CRITICISMS OF CONSTITUENCY SERVICE. Several criticisms have been advanced against heavy congressional involvement in constituent service activities. These evaluations usually assume (1) that constituency

[20] Kravitz, "Case Work by Members of Congress: An Analysis Based on a Survey of Existing Literature," memorandum, Government and General Research Division, Library of Congress, May 1965, p. 1.

service has become the dominant focus of the congressman's work and (2) that congressmen have created a virtual monopoly for processing citizens' grievances at the federal level.

Constituency service detracts from the real, or priority, functions of the Congress, especially legislation. The errand-boy function, according to this evaluation, consumes the individual congressman's potential for contribution to the legislative process. The new congressman, especially, must build up his political reputation in his district. Careful attention to the mail will have its rewards. An incumbent who effectively uses his staff and the resources available to him "can become so deeply entrenched that only a landslide can dislodge him." [21] The system leads American legislators to "absorb themselves so actively in constituents' conflicts with law administrators that they have little time left for thinking about the laws they enact." [22]

Congressional intervention in behalf of constituents is episodic and has little significant effect in changing the patterns of administrative policy and behavior. The current system for processing citizens' grievances through decentralized congressional offices means that "constituents' casework problems rarely come to the notice of the Congress as a whole or even of its standing committees." [23] Walter Gellhorn, in his comparative analysis of grievance procedures, sees this congressional inattentiveness to the root causes of constituents' problems as the basic weakness of the American system:

> Since triumph is its usual goal, casework tends to go no further than the case at hand, leaving untouched the problems that generated it. Ordinarily, investigation is superficial. Implications, if not altogether unperceived, are in any event likely to be ignored. So long as the present case has an appropriately happy outcome, tomorrow's case is left to its own devices; anyway it may involve some other congressman's constituent. Always pressed for time and almost always untrained generalists in a world of trained specialists, congressmen pass on to other things — and so do the administrators.[24]

Related criticisms are the uneven quality of congressional staff assigned to casework and the tendency of congressmen to service all cases regardless of their merits. In sum, constituency service mixes the pro-

---

[21] Gellhorn, *op. cit.*, p. 76. See also "Electronics Give Incumbents an Edge," *Business Week*, September 15, 1962, pp. 31–32.
[22] Gellhorn, *op. cit.*, p. 8.
[23] *Ibid.*, p. 86.
[24] *Ibid.*, p. 128.

cessing of complaints with the politics of re-election with a decided bias in favor of the latter.

Congressional intervention in behalf of constituents undermines good administrative practice within the Executive. In communications with the bureaucracy, congressmen and the staff they have built for processing casework tend to short circuit normal administrative processes by "going to the top" or utilizing friendly contacts. The level of ad hoc congressional intervention diffuses responsibility within the Executive, overburdens superior officials, and contributes to needless duplication. This evaluation argues, "Systematic government — a government whose organizational methods are discoverable and operable — is the best alternative to a government in which knowing the right people is the only reliable way of getting things done." [25]

Constituent casework and service have no upper limit and their continued growth threatens to subvert the professional and institutional staff Congress has created for other purposes. There is no logical or self-enforceable limit to constituency service as Congress has defined it. The rapidly growing complexity of social welfare programs in itself will generate an increased workload that will tax existing congressional resources. In addition, congressmen, inviting more communications and requests from their constituents, have an ever increasing constituency workload. To keep pace with the workload, members have increased their own staffs, borrowed professional committee staff, and turned to the institutional resources of the Library of Congress. Concern about this trend was evidenced in the Report of the Joint Committee on the Organization of the Congress which warned against the dissipation of the research resources of the Legislative Reference Service. Of some 113,628 inquiries handled by the service in 1965, over 50 per cent were reference requests from constituents requiring almost 20 per cent of the service's total staff time.[26]

JUSTIFICATIONS FOR CONSTITUENCY SERVICE. Those who defend a vigorous congressional role in constituency service discount these nega-

[25] *Ibid.*, p. 126.

[26] "Legislative Reorganization Act of 1966," Senate Report No. 1629, 89th Congress, 2nd Session, September 21, 1966, p. 9. For a complete discussion of the Legislative Reference Service and the workload due to constituent inquiries, see Joint Committee on the Organization of Congress, *Hearings: Organization of Congress*, 89th Congress, 1st Session, 1965, pp. 1109–81; and House of Representatives, Subcommittee on Legislative Branch Appropriations, *Hearings: Legislative Branch Appropriations for 1968*, 90th Congress, 1st Session, 1967, pp. 507–41.

tive evaluations and offer positive justifications of their own. The amount of time congressmen actually spend on casework is greatly overstated they argue. Congress can increase and control the use of staff as it sees fit. Any form of congressional intervention imposes costs in terms of administrative efficiency. Such negative effects as there may be are clearly outweighed by positive considerations.

Constituency service is an important form of congressional control of administration and may be justified on the same grounds as the control or oversight function of Congress. Former Senator Joseph S. Clark's defense of constituency case intervention as "an effort to humanize what is inevitably a hardened bureaucratic process" is shared by most members of Congress. "The very knowledge by executive officials that some Congressman is sure to look into a matter affecting his constituents acts as a healthy check," Clark observes, "against bureaucratic indifference or arrogance. Congress performs a useful function in acting as errand boy, correspondent and father confessor." [27]

Congressmen believe that they *do* have a significant effect on bureaucratic behavior. They estimate that they have about a 10 per cent rate of success in achieving favorable outcomes for their constituents.[28] Moreover, members do not lost interest once a case is completed. Charles Clapp reports:

> Through his handling of complaints the congressman feels that he learns about laws that need revision and agencies that would benefit from reorganization. The mail, then, helps the legislator to carry out his legislative responsibilities as well as his representative function. In pointing up weaknesses in the executive branch, it contributes to the strengthening of the administrative process.[29]

The congressman sees himself as the last personal representative of constituents facing an ever more impersonal, incomprehensible bureaucratic government, and he is reluctant to yield that responsibility.

[27] Clark, *Congress: The Sapless Branch* (New York: Harper & Row, 1964), pp. 63–64. A majority of congressmen agree with him. Davidson, Kovenock, and O'Leary report that 78 per cent of their sample of the House membership agreed that casework should be an important part of the congressman's job. *Hearings: Organization of Congress*, p. 775.

[28] Gellhorn, *op. cit.*, pp. 79–80. Clapp reports that some congressmen rate themselves higher, one as high as one success in every three or five attempts. *Op. cit.*, p. 78.

[29] *Op. cit.*, p. 79.

The congressman's perspective and his potential contribution to government are enhanced by his continuing association with constituent problems. The unique contribution that the congressman makes to the legislative and administrative processes in government rests in his sensitivity to the political system and in his capacity to make judgments of political feasibility. Given this interpretation, it is neither possible nor desirable to separate artificially the "legislative" and "nonlegislative" responsibilities of the congressman. As Kenneth G. Olson concludes in his analysis of the service function of Congress:

> A major source of the total knowledge required by the Federal Government to govern effectively resides in the constant press of constituent requests upon members of Congress. That knowledge is essentially indivisible; it can be used for remedial legislation as well as for stimulating administrative changes within the bureaucracy. Knowledge of a constituent's problem can lead to a single, specific solution, or it can be the germ of a creative legislative idea ultimately affecting millions of persons as it is made the law of the land. Certainly, however, such knowledge is a necessary — if not a sufficient — condition of creative legislation.[30]

Thus, to eliminate the service function of Congress would serve not to increase the congressman's legislative productivity by freeing some of his time but rather to limit his effectiveness by reducing his feel of constituents' problems.

Constituency service enhances the independence of the congressman and the autonomy of the Congress. Admittedly, congressmen pay attention to their constituents' problems because failure to serve constituents means risking defeat in a primary or general election. Beyond influencing individual election outcomes, the constituency service function may have important consequences for the organization of power, both within Congress and between the Legislature and the Executive. The development of the constituency service function has probably been a significant factor in the increased tenure of congressmen since the turn of the century.[31] It has thus complemented a weak

30 "The Service Function of the United States Congress," in Alfred de Grazia (ed.), *op. cit.*, pp. 373–74.

31 See Samuel P. Huntington, "Congressional Responses to the Twentieth Century," in *The Congress and America's Future* (Englewood Cliffs, N.J.: Prentice-Hall, 1965), pp. 8–9, 22–25; also Nelson W. Polsby, "The Institutionalization of the U.S. House of Representatives," *The American Political Science Review* (APSR), March 1968, pp. 144–68.

form of party organization in the Congress as well as the development of the seniority-protégé-apprentice system.

Advocates of greater congressional autonomy from the Executive, such as Alfred de Grazia, assign an important function to congressional-constituency relations. De Grazia is concerned that the present active constituency of Congress is too small and that "Congress may be fatally weakened by lack of support from the grass roots." He would emphasize building a larger "nuclear constituency" or *personal* following of the congressman. "It is most unreasonable and anti-congressional to strip the support of congressmen away, leaving them to perform heavy tasks with help that is numerically or quantitatively inferior to that provided for a middle-level bureaucrat." [32]

Donald Matthews confirms the political benefits of an independent following:

> The support gained in this fashion cuts across normal party and factional lines. It is a following, too, which is not likely to be affected by how the senator votes on issues. Good case work can contribute to the senator's maneuverability on matters of policy.[33]

This argument in support of the service function of Congress is thus consistent with normative perspectives that accord the congressman independent initiative in the legislative process. The President cannot automatically assume his support through party regularity. On the other hand, the policy independence the congressman gains through constituency service permits him to take broad, national positions frequently with the President.

RECENT DATA ON THE SERVICE FUNCTION. Before commenting on these conflicting evaluations of casework and constituency service, it will be helpful to review two studies of congressional communications and workload that provide some quantitative estimates. The first of these, the Study of Congress survey on congressional office workload, asked the congressman and each member of his office staff for an estimate of how much time during a "typical work week" was devoted to each of a number of specified activities. Of the 160 congressmen who

[32] *Republic in Crisis: Congress Against the Executive Force* (New York: Federal Legal Publications, 1965), pp. 30–31, 218–19.

[33] *U.S. Senators & Their World* (New York: Vintage Books, 1960), p. 226. See also Bauer, Pool, and Dexter, *American Business & Public Policy: The Politics of Foreign Trade* (New York: Atherton Press, 1963), pp. 418–19.

participated in the survey, 150 provided reasonably complete information.[34] Only 60 offices submitted reasonably complete staff questionnaires. The results are summarized in Tables 6.4 through 6.7.

TABLE 6.4

AVERAGE WORK WEEK FOR A CONGRESSMAN

Activity	Hours per Week (average)	Percentage of Work Week	Standard Deviation [a]
On the floor	15.3	26.0%	44.8%
In committee	7.7	13.1	48.4
Answering mail	7.0	11.9	60.3
On legislative research and reading	6.9	11.7	84.3
Handling constituent problems	5.1	8.6	84.6
Visiting with constituents in Washington	4.2	7.1	76.6
On committee work outside of committee	3.4	5.8	76.8
On writing speeches, articles	2.6	4.4	112.1
On leadership or party functions	2.4	4.1	137.3
Meeting with lobbyists and lobby groups	2.3	3.9	92.4
On press work, radio, and television	2.0	3.4	103.8
TOTAL	58.9	100.0	—

[a] Expressed as a percentage of the mean.

TABLE 6.5

AVERAGE WORK WEEK SUMMARIZED BY FUNCTION

Function	Hours per Week (average)	Percentage
Legislative	38.0	64.6%
Committee work	(11.1)	(18.9)
General	(26.9)	(45.7)
Constituency service	16.3	27.6
Education/Publicity	4.6	7.8

[34] See Saloma, op. cit., pp. 7–11, 25–29. The sample included two noticeable biases. On party breakdown, the expected total of Republicans in a sample of 160 was 51.5; the actual total 65. On seniority the sample was biased toward freshmen (21 expected, 35 actual) and against members with five to ten terms of service (54.2 expected, 42 actual).

TABLE 6.6

AVERAGE STAFF WORK WEEK FOR A CONGRESSIONAL OFFICE

Activity	Hours per Week (average)	Percentage
With the member in committee	1.1	0.5%
Handling constituent problems (casework)	40.6	18.7
Visiting with constituents in Washington	12.9	6.0
With lobbyists and special interest groups	4.9	2.3
On press work, radio, and television	13.9	6.4
Writing speech drafts, floor remarks	11.2	5.2
On legislative research, bill drafting	13.6	6.3
On pressure and opinion mail	34.2	15.8
On opinion ballots (preprinted by organizations)	4.4	2.0
On requests for information	14.6	6.7
On letters of congratulation, condolence	9.2	4.2
On correspondence other than described	26.2	12.1
Mailing government publications	8.5	3.9
Other	21.4	9.0
TOTAL	216.7	100.0

TABLE 6.7

AVERAGE STAFF WORK WEEK SUMMARIZED BY FUNCTION

Function	Hours per Week (average)	Percentage
Legislative support	30.8	14.3%
Constituency service	53.5	24.7
Correspondence (mixed constituency service, education)	88.6	40.8
Education and Publicity	22.4	10.3
Other	21.4	9.9

The principal limitation of this data is its subjective character. Several congressmen and staff members who reviewed the findings considered them high, especially in "time spent on the floor." The congressman probably interpreted "a typical work week during the session" to mean a *full* legislative week (floor and committee sessions). To a degree, the answer given represented an idealized work week of how many hours the member *ought* to be spending on various activities. Although the questionnaire was pre-tested to determine the

best activity categories for data collection, some activities, such as social functions, physical exercise (gymnasium), and travel time between
points on the Hill, were omitted from the "work day" and may appear
as hidden items in other activities.

Despite these limitations there are counterbalancing considerations.
Overall time estimates, with a few exceptions, fell within what appeared to be a reasonable range for a congressional work week. The
anonymity of respondents should have reduced the tendency to make
oneself look good. The variety of time-budget patterns discerned in
further analysis of the data suggested in any event that there was no
consensus among members on what was a "good" work week. Three
activities were weighted most nearly the same by all congressmen (i.e.,
they had the lowest standard deviation of the activities scored): time
spent on the floor, time spent in committee, and time spent answering
mail. There was a wider spread in all other time estimates. We consider the data a reasonably good approximation of the congressional
work week. Even as a rough measure the results are more comprehensive and specific than data that have previously been available.

Returning to our original task — the evaluation of casework and
constituency service — several interesting, if tentative, conclusions
may be drawn from the data. Legislation, constituting 64.6 per cent
of the work week, is clearly the dominant concern of the congressman.
(See Tables 6.4 and 6.5.) Grouping nonlegislative activities arbitrarily,
"constituency service" (broadly defined) accounts for only 27.6 per
cent (16.3 hours) of the average congressional work week while the
information function (narrowly defined) accounts for 7.8 per cent
(4.6 hours). Some "constituency service" activities obviously have educational aspects and should probably be counted in both categories.

The results are somewhat surprising in view of the frequent complaint that congressmen are overburdened with constituency work.
Even when those congressmen who scored significantly high in per
cent of work week devoted to constituent problems were considered
separately, their average per cent of work week devoted to constituency service was only 42.7.[35] The relatively small amount of time
spent by congressmen on the functions of constituency service and
education should not be misread, however, as inattention. The data

---

[35] *Ibid.*, pp. 16, 18. This group, labeled by their time-budget as "Representative," also spent an above average amount of time answering mail and were
below average in time allocated for committee sessions, committee work outside of sessions, and meeting with lobbyists.

on congressional staff suggest that the congressman's office staff, functioning as an extension of the congressman, relieves much of his time burden relating to his constituency.

The average office staff work week was found to be 216.7 hours: 5.1 people worked an average of 42.5 hours. (Part-time workers, summer interns, and volunteers are included in that figure; district office personnel are not.) Staff work activities may be regrouped by function as were the work activities of the congressman. (See Tables 6.6 and 6.7.) "Legislative support" includes activities most directly related to the legislative function of the member. Constituency service and education parallel the functional classifications of the congressman's work week. Correspondence, the largest type of staff activity, has both constituency service and educational components. Since there is no standard definition of case work or of the various categories of mail and correspondence, this functional grouping is only a rough approximation.

Comparing Tables 6.4 and 6.6, it is clear that the average congressman draws his heaviest staff support in answering mail (he spends 7.0 hours to his staff's 88.6) and handling constituent problems (5.1 hours to 40.6). His staff is proportionally less helpful to him (in decreasing order) in press work, radio, and television (2.0 hours to 13.9); speechwriting (2.6 hours to 11.2); visiting with constituents in Washington (4.2 hours to 12.9); and meeting with lobbyists (2.3 hours to 4.9). On legislative research and committee work outside of committee the congressman and his staff spend roughly an equivalent amount of time (10.3 hours to 13.6). These figures suggest strongly that the congressman uses his staff to reduce his nonlegislative work burden (or conversely to increase constituency service), and to screen himself from excessive interruptions from constituents and the public.

A second study, by David Kovenock, based on a communications audit of six members of a House legislative subcommittee (which he names only as the "J subcommittee"), provides some important new data in support of the estimated work week reported above.[36] Kovenock recorded and analyzed the incoming communications or "deci-

[36] Kovenock, "Communications and Influence on Congressional Decision-Making: Employing the Communications Audit Technique in a U.S. House of Representatives Subcommittee," paper delivered at the annual meeting of the American Political Science Association, Chicago, September 1964; and "Influence in the U.S. House of Representatives: Some Preliminary Statistical 'Snapshots,'" paper delivered at the annual meeting of the American Political Science Association, Chicago, September 1967.

sion premises" received by each of the six members. His findings are summarized in Table 6.8.[37]

TABLE 6.8

COMMUNICATIONS AUDIT OF THE J SUBCOMMITTEE:
CLASSIFICATION OF INCOMING PREMISES
BY GENERAL DECISION SCOPE

Scope of Decision	Subcommittee Members						
	Geneva	Stokes	Haskas	Yale	Morris	Armstrong	Total
Legislation and related	49%	54%	45%	25%	56%	52%	49%
Intervention	5	4	9	13	4	4	6
Patronage	3	9	1	2	—	1	2
Political procedure: House and Senate	11	10	11	14	18	15	14
Political procedure: district and related	22	11	21	26	7	11	15
Political procedure: elsewhere	5	7	5	7	8	7	6
Other (including office service and administration)	5	5	8	14	7	11	8
Total	100%	100%	100%	101%	100%	101%	100%
(Number of premises)	(1784)	(1416)	(1846)	(1329)	(2625)	(2530)	(11530)

Suggested by David Kovenock, "Influence in the U.S. House of Representatives: Some Preliminary Statistical 'Snapshots,'" paper delivered at the annual meeting of the American Political Science Association, Chicago, September 1967, p. 20.

On the basis of his analysis, Kovenock points out "how misleading is much of the conventional wisdom on 'time budgets' of Congressmen! Much of the popular literature (and not a few introductory American government textbooks) leaves the reader with the impres-

[37] Kovenock defines a decision premise as "nothing more than a verbally transmitted statement that can be used as a component of an individual (or an organizational) decision." The scope of a decision premise refers to its substantive content. Premises were "characterized in terms of their relevance to one or more of the elements in a typology of substantive decisions made by the subjects in their roles as Congressmen: decisions on specific legislative proposals (i.e., bills and resolutions), legislative policy making independent of specific bills, intervention in executive agency decisions, patronage, political procedures in Congress, procedures in their constituencies, political procedures elsewhere, and a residual category consisting largely of office service and staff matters." "Influence in the U.S. House of Representatives," pp. 8–11.

sion that the Members spend a major portion of their time 'running errands' for their constituents." [38] Kovenock concludes that, in fact, almost 65 per cent of the premises reaching the J Subcommittee members were directly related to the traditional law-making activities of elected representatives (legislation and political procedure: House and Senate). "If we combined the scope categories of 'intervention,' 'patronage,' and 'other' (the last containing a large element of the most routine office service work), the data suggest that messages relating to errands were but a minor fraction of the incoming premises, i.e., 16%." [39] In estimating the relative influence incoming premises had on congressmen, Kovenock found, however, that the premises in these same three "errand" scopes were attributed the most influence; i.e., that members might receive fewer premises in these areas but they paid more attention to them.

SUGGESTED DIRECTIONS FOR REFORM. Suggestions for reform in handling casework and constituency service may be grouped into three broad categories according to Walter Kravitz: (1) those seeking to eliminate all or part of the practice; (2) those seeking to replace, either totally or partially, the congressional office by some other agency or unit; and (3) those seeking to augment the existing facilities of the congressional office for carrying out the service function. [40]

The first category includes a variety of self-denying ordinances and formal prohibitions, the most extreme being a proposed constitutional amendment "which would prohibit a member of Congress, or Senator, from contacting the executive branch of the Government except in regard to legislation." [41] The fundamental assumption of these sugges-

[38] *Ibid.*, p. 21. The Davidson, Kovenock, and O'Leary survey of House members in general also supports this conclusion. Members identified legislation and committee work most frequently (77%) as the most time-consuming portion of the job of a congressman; casework and "errands for constituents," a distant second (16%). *Hearings: Organization of Congress*, p. 775.

[39] Kovenock, "Influence in the House of Representatives." Data for individual members range from 11% to 29%. The high figure (Yale) is misleading, however, for "much of Yale's relatively heavy load of incoming intervention premises concerned his efforts to channel federal aid and federal contracts into the troubled economy of his district. He did not consider this activity as errand running; he was seeking solutions—wherever they might be found—that went far beyond the problems of the lone constituent."

[40] *Op. cit.*, pp. 21 ff.

[41] See testimony of Congressman Robert Ramspeck (D-Ga.), Joint Committee on the Organization of Congress, *Hearings: Organization of Congress*, 79th Congress, 1st Session, 1945, p. 296.

tions is that casework and constituent errands are improper or undesirable extensions of the role of the congressman. The congressman
should not volunteer his services and should politely decline to assume
the personal burdens of his constituents. Congress should educate its
constituents not to look to its members for the variety of assistance
they now do. As one former member of the House complained:

> A Congressman has become an expanded messenger boy, an
> employment agency, getter-out of the Navy, Army, and
> Marines, a wardheeler, a wound healer, troubleshooter, law
> explainer, bill finder, issue translator, resolution interpreter,
> controversy-oil-pourer, glad hand extender, business promoter,
> veterans affairs adjuster, ex-serviceman's champion, watchdog
> for the underdog, sympathizer for the upper dog, kisser of
> babies, recoverer of lost baggage, soberer of delegates, adjuster
> for traffic violations and voters straying into the toils of the
> law, binder up of broken hearts, financial wet nurse, a good
> samaritan, contributor to good causes, cornerstone layer, pub-
> lic building and bridge dedicator and ship christener.[42]

The public expectations of congressional performance in these areas
should be reduced. Not until then will congressmen have the peace of
mind and time to attend to the real work for which they were elected.

Two comments on this suggested direction for reform are called for.
First, as we have suggested, it rests on an unfounded assumption that
congressmen are literally consumed by insatiable constituent demands
on their time. In fact, the real burden falls on congressional office
staff rather than on the member. Constituent service imposes some
costs on the legislative process; it also yields benefits. The issue is one
of degree rather than an either/or choice. Second, the argument gives
insufficient attention to the motivation of the congressman himself.
As our discussion of the educational role of the congressman suggests,
members generate a significant part of their own workload through
mass circulated newsletters and questionnaires. It may be that such
promotional behavior is part of a system that many members and
sympathetic observers of Congress would like to escape. But the important immediate fact is that some undesirable aspects of it simply
cannot be eliminated. The elimination of casework implies significant

[42] Luther Patrick, "What Is a Congressman?" reprinted in *Daily Congressional
Record*, 88th Congress, 1st Session, May 13, 1963, p. A 2978, cited by Clark,
op. cit., p. 62.

related changes in elections and in the relationship of the individual member of Congress to this constituency.

The most popular reforms in the second category are the ombudsman (an external, impartial, nonpolitical critic of administration) and Congressman Henry S. Reuss' (D-Wis.) proposal for an Administrative Counsel of the Congress (a centralized congressional staff adjunct to the individual member's staff).

The concept of the ombudsman, most fully developed in the Scandinavian parliamentary systems, has been suggested for adaptation to all levels of the American federal system.[43] The most persuasive case for its adaptation at the federal level has been made by Walter Gellhorn. Gellhorn credits the United States with "the world's most fully elaborated procedural protections against ill-informed exercises of official judgment." [44] American practice has been to specify the detailed steps administrators are to take. This procedural system is, and should remain as, "a main fortification against lawlessness, negligence, and caprice." Yet the trends toward tremendously enlarged governmental activity and higher educational levels of the public have created new needs and demands for "intercession" with the bureaucratic officialdom. The American response has been to vest the function of intercession with the elected representative; elsewhere there has been "a significant worldwide movement toward reliance on systematized, professionalized critics of administration." [45] The ombudsmen of Sweden, Finland, Denmark, Norway, and New Zealand share the following characteristics:

> 1. All are instruments of the legislature but function independently of it, with no links to the executive branch and with only the most general answerability to the legislature itself.

[43] See, for example, *Report of the Thirty-second American Assembly: The Ombudsman* (New York: The American Assembly, Columbia University, 1967); and the accompanying volume, Stanley V. Anderson (ed.), *Ombudsmen for American Government?* (Englewood Cliffs, N.J.: Prentice-Hall, 1968). See also Walter Gellhorn, *Ombudsmen and Others: Citizens' Protectors in Nine Countries* (Cambridge, Mass.: Harvard University Press, 1966); and the special issue "The Ombudsman or Citizen's Defender: A Modern Institution," *The Annals of the American Academy of Political and Social Science,* May 1968. "The Ombudsman: A Bibliography," Charles Smith (ed.), appears in U.S. Senate, Subcommittee on Administrative Practice and Procedure, Committee on the Judiciary, *Hearing: Ombudsman,* 89th Congress, 2nd Session, 1966, pp. 4045.

[44] Gellhorn, *When Americans Complain,* p. 212.

[45] *Ibid.,* pp. 6–10.

2. All have practically unlimited access to official papers bearing upon matters under investigation, so that they can themselves review what prompted administrative judgment.

3. All can express an ex officio expert's opinion about anything that governors do and that the governed do not like.

4. All take great pains to explain their conclusions, so that both administrators and complaining citizens well understand the results reached.

Gellhorn joins the critics of congressional casework on all the points already noted. But his basic concern is that the critic of administration has been an amateur. Legislators are partisan and interested in re-election; they cannot be neutral. "With that as its underlying assumption, most intercession resembles advocacy more than inquiry." [46] Nothing short of a complete separation of this function from the congressman is really satisfactory to Gellhorn. While he concedes that the Reuss proposal might have some benefits and that it is politically realistic, he fears that congressmen would still corrupt the potential of the reform:

> [T]he Reuss plan would keep congressmen in the very center of the picture — if anything, too much so. Everything would have to pass through them, so that they could squeeze from it the last possible drop of credit. . . . The massive parts of casework — the information requests, the pleadings for special privileges, the job applications — would remain precisely where they are now, on the desks of congressmen's staffs. Hence, the personal touch and the accretions to mailing lists, both of which are so dear to the hearts of constant candidates, would be unaffected. . . . Congressmen are too sure that they gain supporters by seeming to handle grievances themselves. . . .[47]

Gellhorn concedes that the concept of the ombudsman cannot be transplanted to America without modification and that those who admire the idea in principle will have to dilute their enthusiasm. A variety of specific adaptations, including a permanent Office of Administrative Procedure and Organization in the Executive Office of the President, have been suggested.[48]

[46] *Ibid.*, p. 216.
[47] *Ibid.*, pp. 92–93.
[48] See Kenneth Culp Davis, "Ombudsmen in America: Officers to Criticize Administrative Action," *University of Pennsylvania Law Review*, June 1961, pp. 1057–76.

The Reuss proposal for an Administrative Counsel of the Congress attempts to provide central, institutional staff services to strengthen the existing decentralized system of casework. The two basic arguments for creating the counsel are: (1) that information on recurrent problems encountered by citizens and indicating the need for remedial legislation is "only sporadically available and frequently is inadequately developed or fails entirely to reach the appropriate legislative committees"; and (2) that "the necessary and proper efforts of . . . individual Members to deal with these problems have increasingly become so burdensome as to constitute a serious impediment to the discharge of their other legislative duties." [49] The Administrative Counsel, a nonpartisan, professional employee of the Congress, would appoint, subject to the availability of appropriations, such staff as might be necessary to carry on the work of the office. It would review cases only upon the request of a congressman, although it would have discretionary authority to make further investigation into any case. It would be required to make an annual report to the Congress including recommendations for legislation or further investigation.

Congressman Reuss anticipates that the initial size of the staff would be 10 or 20 experts — "just enough so that you would have a real top notch legal or administrative expert on top of each specialized field." [50] The advantages of such a counsel would be: a high quality staff knowledgeable in the major grievance areas (something impossible in any individual congressman's office), a central perspective and capacity for generalization from a large number of cases, and the opportunity to share information and answers to specific problems among offices.

In designing his proposal, Congressman Reuss has been careful to integrate it with the existing system of channels through members of Congress. "I do not believe that Members of Congress, who want to be re-elected, would consent to remove themselves entirely from dealing with constituents' problems," he concludes.[51] Yet he considers his reform a clear alternative to the third suggested direction of reform — further increasing the office staffs of congressmen. This approach, which has been the congressional response to date, should not be continued for two reasons: (1) there simply is no physical room in the five existing House and Senate office buildings for such increased in-

[49] H.R. 4273, 89th Congress, 1st Session, Section 2.
[50] *Hearings: Organization of Congress*, 89th Congress, 1st Session, 1965, p. 87.
[51] *Ibid.*, p. 83.

dividual staffs; and (2) the burgeoning of office staffs would provide at best an unwieldy, costly, and inefficient means of handling the increased volume and complexity of casework.[52]

A SENSITIVITY TO FUTURE REQUIREMENTS. The congressional and public concern with the mounting burdens of casework and constituent problems is not misplaced in our judgment. Some of the assumptions on which criticism and prescription have been based, however, are not supported by empirical data. More important, they involve much broader normative judgments on the proper role of the congressman and the Congress in the American system.

For reasons we shall develop in the following chapters, we believe that the relationship of Congress to its constituents — both in education and service — will become even more important in the future. The mediating role of the congressman will almost certainly be enhanced in an era of rapid technological change that promises to revolutionize the distribution and administration of governmental services.

Apart from a technological era that few have yet perceived, the burden of casework channeled through the Congress will increase sharply over the next decade or two because congressmen will be representing rapidly growing constituencies and because, in Congressman Reuss's words, "federal problems per capita will become more numerous and complex." [53]

When the current size of the House of Representatives was set at 435 members in 1911, the average population of a House district was slightly over 210,000. In late 1967, when the population of the United States reached 200 million, the average stood at slightly over 460,000. By 1980, each congressman will have acquired on the average another 100,000 constituents! And constituents will be both better educated and in closer contact with their congressman because of continued advances in communications and transportation.

The extensive legislative innovation of the 89th (Johnson) Congress is also bound to produce an increase in casework. Medicare and the Social Security amendments, the rent supplement program, the Elementary and Secondary Education Act, the new forms of public-private cooperation embraced in the concept of "creative federalism"

[52] *Ibid.* One response, welcomed by many members, is the establishment of a network of new Federal Information Centers in Atlanta, Kansas City, and around the country, to answer citizen requests for information. A total of 50 were projected for the end of 1968.

[53] *Ibid.*, p. 82.

— all enlarge the active constituency of the congressman. Even if Congress avoids the burden of detailed legislation through grants of broad discretionary authority, it retains the responsibility for control and oversight of massive program innovation.

Rather than limit its role in constituency service, Congress, in our view, will choose to rationalize the continued growth of such activities, probably with an innovation such as the Administrative Counsel. The constituency service function provides Congress with one of its most important sources of feedback information on the impact of governmental programs. A Congress that is sensitive to the present and future requirements of a rapidly changing society will choose to expand and refine constituency contact — not to restrict it.

PART THREE

Congress in the Future

CHAPTER SEVEN

Congress and the Information
Revolution: The Imperative to Adapt*

Our minds are finite, and yet even in these circumstances of finitude we are surrounded by possibilities that are infinite, and the purpose of human life is to grasp as much as we can out of that infinitude. . . .

Those societies which cannot combine reverence to their symbols with freedom of revision, must ultimately decay either from anarchy or from the slow atrophy of a life stifled by useless shadows. . . .[1]

INTRODUCTION: A NEW LOOK AT CONGRESS

The study of Congress has been largely the study of the contemporary Congress, with a few political historians searching out the roots and precedents of congressional forms and procedures. The future of Congress has been left to the polemicists and the reformers.

The late 1960's have witnessed, however, a significant new intellectual concern about social prediction and "alternative futures" for the United States — a concern that can and should include the future of the United States Congress.[2] One acute observer of contemporary

---

* An article adapted from this chapter, "System Politics: The Presidency and Congress in the Future," appeared in *Technology Review*, December 1968, pp. 22–33. Copyright 1968 by the Alumni Association of the Massachusetts Institute of Technology.

[1] Alfred North Whitehead, *Dialogues of Alfred North Whitehead* (Boston: Little, Brown & Co., 1954), p. 163; and *Symbolism: Its Meaning and Effect* (New York: The Macmillan Co., 1927), p. 88.

[2] See Daniel Bell, "The Year 2000 — The Trajectory of an Idea," in *Toward the Year 2000: Work in Progress, Daedalus*, Summer 1967, pp. 639–51. An ongoing summary of futurist research and publications is available in *The*

American life has suggested that this new style of dealing with the future with its "sense of direction, of intelligent, effective choice" will be widely recognized as a salient American characteristic within a decade.[3] As our capacity to manipulate the future has grown tremendously over the past few years, our concern has become much more one of control and anticipation of outcomes than simply of prediction.

Why should the student of Congress be interested in the study of the future? What relevance can social speculation have to an understanding of congressional performance? Several reasons might be given.

First, we have a substantial amount of data on economic, social, and political trends that underline the changing nature of the congressional environment: GNP forecasts, population trends, urbanization, Negro registration in the South, income distribution. Rather than view Congress from a static point in time, we should be aware of the changing inputs into the congressional system. "Futurism" gives our perspective a time dimension.

Second, important new technologies relating to the application of the digital computer have already been developed experimentally and will soon be widely diffused in government. We now have sufficient experience with these technologies to foresee much of their potential as well as the problems that are likely to attend their introduction. By ignoring technological forecasts, we limit our possibilities for anticipating or understanding change. If, as some observers have stated, we are experiencing a technological change of kind rather than degree — from an industrial era to a "cybernetic" era [4] — political scientists who ignore the future risk overstating and overvaluing characteristics of the contemporary political process.

Third, the interdisciplinary, "systems" orientation of the futurists offers the political scientist access to the collateral findings and insights of related disciplines. For example, some of the most imaginative research on the organizational effects of computers — a subject of critical importance to the study of governmental bureaucracies — has come from industrial management. Similarly, the research of scientists

---

Futurist: A Newsletter for Tomorrow's World, published by the World Future Society, Washington, D.C.

[3] Max Ways, "The Road to 1977," *Fortune*, January 1967, p. 94. See also Martin Shubik, "Information, Rationality, and Free Choice in a Future Democratic Society," *Daedalus*, Summer 1967, pp. 771–78.

[4] Cybernetics may be defined as the study of automatic or self-regulating control systems. For a fuller explanation of the term and its historical significance, see Charles R. Dechert (ed.), *The Social Impact of Cybernetics* (Notre Dame, Ind.: University of Notre Dame Press, 1966).

and engineers in communications theory provides valuable insights for the social scientist.[5] The analysis of urban systems in terms of urban transportation, housing, health, communications, education, and environmental quality control is another potentially significant breakthrough that may alter many of our conceptions about local and municipal governmental performance.[6]

There is a danger of seeing Congress in one historical form — abstracted from one moment of time and by implication eternally valid. Political scientists of this generation have viewed Congress in the pluralistic perspective and have interpreted the hidden "rationality" of incremental decision making in highly complicated areas of public policy.[7] This may have been a largely valid description for the recent past, but there is no assurance that it will continue to hold in the age of the computer.

It is our contention that just as congressional structures and functions have changed in the past so will they change in the future. By examining the processes of change we should be able to acquire a much better understanding of that future. Congress cannot escape the necessity for choice that all change implies, but political scientists can help to define the alternatives of choice.

The hypothetical future choices for Congress outlined here reflect certain admitted biases of the author. In the preceding chapters we have emphasized the dynamic character of legislative-executive relations in the American political system as well as the continued vitality of Congress. We can almost certainly expect more significant changes in the technology of American politics and government in the remaining decades of the twentieth century than we have witnessed in the early decades. The application of computer-based technology and information systems to government promises a revolutionary change in governmental decision making. We anticipate that Congress will participate in this change.

Our view of the congressional future is best described as "open" or

[5] For example, see Karl W. Deutsch, *The Nerves of Government: Models of Political Communication and Control* (New York: The Free Press of Glencoe, 1963), Chap. V.

[6] In early 1968, the Urban Systems Laboratory, an interdepartmental laboratory for research in the area of urban systems, was established at M.I.T., Cambridge, Mass., with the assistance of a Ford Foundation grant. Among its first projects was a ground-breaking Summer Studies Group on Urban Information Systems.

[7] See Henry S. Rowen, "Bargaining and Analysis in Government," paper delivered at annual meeting of the American Political Science Association, New York, September 1966.

"possibilist." [8] It is neither heavily optimistic nor pessimistic about the prospects for the adaptation of American political institutions. It combines the dynamics of change, particularly the impetus toward rationalization in governmental decision making, with an appreciation for the structural continuities of the American political system. Daniel Moynihan may be right in his estimate that "the near future is almost sure to be much like the distant past" and that a time-span of thirty-five years is "short" in the history of American government. But that past has been characterized by extensive innovation and flexible adaptation within the apparent structural inertia of the system. Moynihan himself admits, "We have centralized decision-making within a federal structure and thereby greatly reduced pressures to change the latter in order to achieve the former." [9] The imperative to adapt will be even greater in the near future than it has been in the past.

The time-span chosen — up to the year 2000 — is also open in the sense that while it lies within the life expectancy of the majority of Americans living today, it encompasses technological change beyond the imagination of the contemporary citizen. Some observers of Congress will continue to define for themselves a relatively short time-span that excludes much of what we shall discuss here.

Finally, our projection is open in the sense that it counterbalances technological enthusiasm with political evaluation. Frederick C. Mosher has commented on the tendency of the proponents of systems analysis in government to ignore democratic values and processes. "In all the literature I have read about PPBS (Planning-Programming-Budgeting System)," he notes, "only a very few authors have even mentioned the executive and legislative processes of review and decision. The President and Congress seem to be regarded as enemies of rationality." [10] Indeed, the futurists tend to view the contemporary Congress as an artifact that is likely to become even more of a curio piece in the post-industrial society.[11] Zbigniew Brzezinski goes so far

---

[8] The term "possibilist" is from Max Lerner. See his "dream of possibility" and of "a possible emergent man in the American civilization" in "Six Revolutions in American Life," in Thomas R. Ford (ed.), *The Revolutionary Theme in Contemporary America* (Lexington, Ky.: University of Kentucky Press, 1965), pp. 1–20.

[9] Moynihan, "The Relationship of Federal to Local Authorities," *Daedalus*, Summer 1967, pp. 801–2.

[10] "P.P.B.S.: Two Questions," *Public Administration Review*, March 1967.

[11] Peter Drucker, for one, concludes, "The developments of the last two decades have largely pushed Congress out of being a partner in political decision. . . . The complex arrangements of the New Federalism are largely

as to suggest the Presidency itself may become "symbolic" and that we will see a revolution in the concept of representation.

> Legislation will cease to be a cancelling out and balancing of interests, and will become something far more abstracted, involving the weighing of interrelationships within the society and within the technological processes.

> . . . The President will not be able to adjust effectively and interrelate all the functionally specialized interests that will evolve. Such political problems cannot be solved or meaningfully analyzed by people concerned only with the political system.[12]

We accept the proposition that the President and Congress will both have to evolve important new roles by the end of the century, although we question an essentially technocratic projection that reduces either to a merely symbolic status in American society. With this preliminary statement of our perspective in mind, we now turn to the fascinating question of the political world of the future.

CHANGES IN GOVERNMENTAL DECISION MAKING

The central problem facing the contemporary Congress has been the necessity to adapt to the reality of executive-centered government. The effect of the congressional response in this century has not been a diminution in the power of the American Legislature but rather a redefinition of congressional function.

Perhaps the most significant change that will divide the government of today from the government of tomorrow will be a new style of decision making made possible by the revolution in information technology. Already, before computer technology has been developed for, or applied to, most areas of governmental problem solving, significant innovations are evident.

A progressive development of the executive budget as an instrument of government is already being experienced in the management of the defense establishment and the early extension of PPBS to other government agencies, as endorsed by the President in August, 1965. A new planning orientation has been incorporated into the budgetary

---

beyond the power of Congress if not altogether beyond its purview." "Notes on the New Politics," *The Public Interest*, Summer 1966, p. 16.

[12] *Daedalus*, Summer 1967, p. 671.

process that begins with an explicit statement of policy objectives and proceeds to a formal weighing of costs and benefits of alternatives.[13] Economic analysis, cost-benefit and systems analysis are being applied as an increasingly sophisticated extension of traditional decision-making techniques. And policy analysis has yet to be coupled with the breakthrough in computer technology.

One of the first areas of government that is likely to be affected by the availability of computerized information systems is the administration of governmental services. Once the massive records of all levels of government and the statutes and regulations pertaining to eligibility of the public for various services have been converted for computer use, a major rationalization of governmental services will be possible. This will permit both an increase in efficiency and equity of treatment *and* the personalization (i.e., tailoring to meet individual requirements) of service. A part of this rationalization may well be a shift from a "service strategy" to an "income strategy" for social services (in the form of a negative income tax or similar innovation) and a decentralization of services through "contracting out" (i.e., the purchase by government on a contract basis of services from the private sector in lieu of publicly provided services).[14]

Congress will be intimately involved in the rationalization of the welfare state. A conflict between the centralization of governmental files and the establishment of a national data system and infringement upon individual privacy will undoubtedly require political solution. Congressman Cornelius E. Gallagher (D-N.J.) and former Senator Edward V. Long (D-Mo.) have already initiated congressional inquiries into the effect of the computer on privacy. The balance between efficiency and individual treatment will concern Congress. As the Executive moves toward greater professionalism in administration supported by massive information systems, the congressman is likely to gain stature as the citizen's personal link with government. Even

---

[13] See Allen Schick, "The Road to PPB: The Stages of Budget Reform," *Public Administration Review*, December 1966, pp. 243–58. For an evaluation of PPBS in defense policy and foreign affairs, see Paul Y. Hammond, "A Functional Analysis of Defense Department Decision-Making in the McNamara Administration," *The American Political Science Review* (APSR), March 1968, pp. 57–69; and Thomas C. Schelling, "PPBS and Foreign Affairs," memorandum prepared at the request of the U.S. Senate, Subcommittee on National Security and International Operations, Committee on Government Operations, *Committee Print: Planning-Programming-Budgeting*, 90th Congress, 1st Session, January 1968.

[14] Moynihan, *op. cit.*, p. 807.

though the Congress will also rationalize constituency service through automated mail processing and some form of central complaint clearance, such as the Administrative Counsel proposed by Congressman Henry S. Reuss (D-Wisc.), the congressman will retain his personal identity as *the* ombudsman for his constituency. Congress will also have a major role in redefining the levels of administrative responsibility for governmental services in the federal system.

The rationalization of existing services will be a relatively easy demand on the new information technology; it is largely a task of gathering, storing, processing, and making readily accessible large amounts of data. The current "third-generation" computers, which can incorporate scores of terminals using a central computational facility on a time-sharing basis and which can make data available anywhere in the system in "real time" (almost instantaneously or so rapidly that the human user does not notice the intervening time of computer processing), are already technologically equal to the task.

Before more advanced applications of the computer can be widely used, a more adequate data base and framework will be required for governmental decisions at all levels. The National Commission on Technology, Automation, and Economic Progress reported to the President in February 1966:

> We do not have, as yet, a continuous charting of social changes, and we have been ill-prepared (in such matters as housing, education, or the status of the Negro) to determine our needs, establish goals, and measure our performance. Lacking any systematic assessment, we have few criteria which allow us to test the effectiveness of present policies or weigh alternatives regarding future programs.[15]

The early phases of PPBS have indicated a similar deficiency in information for program evaluation and budgetary decisions. We can, accordingly, expect the Executive to develop within a few years a system of "social accounts" in the four areas designated by the National Commission: (1) the measurement of social costs and net returns of economic innovations; (2) the measurement of social ills (i.e., crime, family disruptions); (3) the creation of "performance budgets" in areas of defined social needs (i.e., housing, education); and (4) indicators of economic opportunity and social mobility. One comprehensive system of social accounting has already been suggested

[15] *Technology and the American Economy* (Washington, D.C.: U.S. Government Printing Office, 1966), p. 95.

by Bertram Gross, and the idea has received a significant boost from a group of United States senators, headed by Walter F. Mondale (D-Minn.), who have introduced draft legislation for a Full Opportunity and Social Accounting Act.[16] Since social indicators will become the reference points for a range of governmental decisions, Congress is likely to assume an important role in their definition and testing.

The really significant change in government will come through improved techniques of decision making — operations research, mathematical analysis, systems modeling, and simulation — used in conjunction with the computer and a more adequate data base. The possibilities for analysis of the social system generally open a new area for rationalizing governmental policies. Daniel P. Moynihan, in his testimony during the hearings of the Ribicoff Subcommittee on Executive Reorganization on "The Federal Role in Urban Affairs" cited the research and evaluation (including the careful economic analysis of the Subcommittee on Low Income Families of the Joint Economic Committee) that led to the major social initiative of the War on Poverty and that have been crucial to its ongoing redefinition and improvement. While one "would wish to leave plenty of room for the eventual mysteries of life," Moynihan concludes, "it is fair to state that the first order effects of many social programs are now subject to rudimentary, but nonetheless useful measurement. . . ."[17] Such "rudimentary" measurement, it is also fair to state, will become increasingly refined as we increase our theoretical understanding of the social system through the potential of computer-based analysis.

Most of the subsequent analysis assumes that low-cost, comprehensive information systems will be generally available to governmental decision makers well before the end of the century and that these systems will be steadily adapted for governmental use in the intervening years. In the first two decades of computer technology, the federal government has pioneered in computer innovation and application,

[16] See Bertram Gross, "The State of the Nation: Social System Accounting," in Raymond A. Bauer (ed.), Social Indicators (Technology, Space and Society Series of the American Academy of Arts and Sciences; Cambridge, Mass.: The M.I.T. Press, 1966), pp. 154–271; and Senator Walter F. Mondale, "The Full Opportunity and Social Accounting Act of 1967," Daily Congressional Record, 90th Congress, 1st Session, February 6, 1967, pp. 51534–37. See also Bertram Gross (ed.), "Social Goals and Indicators for American Society I," The Annals of the American Academy of Political and Social Science, May 1967.

[17] U.S. Senate, Subcommittee on Executive Reorganization, Committee on Government Operations, Hearings: Federal Role in Urban Affairs, 89th Congress, 2nd Session, December 13, 1966, p. 2644.

beginning with data processing by the Bureau of the Census and extending through the $1.6 billion Air Force SAGE (Semi-Automatic Ground Environment) system, the most sophisticated real-time computer system yet developed.[18] It is likely that the government will continue to be a pioneer in the use of the new information technology.

The use of this technology will require a restatement of many of the traditional assumptions about communications and decision making in government. The basic invention of the information revolution — the digital computer — will continue to be improved (through large-scale use of integrated circuits and parallel processing), although the central processing unit has long since ceased to be the bottleneck in information systems technology. Revolutionary advances are necessary in input and output devices. Optical scanners, now in prototype development and marketing, will in time be able to code and store printed text far more efficiently than current key-punch operations. Eventually voice communication with computers should be feasible. Machine-independent computer languages will make practicable machine-machine communications. Applications programs will be continually extended, refined, and internalized, although there will be a continuing and increasing demand for systems programs (i.e., monitors, operating systems, compilers). The costs of data transmission will fall rapidly. As the net costs of acquiring, processing, storing, retrieving, and using information decline to a fraction of their current total, computer applications will multiply at a bewildering rate. Some futurists, such as Herman Kahn, expect advances in computer technology by five, ten, or more orders of magnitude over the next 30 years, effectively eliminating the economic constraint to computer application.[19]

[18] For a summary of federal agency uses of automatic data processing and congressional interest in the subject, see Robert L. Chartrand, "Automatic Data Processing for the Congress" (Washington, D.C.: Library of Congress, Legislative Reference Service, 1967), reprinted in *Daily Congressional Record*, 90th Congress, 1st Session, January 30, 1967, pp. H-728–31. A discussion of SAGE and related uses of real-time systems in the private sector is included in Gilbert Burck and the editors of *Fortune* magazine, *The Computer Age and Its Potential for Management* (New York: Harper & Row, 1965), Chap. II. Also see James Martin, *Programming Real-Time Computer Systems* (Englewood Cliffs, N.J.: Prentice-Hall, 1965).

[19] See Herman Kahn and Anthony J. Wiener, *The Year 2000: A Framework for Speculation on the Next Thirty-Three Years* (New York: The Macmillan Co., 1967), pp. 86–91. Another set of projections is developed by Paul Armer, *Computer Aspects of Technological Change, Automation, and Economic Progress* (Rand Memorandum P-3478; Santa Monica, Cal.: The RAND Corporation, 1966). Armer notes that between 1955 and 1965 the size of a central processing unit with its storage has decreased by a factor of about ten. The decade through

No matter how conservatively one views the future, computers, by virtue of their ability to store and process enormous amounts of data, to calculate at lightning speeds, and to simulate human and organizational decision-behavior, provide man with an intellectual tool of almost inconceivable power. Almost certainly the application of the computer will introduce a new era for both the social and political systems. For our purposes, we need assume only that there will be cumulative improvement in information processing and computer-assisted techniques for analysis. Together, these advances will dramatically alter the decision-making context. What effect the new information technology will have on the political process itself (i.e., on the kinds of decisions made) is another question. A preliminary review of information problems in government today suggests the potential.

INFORMATION, COMMUNICATION, AND POLITICAL DECISION MAKING

Will the computer significantly alter decision-making behavior? Will the availability of comprehensive information systems improve the quality or rationality of decisions reached in the political process? Skeptics abound. First, there is the opinion that the decision maker is inherently limited by a world of imperfect and partial information. But even among those who concede that data systems may yield impressive technical payoffs in improved information, there are the "realists" who question how significant the "final payoffs" of "actual improvements in government or private action" will be.[20] This section of our analysis offers an affirmative argument to both of these positions.

SOME CURRENT LIMITATIONS ON INFORMATION AND DECISION MAKING. Information provides the premises for decision or action. By one definition, decision making is simply "the process of converting informa-

---

1975 is expected to produce a further reduction of size by a factor of about 1000. In the two decades through 1975, the cost of computing power will decrease to less than one 200-thousandth of its 1955 value. The internal speed of computers has increased by a factor of about 200 between 1955 and 1965 and should experience a similar increase in the next decade. Total installed computing power in the United States in 1965 amounted to about 200 million additions per second, an increase in capability of about 400-fold over 1955.

[20] See Anthony Downs, "A Realistic Look at the Final Payoffs From Urban Data Systems," *Public Administration Review*, September 1967, pp. 204–10.

tion into action." Policy or decision rules guide the decision maker in relating information sources to resulting decision flows.[21] A number of typologies of the decision-making process have been suggested. For simplicity, we shall assume Herbert Simon's definition of a three-phase decision process: finding occasions for making decisions (*intelligence* activity); finding possible courses of action (*design* activity); and choosing among courses of action (*choice* activity).[22] Information — intelligence, news, facts, data — is essential at all phases of the process. The political decision maker needs, broadly speaking, two types of information: *technical* information defining the content of a policy issue and *political* information concerning the relative strength of competing claims and the consequences of alternative decisions.[23] It is a common assumption that "bad" or "wrong" decisions in politics as in business stem from insufficient or improperly processed information. What are some of the current limitations in information processing as a basis for decision making?

One group of limitations centers on the capacity of the individual decision maker. Anthony Downs cites six "inherent" limitations of human decision making — all of them linked to a world of "imperfect" information:

> 1. Each decision-maker can devote only a limited amount of time to decision-making.
>
> 2. Each decision-maker can mentally weigh and consider only a limited amount of information at one time.
>
> 3. The functions of most officials require them to become involved in more activities than they can consider simultaneously; hence they must normally focus their attention on only part of their major concerns, while the rest remain latent.
>
> 4. The amount of information initially available to every decision-maker about each problem is only a small fraction of all the information potentially available on the subject.
>
> 5. Additional information bearing on any particular problems can usually be procured, but the cost of procurement and utilization may rise rapidly as the amount of data increases.

[21] Jay W. Forrester, "Managerial Decision-Making," in Martin Greenberger (ed.), *Computers and the World of the Future* (Cambridge, Mass.: The M.I.T. Press, 1962), pp. 37–38.

[22] Simon, *The Shape of Automation for Men and Management* (New York: Harper Torchbooks, 1965), pp. 53–56.

[23] David B. Truman, *The Governmental Process: Political Interests and Public Opinion* (New York: Alfred A. Knopf, 1951), p. 334.

6. Important aspects of many problems involve information that cannot be procured at all, especially concerning future events: hence many decisions must be made in the face of ineradicable uncertainty.[24]

Moreover, communication of information requires definite resource costs in time, money, and effort as well as costs of delay. But the central problem is that "every individual has a saturation point regarding the amount of information he can usefully handle in a given time period." [25]

The limited capacities (and information) of the individual decision maker have led some political scientists to ask how does man actually make decisions. If a "rational-comprehensive," or "synoptic," ideal of decision making is not possible, what is? [26] Charles Lindblom has suggested that most administrators rely on a method of "successive limited comparisons" in arriving at decisions. By focusing on marginal or incremental values and neglecting many important possible outcomes, alternative policies, and affected values, the decision maker's need for information on values and objectives is drastically reduced. Aaron Wildavsky has extended Lindblom's method to the politics of the budgetary process, illustrating many of the techniques budget officials and congressmen use to reduce "the burden of calculation." Participants in the budget process experiment, simplify, "satisfice" (satisfy and suffice), and deal in increments. In reviewing the alternatives to incremental decision making, Wildavsky concludes, "Comprehensive calculation and formal coordination turn out to be unfeasible, undesirable, or both." [27]

A second set of limitations in information processing relates to the complexity of human organizations. By its very definition, organization implies and "requires the introduction of constraints and

[24] Downs, *Inside Bureaucracy* (A RAND Corporation Research Study; Boston: Little, Brown & Co., 1967), p. 75.

[25] *Ibid.*, p. 112.

[26] For a detailed criticism of the synoptic ideal see Charles E. Lindblom, *The Intelligence of Democracy: Decision Making Through Mutual Adjustment* (New York: The Free Press, 1965), pp. 138–43. A comparative analysis of the rational-comprehensive method and the method of successive limited comparison is given in "The Science of 'Muddling Through,'" *Public Administration Review*, Spring 1959, pp. 79–88. Lindblom's most recent statement of these ideas is found in *The Policy-Making Process* (Foundations of Modern Political Science Series; Englewood Cliffs, N.J.: Prentice-Hall, 1968).

[27] Wildavsky, *The Politics of the Budgetary Process* (Boston: Little, Brown & Co., 1964), p. 178.

restrictions to reduce diffuse and random communication to channels appropriate for the accomplishment of organizational objectives." [28] A network of human communicators introduces some immediate inefficiencies to organizational decision making, such as distortion, errors in transmission, resources absorbed in internal communication, and short-run communications overload.[29] Hierarchy and specialization introduce more serious problems to information processing. Hierarchy is conducive to "concealment and misrepresentation" in systems where subordinates are upwardly mobile or advocates of subprograms.[30] Specialization intensifies blockage and distortion. Communication of information is limited by several types of separation in "organizational space": geographical, functional, status or prestige, and power. Katz and Kahn conclude that the most general limitation to information coding and processing in human organizations is that "the position people occupy in organizational space will determine their perception and interpretation of incoming information and their search for additional information." [31]

One critical problem in organizational communication is the strong tendency to overload certain decision makers with information. Individuals working under conditions of information overload have exhibited a number of often maladaptive reactions: (1) *omission*, failing to process some of the information; (2) *error*, processing information incorrectly; (3) *queuing*, delaying during periods of peak load in the hope of catching up later; (4) *filtering*, neglecting to process certain types of information, according to predetermined priorities; (5) *approximation*, or eliminating categories of discrimination (a blanket and imprecise way of responding); (6) employing *multiple channels*, as in decentralization; and (7) *escape* from the task.[32] In the specific case of communications from constituents, Dexter found that congressmen had developed a number of similar techniques for coping with overload.[33]

[28] Daniel Katz and Robert L. Kahn, *The Social Psychology of Organizations* (New York: John Wiley & Sons, 1966), p. 225.

[29] Downs, *Inside Bureaucracy*, p. 178.

[30] *Ibid.*, pp. 116–18.

[31] *Ibid.*, p. 228.

[32] J. G. Miller, "Information Input, Overload, and Psychopathology," *American Journal of Psychiatry*, 1960, pp. 695–704, cited in Katz and Kahn, *op. cit.*, pp. 231–35.

[33] Raymond A. Bauer, Ithiel de Sola Pool, and Lewis A. Dexter, *American Business and Public Policy: The Politics of Foreign Trade* (New York: Atherton Press, 1963), pp. 403–50.

Sociologists have begun to integrate the research findings on communications in complex organizations. Harold Wilensky, in an excellent study of the function of *organizational intelligence* (which he defines as "gathering, processing, interpreting, and communicating the technical and political information needed in the decision-making process"), concludes that there are several roots of "intelligence failure" in governmental and industrial organizations. Among these he includes structural problems, intelligence doctrines, and problems of organizational growth.[34] Intelligence failures occur when there is adequate information in the organizational system but it is poorly integrated or lost at subordinate levels or when the relevant information is not in the organizational system due to inadequate or inappropriate search procedures. When "high quality" intelligence (information that is clear, timely, reliable, valid, adequate and wide ranging) does reach the decision maker, but he is not in a position to act or will not act on the basis of that information, it is more appropriate to speak of a deficiency in power or motivation than of an intelligence failure.

THE INFORMATION PROBLEMS OF CONGRESS. The contemporary Congress and individual congressman are subject to all these current limitations of information and communication, accentuated by several additional or more specific constraints.

Dependence on executive bureaucracy. While Congress may be viewed as an open system receptive to information from a variety of sources and at numerous stages in the decision process, it is dependent on information provided by executive agencies for many of its decisions. The House Appropriations Committee, for example, considered one of the major channels of information for congressional decision making, operates under serious "information disadvantages" concerning the budget. One of the most important political resources that executive agencies can draw upon but *both* the Bureau of the Budget and the relevant congressional committees cannot is "their ability to manipulate complex bodies of information relative to their own area of expertise." [35] Top decision makers are dependent on the informa-

---

[34] *Organizational Intelligence: Knowledge and Policy in Government and Industry* (New York: Basic Books, 1967), pp. 175–78.

[35] Richard F. Fenno, Jr., *The Power of the Purse: Appropriations Politics in Congress* (Boston: Little, Brown & Co., 1966), p. 265. "The [Appropriations] Committee's sense of information inferiority . . . is sufficiently widespread so that agency officials are well advised when they warn their witnesses not to talk down to the Committee" (p. 347). One study of state legislatures similarly

tional resources of the bureaucracy. While the President and Congress may develop independent staff resources, the basic dependency continues. In a system of separated power, each agency must decide what informational relationships it will develop with which political actors. As Norton Long observes, "The bureaucracy under the American political system has a large share of responsibility for the public promotion of policy and even more in organizing the political basis for its survival and growth." [36] It follows that agencies will exchange information for support at the best exchange rates they can establish. The result, for Congress, is "mutual dependence" where "both sides generally regard their contacts as prerequisites to doing their best work." [37]

Access to information: the problems of executive privilege and executive secrecy. Increasingly large bodies of information within the Executive are screened from Congress entirely. One basis for withholding information is the right of the President to confidential advice in executive deliberations. This right is interpreted by the Bureau of the Budget as comprehending the entire process of executive budget formulation. In budget review, Congress must "second-guess" the Executive without full information on how decisions were reached. The President's Budget Message "too frequently . . . merely declares the Presidential decision with an implied challenge to the Congress to amend — if it dares." [38] Much of the committee work of Congress, accordingly, involves an effort to unearth and evaluate the informational premises of executive decision. An elaborate subterfuge has evolved in the appropriations process which permits dissatisfied agencies to "tell it all" when it is to their advantage, while applying lip service to the canons of the program of the President.

A second basis for withholding information from Congress is the

---

concludes, "The biggest limitation on the use of the power of administrative surveillance is in the *quality of information* that the legislature is able to command. In nearly every case, the administrative official who is to be examined will be superior in the amount and quality of information that he possesses." Wilder Crane, Jr., and Meredith W. Watts, Jr., *State Legislative Systems* (Foundations of State and Local Government Series; Englewood Cliffs, N.J.: Prentice-Hall, 1968), p. 12.

[36] "Power and Administration," *Public Administration Review*, Autumn 1949, p. 259.

[37] Wildavsky, *op. cit.*, p. 56.

[38] Arthur Smithies, *The Budgetary Process in the United States* (Committee for Economic Development Research Study; New York: McGraw-Hill Book Co., 1955), p. 204.

need for secrecy in national security affairs. Much of the relevant information for decision making in the foreign and defense policy areas has been "classified" by the Executive. This means that most members of Congress are deprived of adequate information in increasingly important sectors of national policy. They may receive occasional briefings from State and Defense Department officials on a confidential basis, only to find more detailed information and analyses available in the public press. In one area, atomic energy, Congress has specified for itself coordinate access to some of the most highly classified governmental information, albeit for a limited number of members. The basic atomic energy legislation authorizes the Joint Committee on Atomic Energy "to utilize the services, information, facilities, and personnel of the departments and establishments of the Government." [39] Yet Congress has been reluctant to extend the JCAE model to other national security areas, such as the intelligence community.

Decentralized information and committee power. Since the early nineteenth century Congress has relied on a decentralized system of standing and special committees to perform its intelligence function. (More recently the institutionalization of the congressman's office and the development of congressional agencies, such as the Legislative Reference Service of the Library of Congress, have supplemented the intelligence function of the committee system.) Within this system of specialization in intelligence, "the dominant expectation is that the (individual) Committee should disseminate most of the information it has assembled to the other ˙nembers of the House to form the basis on which their authoritative decisions can be made." [40] The committee disseminates information through its published hearings and reports, the speeches of committee spokesmen on the floor, and word-of-mouth communications between congressmen and individual committee members.

Yet in a political system where information is a form of power, individuals and committees that have access to information have an immediate interest in limiting the dissemination of information. The decentralization of information to relatively autonomous committees or subcommittees means that a very limited number of individuals have the opportunity to develop broad enough perspectives to process and use information, usually only the committee or subcommittee

---

[39] Harold P. Green and Alan Rosenthal, *Government of the Atom: The Integration of Powers* (New York: Atherton Press, 1963), pp. 80–81.

[40] Fenno, *op. cit.*, p. 23.

chairman and ranking minority member.[41] Overseeing staff, the intelligence arm of the committee, is frequently the prerogative of the chairman and ranking minority member. Other procedures enhance the control of the committee leadership over information: limited advance circulation of reports in subcommittee and full committee; extensive, complicated, and poorly indexed committee hearings; unanimous committee findings; expeditious routing of legislation to the floor; allocation of time on the floor. In sum, the individual member operates at a decided information disadvantage to the committee and committee member in the legislative process. Former Congressman Thomas B. Curtis (R-Mo.) sees this information problem as a major obstacle to congressional reform:

> Instead of fulfilling their function, namely to gather facts and arguments concerning issues so the House itself could intelligently reach a decision, [the committees] have usurped the prerogatives of the House and sought to make the decision themselves, each in their own little kingdoms.
>
> This usurpation of the power to make decisions has corrupted the study and deliberative process from one of gathering as much information as possible and spreading it out on the record for the rest of Congress . . . and the people . . . to see, to one of squirreling away what information the senior members of the committee have acquired . . . to make of the committees the "experts" on the subject . . . so that the committee's decision, made behind closed doors, becomes the decision the full Congress adopts . . . without full debate or discussion.[42]

Multiple information channels. A number of factors combine to provide Congress multiple information channels for any major policy issue. As a result the range of information and the potential for innovative approaches to problems is broadened, but the liabilities are

[41] Fenno notes that in the appropriations process "where jurisdictions are splintered, where information is decentralized, and where decision-making units operate autonomously, only the Chairman and ranking minority member comprehend the whole. They and only they can possess a breadth of vision, sources of information, and a degree of participation that encompasses the full scope of the Appropriations Committee's work." *Ibid.*, p. 157.

[42] "Role of Congress in the Decisionmaking Process," report to constituents, reprinted under Extension of Remarks of Hon. Donald Rumsfeld, *Daily Congressional Record*, 90th Congress, 2nd Session, March 27, 1968, pp. E-2368–69.

increased also. Members may receive contradictory information signals, biased by the specialized channel that is processing the information. Decisions reached on the basis of different informational premises may be inconsistent. The differentiation of appropriations subcommittees and substantive legislative (or authorization) committees provides two different channels of information. The trend toward increased use of the technique of annual authorization has given Congress new access to information and an expanded information base at the cost of some delay in the authorization-appropriation cycle.[43] Overlapping subject-matter jurisdictions among legislative committees are another source of complication and dissonance in communication. Finally, separate investigating committees or subcommittees (such as the Government Operations Committees) provide additional and often unutilized information feedback for congressional decision making.

The information problems of the individual member of Congress. Within the congressional system, the individual member has acute information problems. In a survey of members' complaints, Davidson, Kovenock, and O'Leary found that "the most frequently mentioned problems were associated with the complexity of decision-making: the lack of information, the volume of legislation to be considered, and the difficulty of making a rational choice among conflicting alternatives." The decision-making, information-deficiency problem was cited by 62 per cent of their sample, the highest complaint frequency.[44] Apart from the specific deficiencies noted above, congressmen have a surfeit of information, including internal congressional documents, publications of executive agencies, and reports from private sources. David Brinkley opened a November, 1965, NBC-TV News Special Report, entitled "Congress Needs Help," standing next to mountainous piles of paper that passed through a typical congressman's office in a single session. The congressman may utilize his legislative assistant, office staff, committee staff, the Legislative Reference Service, and staff assistance from other sources to help him process this glut of information, but in the real work of legislation — committee and floor action — he must rely primarily on himself. The Study of Congress

---

[43] For an example of the development of new information channels through annual authorization, see Raymond H. Dawson, "Congressional Innovation and Intervention in Defense Policy: Legislative Authorization of Weapons Systems," *APSR*, March 1967, pp. 42–57.

[44] Davidson, Kovenock, and O'Leary, *Congress in Crisis: Politics and Congressional Reform* (Belmont, Cal.: Wadsworth Publishing Co., 1966), pp. 75–78.

survey of House offices found that members did 30 per cent of their own general legislative research and 60 per cent of their own preparation for committee meetings and hearings and for floor debate and voting.[45] Considering the range of policy issues on which congressmen must act and the heavy pressures on their time, the national legislator faces problems of information processing as acute as any other individual in the political system except for the Chief Executive. Not surprisingly, a variety of simplifying devices are utilized: following the party leadership, deferring to the judgment of the responsible committee, voting with the state delegation, consulting members who are expert on the subject under consideration.

In view of the complexity of the legislative process and especially the chaos that can erupt at any moment during floor debate, members rely heavily on the exchange of information or advice about voting. Robert Peabody considers information exchange one of the basic means of influence in the legislative process:

> There is no lack of information, but it is almost inevitably contradictory. Who does the representative seek out? A member turns to the most informed and reliable sources of all — other representatives. A freshman member coming from a large state delegation is likely to look, first, to members of his party in his state who have examined the bill in committee. As he gains more experience, his reference group is likely to be extended to committee experts in other states. He has many opportunities for consultation — on the floor, at lunch, over the phone, walking to and from the House Office Buildings to the floor. Not only will these members provide him with informed technical knowledge, but the best ones will see things from his point of view. They will give him political advice as well as technical knowledge. . . . These are the conditions which lead almost all members of Congress to make investments in other members, permitting these other members to have influence on them. . . .[46]

Some recent research by David Kovenock confirms the hypothesis that the most important direct source of information for the individual member of Congress is other congressmen. Forty per cent of the

---

[45] John S. Saloma III, "The Job of a Congressman: Some Perspectives on Time and Information," unpublished paper, February 1967.

[46] "Organization Theory and Legislative Behavior: Bargaining, Hierarchy and Change in the U.S. House of Representatives," paper delivered at the annual meeting of the American Political Science Association, New York, September 1963, p. 5.

decision premises received by the six subcommittee members studied by Kovenock (see pp. 187–89) came directly from members of the House, almost three times as many as from any other single source. (Fifteen per cent originated with staff employees of individual members.) [47]

Most of the limiting conditions to individual and organizational decision making in a world of imperfect information are abundantly present in the contemporary congressional milieu. Congressmen are left to make their decisions in the dark — to develop coping or defensive strategies in the face of overwhelming complexity. The realist students of political decision making, whom we might describe as the "incrementalists," emphasize these current limitations of information. The question of interest to us is what difference will the new information technology make for the decision-making process in government. First we shall examine a range of technically feasible change; then, some of the political factors that will condition such change in the American political system.

POTENTIAL USES OF NEW INFORMATION TECHNOLOGY. With new information technology, many of the limitations of a world of imperfect information will be overcome. This does not mean that governments will operate in an environment of perfect information or that reaching political decisions will necessarily be any easier. As the information constraints on decision makers are eased, other limiting factors and tensions will come into play. There may well be a social disutility in greater knowledge. But this is a cost man has been willing to incur since the Garden of Eden. The following projection of governmental decision making in the future, based in good part on the contemporary application of computers in industrial organizations, is technologically expansive. We do not consider it to be an exaggerated or unrealistic claim for the *potential* of the new information technology.

Improved quality of information and information processing. The first two technical payoffs of computerized information systems are essentially mechanical (i.e., they involve no application of techniques of analysis, simply the more efficient processing of information) but are nonetheless significant.

One of the most obvious advances that will be made possible by the new information technology is increased quality of information (in-

[47] Kovenock, "Influence in the U.S. House of Representatives: Some Preliminary Statistical 'Snapshots,' " paper delivered at the annual meeting of the American Political Science Association, Chicago, September 1967, p. 22.

cluding factors such as relevance, precision, completeness, and timeliness) and quality of information processing (accuracy, speed, ability to handle complex relationships, flexibility, and potential for codification in standard rules).[48] The resource and delay costs to the individual decision maker who has access to governmental information systems will in time be minimal. Assuming no political restraints on access, the decision maker should be able, through proper specification, to locate all relevant information anywhere in the system almost instantaneously. Geographical and other forms of information "isolation" will end with a nationally (and eventually internationally) integrated information system. The inefficiencies and cost of information communication within human systems will be largely eliminated as many of the information processing functions of bureaucracies are assumed by programmed machines. The elimination of middlemen between top officials and data gatherers or their replacement by top-level data analysts will effect a major reduction in hierarchical distortion.[49]

A vivid example of the potential of the computer to eliminate inefficiencies in information processing and retrieval is in compiling the "government dossier." Each individual citizen leaves behind him a trail of public and private records from the time of his birth. Much of this information is retained in the files of government agencies scattered around Washington and the country: income tax returns, applications for government employment, security-clearance checks, social security and unemployment benefits, and census data.[50] Although there are restrictions of confidentiality and limits of disclosure on some files, it is still technically feasible to collect an enormous amount of information on a single individual. In the estimate of former Senator Edward V. Long (D-Mo.), "There is very little that some agency of the Federal government does not know about us from the cradle on. . . . [T]he proposed government computer or so-called Federal data bank will make it easier and cheaper to put your whole life his-

---

[48] These definitions of information and information processing are taken from Melvin Anshen, "Managerial Decisions," in John T. Dunlop (ed.), *Automation and Technological Change* (The American Assembly, Columbia University; Englewood Cliffs, N.J.: Prentice-Hall, 1962), p. 68.

[49] See Downs, *Inside Bureaucracy*, pp. 123–26.

[50] See U.S. Senate, Subcommittee on Administrative Practice and Procedure, Committee on the Judiciary, *Committee Print: Government Dossier (Survey of Information Contained in Government Files)*, 90th Congress, 1st Session, November 1967.

tory no further than the push of a button away." [51] The conflict with individual privacy posed by the elimination of inefficiency in information processing goes well beyond the governmental sphere.

On the positive side, the computer will give man the capacity to interrogate and reorganize massive data files almost instantaneously for social science research.[52] In sum, the usable information accessible to decision makers acting under time pressure should be increased significantly. But will this not simply accentuate the problem of information glut? Haven't decision makers more than enough information as is? The answer lies in a second technical payoff of the computer.

Improved channeling of information: easing the problem of information overload. The time and personal stamina of the individual decision maker will always be a limiting factor. In our foreseeable future there will always be more problems calling for the attention of a congressman than he can possibly consider. As long as he listens, there will be a communications and an information overload.

But with the use of the computer, information overload will be more subject to the control of the individual decision maker. He will have the potential to direct more of his work. The computer can be programmed to screen routine data with reference to predetermined critical variables and to provide top decision makers with exception information demanding attention or action. The problem of management information, according to Gilbert Burck, is "not how to get information to the top, but how to keep useless information from coming to the top." Automatic data processing will relieve the decision maker of "the necessity of valuing all information that comes his way" and will set him free from unnecessary, time-consuming detail.[53] Decision makers may specify in advance what types of information they wish to receive on given subjects of interest as new information becomes available. Central libraries or document centers can then service the individual decision maker according to his "interest profile" through a technique of "selective dissemination of information" (SDI).[54]

[51] Statement dated February 5, 1968.

[52] The M.I.T. Project MAC includes development of a computer-based management system for social data. See David Griffel and Stuart McIntosh, "The Current ADMINS System," paper prepared for Project MAC Seminar, Cambridge, Massachusetts, January 31, 1967.

[53] Burck, *op. cit.*, pp. 103, 116.

[54] See Carl F. J. Overhage and R. Joyce Harman (eds.), INTREX: *Report of a Planning Conference on Information Transfer Experiments* (Cambridge, Mass.: The M.I.T. Press, 1965), pp. 43–51.

Another means for improving the channeling of information to decision makers will be the use of new data structures and analytical frameworks. The impact of PPB on Defense Appropriations decisions within the House Committee on Appropriations affords an early example of this potential. In a comparative analysis of Department of Defense hearings before the subcommittee on the fiscal year 1954 budget versus the fiscal year 1968 budget, Ellen Nadler concluded that the new PPB format had: (1) restructured committee hearings along more programmatic lines; (2) facilitated the ability of decision makers to view budget decisions in terms of competing alternatives; (3) increased the flow of information to Congress; (4) enhanced the quality of information inputs into the budgetary process; and (5) led to more rational (i.e., comprehensive) decision making. Committee questions, after the introduction of the new budget, were more oriented toward direct comparisons of alternatives in terms of cost-effectiveness and evinced a greater awareness of the notion of weapons as "systems." Department responses to questions were more detailed, more quantitative, and evoked further similarly detailed and quantitative questions from committee members.[55] The implication is clearly that Congress is both getting and using more effectively *more* information on the defense budget with the aid of a new budget framework.

The computer will enable the decision maker to specify one or more of several information formats and to reorganize data in terms of a desired format. Instead of being a largely passive recipient of information, the decision maker will be able to interact with the data system, using it as an active search mechanism.

Congressmen may continue to tap a variety of information sources on a random basis to obtain political information, but improved selective processing of relevant technical information (and even political information on their constituency) should significantly change the problem of information overload. The individual legislator will have an important degree of control over the amount and nature of information he receives. Whether he uses such control to enhance his legislative performance will depend on such human factors as courage, perception, imagination, sensitivity, and achievement motivation.

[55] Nadler, "The Congressional Appropriations Process: Retrospective and Prospective Study of the Political Implications of the Planning-Programming-Budgeting System," unpublished *summa cum laude* B.A. thesis, Harvard University, Cambridge, Mass., 1968.

Improved quality of the human decision process. The computer has already demonstrated its capacity to discipline human thought processes. It requires clear and precise instructions. It must be told in every detail what it is to do; it follows orders — even incorrect orders — with exactitude. The computer is not only enabling but forcing the modern executive "to think more explicitly and analytically — to formalize his decision-making process and spell out his judgments." [56] Even the critics of related analytical techniques, such as cost-benefit analysis, concede that "some implicit judgments are made explicit and subject to analysis." [57]

More advanced computer programs reduce the amount of necessary detailed instruction but reprimand the programmer when he makes an error. Eventually, as computer languages are continually simplified, men will "tell" the computer what they want and delegate to the computer the authority to "tell" them what they must do to get it.[58]

The computer and programmed instruction have further revolutionary implications for the educational process as we have known it — both in the schools and in training programs in government and industry — and the massive multi-billion dollar education industry. Most of the routine information transfer of elementary and secondary education will be handled by computer-assisted instruction. The function of the teacher or instructor will be increasingly to instill motivation in the student, to assist him when he is having difficulty advancing to the next level of proficiency, and to interact with the student in those areas where instruction cannot be or deliberately is not programmed, such as the communication of societal values. The computer will force us, perhaps for the first time, to think through the meaning of education in contemporary American society.

The capacity for systems thinking and systems analysis. What is new about information technology is not the analytical concepts and techniques — systems analysis and program budgeting — but rather the capacity of automatic data processing to make "operational" concept of an organization as a total system.[59] "Men are not good calculators

[56] Burck, *op. cit.*, p. 109.

[57] Aaron Wildavsky, "The Political Economy of Efficiency: Cost-Benefit Analysis, Systems Analysis, and Program Budgeting," *Public Administration Review*, December 1966, p. 297.

[58] Thomas L. Whisler, "The Impact of Information Technology on Organizational Control," in Myers (ed.), *The Impact of Computers on Management* (Cambridge, Mass.: The M.I.T. Press, 1967), p. 46.

[59] See Charles A. Myers, "The Impact of EDP on Management Organization and Managerial Work," working paper 139-65, Sloan School of Management, M.I.T., Cambridge, Mass., September 1965, pp. 3–4.

of the dynamic behavior of complicated systems," says Professor Jay W. Forrester, who has pioneered research in industrial dynamics. "The intuitive judgment of even a skilled investigator is quite unreliable in anticipating the dynamic behavior of a simple information-feedback system of perhaps five or six variables." [60] A computer can handle such a problem with relative ease.

Melvin Anshen considers this "enlargement of the total range of decision-making" as potentially the most valuable contribution of the new information technology to management practice. It is now possible for the first time for the human decision maker to consider the total activity of an organization as "a single integrated system."

> Within this system, a dynamic network of relationships can be discerned and measured, with feedback loops and forces for multiplying and dampening the effects of actions at earlier stages in the continuous process. Analytic techniques based on the programmed computer permit managers to simulate the performance of such a system and to test its output under a range of changing variables within and outside the system. This technical advance is only one among many possibilities now available for extending the scope of decision-making.[61]

The research in and application of industrial dynamics and systems analysis to the individual firm will be generalized to larger social systems. Forrester has already developed a prototype simulated city for the new M.I.T. Urban Systems Laboratory.[62]

One important side benefit of systems analysis will be the development of new conceptual frameworks for more effective data collection and interpretation.[63] Systems thinking in government will generate new and more specific information requirements. With his new ability to understand the dynamics of complex organizations and systems, the decision maker of the future will explore a new range of problems previously unknown. Computer-based analysis will make possible an advance in human intellectual capacity comparable to the invention of language, arabic numerals, and the calculus.

[60] *Op. cit.*, pp. 51–52.

[61] *Op. cit.*, p. 78.

[62] Forrester, *Urban Dynamics* (Cambridge, Mass.: The M.I.T. Press, 1969). Also see John P. Crecine, "Computer Simulation in Urban Research," RAND Memorandum P-3734, The RAND Corporation, Santa Monica, Cal., November 1967.

[63] See Bertram Gross and Michael Springer, "A New Orientation in American Government," *Annals*, May 1967, pp. 11–12.

A lengthened time-perspective with greater opportunity for strategic planning. The new information technology should effect important changes in the time perspective of the decision maker. The amount of crisis decision making (i.e., time spent in reacting to unanticipated crises) should be decreased by the development of better warning indicators and monitoring systems. Simulation will permit the economic preparation of major contingency plans. The management information cycle (i.e., the time between management determination of a need for information for an operational decision and the provision of such information) will be reduced significantly by real-time information systems. The concept of "feedback," defined as "the decision response to the *state* of the system," will be supplemented by a new concept of "feedforward," or control by the decision maker of "decision responses to *anticipated future disturbances* of the subsystem." [64]

The programming of routine decisions and the control of information overload through techniques of selective dissemination will free the decision maker from the burden of both repetitive operations and detailed information. The remedial orientation of incremental policy making will be replaced by an orientation toward the future.[65] The policy making, as opposed to the administrative, role of the public official will be enhanced. The new information technology will draw the attention of analysts and decision makers to higher-level, longer-term problems.

The breakthrough in collaborative research. The computer will help to effect two significant advances in collaborative research — which in the long run may well be its greatest contribution to man's capacity for problem solving — the cumulative storage and preservation of solutions, a kind of division of intellectual labor, and the potential for man-machine-man interaction.

New and more refined computer programs are constantly being developed, tested, and stored. A "program," in computer terminology, is a routine procedure worked out for solving a particular recurring problem. It is "a rule for making a decision in a particular problem situation" or, alternatively, "a detailed prescription or strategy that governs the sequence of responses of a system to a complex task environment." [66] Gains in the processing of information as in industrial and economic organizations have been achieved by specialization and

---

[64] Greenberger (ed.), *op. cit.*, p. 7.

[65] For Lindblom's description of the remedial orientation see *The Intelligence of Democracy*, p. 147.

[66] These definitions are from Anshen, *op. cit.*, p. 72; and Simon, *op. cit.*, p. 59, respectively.

the division of labor but, in this case, *within* the machine itself. The programming capability of the computer has been steadily increased by adding new and more specific routines and subroutines.[67] The *compiler* allows the computer programmer to call, combine, coordinate, and use routines or programs that are already perfected and stored in the computer. In theory, once a particular problem situation is solved, it is solved for all time. Other users of the computer network can draw on any approved program that is in the system. Given the virtually infallible memory of the computer, all gains or improvements in techniques of computation and analysis, no matter how incremental, are preserved until better techniques are perfected and may be retrieved, used, and refined by contemporary and future generations of decision makers.

Computers will rapidly take over most of the routine, repetitive decisions that can be programmed at the lower levels of government and other large organizations. Even for nonspecifically programmed, or ill-structured, novel problems, the computer will become a powerful tool. Herbert Simon and others have shown that such intangibles of executive talent as "judgment, intuition, creativity, and rules of thumb" can be reduced to "heuristic" computer programs. Such programs incorporate the less systematic, more selective processes that human beings use in handling complex information processing problems that cannot be reduced to mathematical or symbolic rules of procedure or program routines (algorithms). Simon, who considers himself a "technological radical," sees the economic law of comparative advantage (i.e., that computers will always be relatively less economical for some purposes than for others) as the only limitation to computer application. He is among a minority of computer experts who believe that "in our time, computers will be able to do anything a man can do." [68]

One does not have to be a technological radical to appreciate the cumulative potential of computer programming. If most human decisions have an underlying structure — as disjointed, incremental,

[67] Martin Greenberger compares the acquisition of new programs by the computer system with learning in the human being. "A new program in interpretive form is similar to a response or behavior pattern that is being tried out tentatively. A compiled program resembles a habit, although it is generally not 'hard to break' unless it is deeply ingrained in the system's central core." "Computer in the Organization," working paper 207-66; Sloan School of Management, M.I.T., Cambridge, Mass., September 1966, p. 36.

[68] *Op. cit.*, pp. xii–xiii, 76–92. See also Simon and Allen Newell, "Simulation of Human Thinking," in Greenberger (ed.), *Computers of the World of the Future*, pp. 94–131.

restricted in scope as that structure may be — in time computer programmers and analysts will discover and program the implicit decision techniques, rules, and coefficients.[69] Already computer programs based on the analysis of past managerial behavior have proved more efficient than continued management practices (i.e., rules of thumb) based on experience.[70] Most computer experts do not expect the computer to replace the human decision maker but rather to extend his planning and decisional capacities through the continued refinement of man-machine interaction. The computer will thus absorb the incrementalists in its inexorable accumulation of intellectual power.[71]

Even more significant than the steady development of computer programs is the advent in prototype form of "the on-line intellectual community" based on man-computer interaction and computer-facilitated cooperation among men in a university setting. (In an "on-line" system, users are connected directly to the central processing unit and have a capacity to respond to, and interact with, the system.) Carl F. J. Overhage and R. Joyce Harman describe the potential breakthrough based on the experience of Project MAC (research and development of Machine-Aided Cognition and Multiple-Access Computer systems) at M.I.T.:

> Because communication among men is fallible, and because heretofore men did not have effective ways of expressing com-

---

[69] Decision situations may be arranged in a hierarchy from "automatic," easily programmed decisions at the base, to situations at the top where there is no basis for action in either experience or intuition. Forrester expects computers to assume decisions at the lower levels of this hierarchy rapidly and to progress up the hierarchy steadily, "Managerial Decision-Making," pp. 49–51. For a discussion of the hierarchy of decisions and analytic techniques, see William M. Capron, "The Impact of Analysis on Bargaining in Government," paper delivered at the annual meeting of the American Political Science Association, New York, September 1966, pp. 3–5.

[70] Edward H. Bowman, "Consistency and Optimality in Managerial Decision-Making," unpublished paper, 1961; also *Management of Science*, January 1963, cited by Myers, "The Impact of EDP on Management Organization and Managerial Work," p. 19.

[71] Greenberger describes this process as "an intriguing interplay of centripetal and centrifugal forces. Tasks that show the computer to comparatively best advantage are drawn inward into the body of programming; tasks that prosper more from the human touch drift outward to men at consoles (and beyond). Many of these tasks would not be identifiable today. The environment from which they emerge will be shaped by a new kind of commerce among new kinds of organizations." "Computer in the Organization," p. 35. Wildavsky, conceding that systems, cost-benefit, and program analysis are getting better in their calculations, concludes: "Alas [the analyst] is an imperialist at heart." "The Political Economy of Efficiency," p. 308.

plex ideas unambiguously — and recalling them, testing them, transferring them, and converting them from a static record into observable, dynamic behavior — the accumulation of correlatable contributions was opposed by continual erosion; and the melding of contributions was hampered by divergencies of convention and format that kept one man's ideas from meshing with another's. The prospect is that, when several or many people work together within the context of an on-line, interactive, community computer network, the superior facilities of that network for expressing ideas, preserving facts, modeling processes, and information and the same behavior — those superior facilities will so foster the growth and integration of knowledge that the incidence of major achievements will be markedly increased.[72]

Comparable networks will in time be available in business and government and between sectors of each of these communities with overlapping research interests. The potential of man-machine-man interaction for pure and applied research is one of the scarcely realized, but most staggering, potentials of the new information technology.

THE INFORMATION REVOLUTION: SOME RESERVATIONS. Lessening the information constraints on, and increasing the potency of, the analytical tools available to decision makers will *not* remove many of the current dilemmas of decision making. These are limitations that go well beyond information.

The problem of values. If we define politics as a struggle for control stemming from "conflict over the direction of social life, over public policy," [73] it is clear that the central problem of politics is one of values, not information. Decision making involves values at all stages. Choice activity especially requires value criteria for decision.

It may be possible at certain program levels to compare alternatives and choose a more efficient means for achieving an agreed-upon objective such as disease control, improved maternal and child health care,

---

[72] *Op. cit.*, p. 26. One of the main features of the concept of the "on-line intellectual community" is that "the system delivers much of its help 'inside the thought cycle' and ready for integration within the structure of the user's thinking. That is the essential advantage of being on-line. That is what so greatly facilitates the melding of the heuristic guidance and evaluation provided by the man and the precise memory and rapid processing provided by the computer" (p. 31).

[73] David Easton, *The Political System: An Inquiry into the State of Political Science* (New York: Alfred A. Knopf, 1953), p. 117.

or improved income maintenance.[74] (Even this approach, it should be noted, ignores the problem of interpersonal comparison of utility; i.e., how to weigh the values of individuals in determining social goals and priorities. . . .) But can improved information help a decision maker weigh major dissimilar program alternatives such as an antiballistic missile system or a domestic Marshall plan for the nation's urban centers? Only insofar as such information gives the President, the Budget Director, or the congressman better understanding of what x million dollars allocated to program A or B will actually buy in benefits. In government, budgeting is a political activity, and the problem of choice or allocation ultimately remains one of values.

The decision maker's values will also shape his intelligence activity; i.e., finding occasions for making decisions, and how he structures alternatives for choice. Data must be structured or organized before it becomes meaningful. Predetermined data-structures can help, but the decision maker himself must constantly synthesize knowledge in an interdisciplinary fashion. He must interpret, project, and interconnect fragmented information. The political decision maker has a natural tendency to select and adapt information and to screen out that which is "politically undigestible." [75]

In a decision-making environment where resources are relatively plentiful (i.e., where economic criteria for resource allocation are less relevant) and where the decision maker has the analytical and information-processing capabilities to structure in advance innumerable alternative solutions, the value perspective of the decision maker will become increasingly important.

With these reservations, information can be an effective contribution to decision making. Katz and Kahn, in their discussion of information as a method of change in organizations, note that while information is not itself a prime mover, techniques of influence that rely primarily on information giving may be "effective in ambiguous situations, where the lack of information is the obstacle to appropriate performance." [76] If we are correct in our estimate that computer-based

[74] See Elizabeth B. Drew, "HEW Grapples with PPBS," *The Public Interest*, Summer 1967, pp. 9–29.

[75] See Amitai Etzioni's discussion of the "political elements of knowledge" in "How May Congress Learn," *Science*, January 1968, pp. 170–72. Richard T. Loomis of the MITRE Corporation, formerly with the Stanford Research Institute, is undertaking a systematic analysis of information resources and requirements of Congress, beginning with a study of three or four congressional committee hearings.

[76] *The Social Psychology of Organizations*, pp. 392–93.

techniques such as systems analysis and simulation will afford decision makers in the Executive and Congress much greater understanding of complex problems, such as those of our urban centers, then the gains may be substantial. As social problems appear more susceptible to rational solution, it should be easier to develop a political consensus to do so. As to the final judgment on values, the American political system will continue to specify the goals and objectives toward which political decision makers must move.[77]

The political use and abuse of information. It follows from the preceding remarks that information systems in government may be used to serve the political purposes of the political actors who have the resources to control them. Information may be processed with conscious policy or partisan biases.[78] Both information and analysis may be abused in the advancement of specific political objectives. Bargaining and compromise will remain a principal feature of the democratic process, although, with the new information technology, different participants and a new language may appear.[79]

Decision making in government cannot be abstracted from the political system within which the decision maker operates. How then can one prevent the President or program-oriented bureau chief from consciously or unconsciously biasing an information system that Congress must use? Can the same information system in Congress serve both Democrats and Republicans?

There are two possible precautions to take against bias and abuse. First, major data sources of the federal government, with multiple users, could be kept as neutral as possible through statutory control, reinforced by regular checks by inspecting authorities such as the General Accounting Office. Second, specialized users including the President, the Congress, and the party leaders within Congress could develop their own private information systems paralleling the central data system and in accord with their own needs. Through this differentiation, it should be possible to keep the policy and partisan biases

[77] Use of the political process for interpersonal comparisons of values also serves to reduce the burden of calculation (or scope of analysis) for decision makers. See Wildavsky, *The Politics of the Budgetary Process*, pp. 130–131.

[78] Wildavsky cites water resources projects as a classic example of agency–interest group distortion and manipulation of prevailing cost-benefit criteria. "The Political Economy of Efficiency," pp. 297–98.

[79] Capron asserts that "the *dialogue* between the parties involved (the bureaus, the departments, the Executive Office of the President, the Congress, the private interest groups and 'constituencies') will be conducted differently and will certainly be 'impacted' by PPB." *Op. cit.*, p. 2.

of central governmental information systems under control and to recognize the use of competing information systems for some adversary situations.

Additional cost factors. The introduction of information systems will entail increased costs as well as increased capabilities.[80] The obvious immediate need is that of capital, both for hardware (the basic computational facility) and software (the development of programs appropriate to the specific user). We have previously suggested that this economic cost factor will rapidly decline in the coming decades and be minimal by the end of the century. A second cost factor is the need for much more highly skilled personnel — a new profession of analysts. However, the computer will not necessarily become more foreign to the lay-user, including the congressman. The educational and skill levels of the general population and familiarity with computers should also arise. And more advanced computer technology and programming should lead to the development of some computers that can be operated with relatively low skills. The decision maker who wants to use the full potential of the computer of the future will probably employ and work with a specialized analyst staff.[81]

Other technical costs must be anticipated in the adaptation of information systems for government. These include: (1) a natural tendency towards greater reliance upon quantifiable data; (2) programming bias that may reduce the sensitivity of the system to new types of data and significant changes in the environment; and (3) the elimination of inputs — interpretations, opinions, and statements of self-interest — previously provided by intermediate-level officials replaced by the information system. All of these tendencies, we shall argue below, suggest a new need for congressional oversight, or review, of the Executive. The computer improperly used could well lead to new rigidities in official behavior that would be inimical to an open system of decision making.

The problem of final payoffs. Anthony Downs, in a searching critique of the expectations of "urban information system" enthusiasts, questions "the intuitively plausible but actually misleading assump-

[80] See Downs, "A Realistic Look at . . . Urban Data Systems," pp. 205–6.
[81] John Dearden has questioned the utility of real-time information systems for top management. Most executives can spend only a limited amount of time on operating functions and most work on the "exception" principle. Under most conditions, therefore, it would seem more economical for a subordinate to monitor the real-time information and inform the top executives when a decision has to be made. "Myth of Real-Time Management Information," *Harvard Business Review*, May–June 1966, pp. 123–32.

tion" that "better data in urban decision-making would have huge final payoffs, because . . . better information would reduce both the frequency and the magnitude of planning mistakes." [82] Downs argues that three factors make it difficult to prove that better data will lead to more effective decisions: (1) the extreme difficulty of measuring the effectiveness of decisions; (2) variances in measurable effects caused by factors other than data inputs; and (3) the problem of whose values to use in calculating payoffs. He concludes that many urban decision makers will be reluctant to make large initial investments for what will "probably seem like only marginal gains in final payoffs."

The basic point is well taken — one must go beyond the technical payoffs of improved information in assessing the value of information systems in government. The author is more optimistic than Downs on three points: (1) the assumption that capital costs to users will steadily decline; (2) the possibility for controlled simulation of systems behavior; and (3) the cumulative effect of marginal gains over time.

The power consequences of information systems. Information systems have important power payoffs as well as technical payoffs.[83] Their introduction involves power shifts among political actors which in turn greatly influence the form in which they are adopted and how they are used. For some, the threatened loss of power may be sufficient to lead to active resistance to the new systems. We shall consider the influence of the new information technology on "system politics" in the following section.

Summary. Acknowledging these reservations, we still believe that the combined and cumulative impact of the new information technology suggests some radical changes in the environment of governmental decision making. The shift will be from a negative to a positive orientation toward problem solving. The incrementalist's view that "public policy problems are too complex to be well understood, too complex to be mastered" and that decision makers develop "a strategy to cope with problems, not to solve them" will be replaced with a more optimistic perspective.[84] The decision maker will have analytical techniques and information-processing capabilities that will

[82] "A Realistic Look at . . . Urban Data Systems," p. 204.
[83] *Ibid.*, pp. 207–9.
[84] Lindblom, *The Intelligence of Democracy*, p. 148.

give him new understanding of governmental and social systems and confidence that he can manipulate and control them. Where the incrementalists have rejected "the impossible prescription to be comprehensive" in favor of a more manageable strategy of "outright neglect," [85] the new information technology will enable the decision maker to develop a *more rational* and *aggressive* strategy of problem solving.[86] The distinction is fundamental.

SYSTEM POLITICS: THE PRESIDENCY AND CONGRESS IN THE FUTURE

Already political scientists have begun to discuss the impact of systems analysis on the American political system. Aaron Wildavsky has suggested that a threefold distinction of *policy politics* (which policy will be adopted?), *partisan politics* (which political party will be assisted in gaining office?), and *system politics* (how will decision structures be set up?) is useful in analyzing the political consequences of program budgeting. Much of the literature on program budgeting assumes that it is a neutral tool. Wildavsky concludes, however, that the program budget is suffused with policy politics, has been used by the President to a lesser extent to advance partisan politics, and leans significantly towards system politics. Program budgeting affords the top executive a powerful tool for coordinating subordinates. Wildavsky expects that its full implementation "will unleash great struggles" among the executive agencies for control of program activities that cut across traditional jurisdictions.[87]

Information technology in government: 1975. The trends in information technology we have outlined have almost unlimited possibilities for application in government. Already certain state legislatures have utilized the computer for scheduling, determining the status of bills, and searching legislative statutes.[88] The Executive

---

[85] *Ibid.*, p. 146.

[86] Karl Deutsch has aptly described politics as "a decisive sphere of social learning." "All studies of politics, and all techniques and models suggested as instruments of political analysis, have this purpose: that men should be more able to act in politics with their eyes open." *The Nerves of Government: Models of Political Communication and Control* (New York: The Free Press of Glencoe, 1963), p. 255.

[87] "The Political Economy of Efficiency," p. 305.

[88] See, for example, Earl W. Brydges, "The Electronic Solon," *National Civic Review*, July 1965, pp. 350–53. Senator Brydges, now Majority Leader of the

branch was utilizing 3,000 electronic computers during fiscal year 1968, on appropriations of over $1.2 billion.[89] In national party politics, a simulation model of the electorate was available to Senator John F. Kennedy in 1960.[90]

Paul Armer of the RAND Corporation has projected the following computer achievements for the 1970's:

> Computers will be readily available as a public-domain service (but not necessarily as a regulated monopoly)
>
> Information per se will be inexpensive and readily available
>
> Large and varied data banks will exist and be accessible to the public
>
> Computers will be used extensively in management science and decision making
>
> Computers will be economically feasible for firms and activities of all sizes
>
> Computers will process language and recognize voices
>
> Computers will be used extensively at all levels of government
>
> Computers will increase the pace of technological development.[91]

A RAND associate of Armer, W. H. Ware, expects that "beginning in the early 1970's, computers will be small, powerful, plentiful, and inexpensive. Computing power will be available to anyone who needs it, or wants it, or can use it. He may have it by means of a personal console connected to some large central facility, or he may own a small personal machine." [92] Some additional projections for innovation in

---

New York State Senate, concludes that the computer has become the means of restoring the Legislature to its "proper equal status" with the Judicial and Executive branches. "Today and in the future, control over facts — the ability to do research in depth and quickly — can gain for legislatures some of the capabilities for leadership they have lost over the years" (p. 351). For a summary of research and applications, see Robert L. Chartrand, "Applications of Automatic Data Processing in Legal Information Handling" (Washington, D.C.: Library of Congress Legislative Reference Service, 1966).

[89] Estimates provided by Congressman Robert McClory (R-Ill.).

[90] See Ithiel de Sola Pool, Robert P. Abelson, and Samuel Popkin, *Candidates, Issues & Strategies: A Computer Simulation of the 1960 and 1964 Presidential Elections* (rev. ed.; Cambridge, Mass.: The M.I.T. Press, 1965).

[91] *Op. cit.*

[92] W. H. Ware, *Future Computer Technology and Its Impact* (RAND Memorandum P-3279; Santa Monica, Cal.: The RAND Corporation, 1966), pp. 15–16.

automation, obtained by the so-called Delphi technique, the systematic solicitation of expert opinions, are: automatic libraries, looking up and reproducing copy (1975); automated looking up of legal information (1978); and widespread use of automatic decision making at management level for industrial and national planning (1978).[93] By the mid-1980's, the computer will begin to realize its potential as a research tool through modeling and experimentation, as an integral part of the educational system, and in areas such as medicine and the biological sciences.[94]

By the mid-1970's, political parties, at both the national and state levels, will operate political data banks, and simulation of alternative strategies will be an accepted technique of campaigning. Individual candidates will have the option of using computer facilities apart from those provided by the parties, and incumbent congressmen will maintain computerized data files for their constituencies.

The rate of innovation in basic computer technology — in both hardware and software — is, of course, a function of the rate of investment and to an important degree the rate of public investment. Leading scientists have recently expressed concern at the sharp decline in the rate of growth of federal support for research and development. (After a decade of expansion at an average annual rate of 22 per cent, the federal research and development budget, since 1964, has been cut back to a growth rate of 2.5 per cent.) "If Congress continues to do what it is now doing, we'll wake up with another sputnik in a decade," warns M.I.T. Provost, Dr. Jerome B. Wiesner.[95] This change in congressional mood took place well before the Vietnam war assumed its current budgetary significance, according to some observers.

Besides controlling public investment and in turn the rate of innovation, the federal government, and especially the Congress, can control the rate of diffusion of computer advances both in the private sector and within government. An obvious example is the rate of progress toward establishing a Federal Data Center.[96] Paul Baran has argued that the technological growth of computers may be limited by

---

[93] T. J. Gordon and Olaf Helmer, *Report on a Long-Range Forecasting Study* (RAND Memorandum P-2982; Santa Monica, Cal.: The RAND Corporation, 1964), p. 21.

[94] Ware, *op. cit.*, pp. 18 ff.

[95] "Research Aid Cuts Upset Scientists," *The New York Times*, June 21, 1968, pp. 1, 25.

[96] See Robert L. Chartrand with Louise Giovane Becker, "The Federal Data Center: Proposals and Reactions" (Washington, D.C.: Library of Congress Legislative Reference Service, 1967).

the regulatory structure for data transmission unless new regulatory doctrine is created.[97] Other examples of control are congressional funding of specialist posts within the Executive and congressional funding of specialist staffs within the General Accounting Office and the Congress itself.

For the purpose of analysis we shall assume that the projected technology is largely realized within the Executive branch by the mid-1970's. After examining some of its consequences within the Executive, we shall examine the potential impact on Congress.

THE IMPACT ON THE EXECUTIVE. The new information technology will have its greatest immediate political impact within the Executive branch because in comparison with the Congress most operating executive agencies will have had more first-hand experience with computers. PPBS has already effected a major change in decision making within the Department of Defense, and Henry S. Rowen, who as Assistant Director of the Budget Bureau helped to introduce the system on a government-wide basis, predicts that "results throughout other parts of government will, in time, be at least as impressive." [98] The President, with his current responsibility for budget formulation and "legislative clearance" (review and coordination of all agency legislative proposals submitted to Congress) has the necessary authority to revolutionize the executive bureaucracy. Several consequences of the new information technology may be suggested.

Centralization of effective decision-making authority at the presidential and departmental levels. The rationalization of program choice,

[97] "The Future Computer Utility," *Public Interest*, Summer 1967, pp. 75–87; and *The Coming Computer Utility: Laissez-Faire, Licensing or Regulation?* (RAND Memorandum P-3466; Santa Monica, Cal.: The RAND Corporation, 1967).

[98] "Bargaining and Analysis in Government," U.S. Senate, Subcommittee on National Security and International Operations, Committee on Government Operations, *Committee Print: Planning-Programming-Budgeting*, 90th Congress, 1st Session, January 1968. Robert A. Levine, Chief of the Office of Economic Opportunity's Office of Research, Plans, Programs and Evaluation has compared the problems of implementing PPBS in his agency with those experienced in the Defense Department: (1) Welfare is easier to measure than national security, i.e., improvement defined by income and other variables; (2) OEO had better data to begin with, including 20 years of economic data gathered and tabulated under the Employment Act of 1946; and (3) Unlike DOD, OEO plays "a game against nature" which makes its task considerably easier. See speech by Congressman F. Bradford Morse (R-Mass.), "Congress Views the Application of the Systems Approach to Public Problems," under remarks of Hon. John V. Tunney (D-Cal.), *Daily Congressional Record*, 90th Congress, 2nd Session, February 8, 1968, pp. E643–45.

through greater availability of information and a more careful and explicit statement of program objectives, alternatives, and results will move the locus of program decision toward the department secretaries and the President. More adequate information systems will permit some functional decentralization of subordinate program decisions, although the thrust will be toward more effective policy control from the top.[99] As the compartmentalized information resources of individual agencies are integrated into comprehensive information systems, political executives will have greater leverage over the bureaucracy. At the same time fewer people will be involved in policy decisions.

> The checks and balances on the decision-maker will be reduced, since he is then a member of a group with fewer total members to criticize and restrain his actions. Subordinate individuals in an organization who are directly affected by the decisions rendered will be in a weaker position than they are today. Their ability to detect and counter undesirable actions will be reduced, since they will *not* have an increased ability afforded by the computers to understand the more complex problems comprehended by centralized management.[100]

In the past it has been appropriate to describe both an executive process *and* a legislative process within the executive bureaucracy.[101] The new information technology will accentuate hierarchical control and reduce legislative bargaining within the Executive. The decision-making process will accordingly become more closed. Within a given department, such as Defense, control may be consolidated with a minimum of reorganization. In other cases interdepartmental reorganization will be required.

The consequences of this development for the American system of checks and balances are fundamental. Congress will face the necessity of defining new points of access and review in the decision-making process if the historical concept of balance is to be maintained.

[99] Capron feels that improved information systems will make possible a "rationalization of centralization-decentralization relationships," and "can be a powerful force for decentralization." *Op. cit.*, pp. 7–8. We still anticipate a centralization of *program* decision.

[100] Paul Ginsberg, quoted in Donald N. Michael, "Some Long-Range Implications of Computer Technology for Human Behavior in Organizations," *The American Behavioral Scientist*, April 1966, p. 32.

[101] See Katz and Kahn, *op. cit.*, p. 45; also Samuel P. Huntington, *The Common Defense: Strategic Programs in National Politics* (New York: Columbia University Press, 1961).

The rise of the general analyst as a new governmental profession.
The advent of PPBS has been accompanied by the explicit recognition
of a new governmental skill — the program analyst. Slightly under
1,000 federal employees now occupy PPB positions (including both
analysts and program monitors–data handlers) about evenly divided
between central staffs attached to the Office of the Secretary and
bureau-level staffs. The Bureau of the Budget has initiated special one-
year, postgraduate courses with various academic institutions, as well
as shorter training courses in Washington, in order to develop the
requisite skills for these positions. The U.S. Civil Service Commission
also sponsors courses with the University of Maryland for federal government personnel. At a later date when computer-assisted analysis is
added to the more rudimentary analytical techniques of PPBS, even
more specialized information-program analysts will be recruited and
trained.

The experience of the computer in industry suggests that "the decision to locate computer responsibility in a specific part of an organization has strong implications for the relative authority and control
that the segment will subsequently achieve." Computer responsibility
has tended to move upward in an organization and away from traditional functional departments to a neutral or independent staff
position.[102] Anthony Downs considers the increase in the power of
high-level staff officials one of the significant power shifts caused by
automated data systems in government.[103] Politicians and line executives at the top simply cannot cope with the increase in information
without relying on expanded staffs. The growth of staff at this level,
however, does *not* undercut the net gain in power of the top policy
maker. The information system gives the top-level official new and
more timely information. Staff at this level owe more direct loyalty to
the official than did lower-level operating officials. And expanded top-
level staff afford the policy maker additional channels of information
to check operating departments. The likely long-term trend in the
federal government, then, is toward the development of highly trained
professional "analyst" staffs within the Budget Bureau and for the
department secretaries.

The power of the analyst within the Executive branch will pose new
problems for congressional oversight. At a minimum Congress will
have to develop its own analytical staff if it is to monitor executive
decision making. More important, it will have to watch for and cor-

[102] Whisler, *op. cit.*, p. 48.
[103] "A Realistic Look at . . . Urban Data Systems," p. 208.

rect new biases of specialization. Harold Wilensky suggests that "information technologists," as they refine the techniques of their job, will be restricted by limited political and social sensitivities.

> The integration of values, theory, and practice nowhere depends more on the supply of talent. The danger of technicism is in direct proportion to the shortage of educated men. Too often the new technologists are methodological and exact in their specialized fields, but impressionable, naive, and opinionated on broader issues of policy. Like the executives they advise, they lack a sense of relevance and analogy — the critical common sense and trained judgment that make an educated man.[104]

Other observers have similarly questioned whether the new profession of systems analysis, drawing on the multiple backgrounds of economics, physics, and engineering, can adequately deal with political decisions, overall strategic planning, and public policy making. Instead, a more advanced type of professional knowledge and training that integrates the disciplines of political science and public administration with systems analysis, decision theory, and economic theory — *policy analysis* — may be required.[105]

One of the implicit dangers of the new information technology is that data systems and analysis will be given an uncritical evaluation by the policy maker. There may be too great a demand for *the* answer, and when the previously incomprehensible is reduced to black and white, too great a readiness to accept it. There is a compelling appeal to analysis. Congress may increasingly find itself questioning the premises, logic, and broader relevance of major executive analyses.

The problem of achieving consensus. The new information technology will effect other more subtle changes in the political process. As old styles of communications and decision making give way to new styles, power will shift at all levels of the political system — even within the Congress.[106] Well-organized and technically sophisticated groups will gain power at the expense of less well-organized and less sophisticated groups. Political leaders who combine technical education and sophistication with good political judgment will gain at the

---

104 *Op. cit.*, p. 190.
105 For a comparison of systems analysis and policy analysis see Yehezkel Dror, "Policy Analysts: A New Professional Role in Government Service," *Public Administration Review*, September 1967, pp. 197–203.
106 Downs, "A Realistic Look at . . . Urban Data Systems," pp. 207–10.

expense of old-line politicians. The government bureaucracy, with continuous inside access to information systems, will enjoy an initial power advantage over the Legislature, the general electorate, and nongovernmental groups.

As it becomes more pervasive, the new information technology will introduce qualitative changes — beginning in the Executive branch and extending outward — in the nature of American pluralism. The necessity of making one's political objectives or goals more explicit within the budgetary process will expose more conflict and disagreement than Americans have been accustomed to. Considered in light of the possible political trends discussed in Chapter Eight this may not be an inconsequential cost.[107] Assuming that the system will progressively eliminate intentional and unintentional bias in the reporting of subordinate units of the bureaucracy (i.e., that quality controls on reporting information and program objectives are instituted), we shall have to learn to live with greater candor in our politics. The gains and costs of alternative policies to the major parties involved in a decision will be much more evident to all the participants. The "who gets what, when, how" of politics will be more nearly a matter of public record. This may lead to one of several alternatives: a centrally enforced and popularly supported decision (in terms of some definition of the public interest); more intelligent, explicit bargaining based on an awareness of the costs and benefits to participants of alternatives under consideration; or irreconcilable differences that preclude any working consensus. The chances are that we shall know a good deal more about ourselves and our politics and that this will complicate the problem of building political consensus.[108] If rationalized decision making in the Executive limits interest bargaining within the bureaucracy (which is important for building political consensus), Congress will have to compensate for this loss through interest representation and education of its constituency.

THE IMPACT ON CONGRESS. During the early phases of the new information technology Congress has generally been content to fund automatic data processing (ADP) for the Executive and to establish

[107] Wildavsky notes, "Mitigation of conflict is a widely shared value in our society, and . . . we ought to realize that program budgeting is likely to affect that value." *The Politics of the Budgetary Process*, p. 138.

[108] For a discussion of the positive functions of symbol-oriented activity and imperfect information in achieving interest group equilibrium, see Murray Edelman, *The Symbolic Uses of Politics* (Urbana: University of Illinois Press, 1964).

general policies and procedures on procurement and use of ADP equipment. Little attention has been given by Congress to the problem of information systems development in the Executive or to the potential and problems that the new information technology poses for Congress itself. In fact, several state legislatures have been well ahead of Congress in developing applications for the computer in the legislative process.

Current congressional interest in information technology. The first serious public and congressional discussion of the problem was held at the hearings of the Joint Committee on the Organization of the Congress during the 89th Congress (1965–66). A series of studies prepared by Robert L. Chartrand, the new "Information Sciences Specialist" of the Science Policy Research Division of the Library of Congress (Legislative Reference Service), and a significant paper by Dr. Kenneth Janda of Northwestern University, entitled "Information Systems for Congress," constituted the major academic contributions to the discussion.[109] During the 90th Congress a number of bills authorizing an automatic data processing facility for the Congress have been introduced by members of both parties. Congressman Robert McClory (R-Ill.), who during the 89th Congress introduced the first such bill in either the House or the Senate that would directly apply ADP techniques to the work of Congress, has been the most articulate spokesman for congressional action.

> The growing dilemma of the Congressman and his staff centers about the voluminous written information — reports, books, periodicals, specifications, memoranda — that must be screened, reduced to a useable length, filed, and later used as reference. Decisions ideally are made on the basis of that information which is timely, accurate, complete, and relevant. All too often it is a case of too much information, not too little. . . .
> The thinking Congressman continually seeks to function in a more effective way. His overburdened staff also looks for

[109] Janda's paper is reprinted in Alfred de Grazia (ed.), *Congress: The First Branch of Government* (Washington, D.C.: American Enterprise Institute, 1966), pp. 414–56. An extended discussion is included in *Information Retrieval: Applications to Political Science* (Indianapolis: The Bobbs-Merrill Co. Inc., 1968). See also Chartrand, "Automatic Data Processing for the Congress," and "The Congressional Milieu: Information Requirements and Current Capabilities," in Robert L. Chartrand, Kenneth Janda, and Michael Hugo (eds.), *Information Support, Program Budgeting, and the Congress* (New York: Spartan Books, 1968).

shortcuts and strives to cope with the flood of paperwork. The Congressman needs to know the status of many bills, the schedule of committee hearings and meetings in which he is involved; he seeks quick access to facts and figures on a broad spectrum of subjects ranging from "What are the Federal expenditures on welfare projects in his district?" to a request for information on unidentified flying objects.[110]

Congressman McClory, obviously concerned by the growing "information gap" between the President and Congress, proposed to equip the Congress with "an identified capability, based on automatic data processing devices and procedures, to retrieve selected information that is of priority value to the Members and committees." During the Senate debate on the Legislative Reorganization Act of 1967 (S. 355) an amendment (No. 63) offered by Senator Hugh Scott (R-Pa.) was adopted authorizing the Legislative Reference Service to acquire automatic data processing equipment and retain the necessary personnel for such a service.[111]

While Congress delayed action on a new Legislative Reorganization Act through 1968, some significant innovations were put into effect. In November, 1967, the General Accounting Office (GAO) created a Systems Analysis Section in its Office of Policy and Special Studies. (A key proposal of S. 355 was that the GAO collect and place in machineable form preliminary budget data from the agencies.) The Comptroller General has also been asked by Congress in a 1967 amendment to the Economic Opportunity Act to assess generally the efficiency with which the act is being administered and the extent to which programs authorized by the act achieve the objectives of the act — an obvious involvement in program analysis and evaluation. Over 200 GAO employees have already taken special PPBS training courses.

In January, 1968, the legislative branch acquired its first ADP installation directly aiding the legislative process.[112] The new on-line

[110] "An Automatic Data Processing Facility to Support the Congress," *Daily Congressional Record*, 89th Congress, 2nd Session, October 19, 1966, p. 26787.

[111] See *Daily Congressional Record*, 90th Congress, 1st Session, February 16, 1967, pp. S2124–25. The wide variety of related bills introduced in the 90th Congress are too numerous to cite. One worth noting, as an example of conservative interest in PPBS, is H.R. 12998, 90th Congress, 1st Session, introduced by Congressman Jackson Betts (R-Ohio).

[112] Statement of Congressman Robert McClory, 12th District of Illinois, at the Washington Operations Research Council's Meeting, January 17, 1968, reprinted under Remarks of the Hon. Tom Railsback (R-Ill.), *Daily Congressional Record*, 90th Congress, 2nd Session, January 29, 1968, pp. E275–77.

terminal system, installed in the American Law Division of the Legislative Reference Service (LRS), now enables LRS to record and store on magnetic tape descriptions of all bills and resolutions introduced in the 90th Congress. The system will compile by computer the "Digest of Public Bills" and eventually allow random recall of bills by number, title, and word descriptions, at the request of a congressional office or committee. (More than 26,000 bills and resolutions were introduced in the 89th Congress — an indication of the scale of the project.) Congressman McClory, after viewing the new system, anticipated that some of the next ADP applications might be:

1. Daily printouts summarizing the previous day's congressional action;
2. An automated index of congressional documents and legal periodicals;
3. Up-to-the-minute information on legislative issues scheduled for debate;
4. Vote summaries on bills already passed;
5. The status of legislation pending in committee;
6. Description of information stored on computer files in the executive departments.[113]

The first congressional committee and staff to tie into the LRS system has been the House Banking and Currency Committee. Early in the 91st Congress (1969), the committee announced that it would provide within seconds a status report and background information

[113] *Ibid.* A number of possible applications of information systems for Congress have been suggested, but there has been relatively little discussion of the consequences of new information systems on the distribution of political power within Congress or between Congress and the Executive. Kenneth Janda develops an extensive list of applications at four levels: (1) for Congress as a whole: informing congressmen of relevant bills, disseminating information about lobbyists, communicating with the Legislative Reference Service, searching the U.S. code; (2) for each Chamber of Congress: locating bills in the legislative process, providing information about votes, providing for automated voting; (3) for individual congressmen: deciding how to vote, maintaining relations with his constituency, reading and analyzing written material; and (4) for congressional committees: compiling histories of committee action, processing data on subjects under committee jurisdiction, and controlling the administration. Janda's proposal "studiously avoids concentrating remote terminals [computer consoles] in the hands . . . of the elected leadership or perhaps party committees" for fear that such a system "would accelerate centralization of power within Congress" and in turn greater presidential party control of Congress. With this proviso Janda feels that his recommendations "harbor no great or systematic alterations in the present distribution of power within Congress." *Op. cit.*, p. 454.

(as of the day the request is received) on any of the several hundred bills before the committee.

A quiet revolution in thinking appears to be taking place on Capitol Hill. Members privately express the desire to be aware of coming problems so they can "gear up" for them. A few senators and representatives already sense that information technology is the "coming thing" and are investing their own time as well as that of their committee staff and office staff in developing a greater familiarity with information systems.

The ferment is evident at numerous points. A wide range of congressional committees, too numerous to recount here, have been studying a variety of related problems (and educating their members in the process): the implementation of PPBS; the development of social indicators and a system of social accounts for analysis of social data comparable to those now available to economists; copyright legislation relating to information retrieval; the application of the systems approach to urban problems and environmental pollution; and the consequences of computer technology for individual privacy. The committee publications of the Congress — hearings, staff reports and memoranda, selected documents — already have become one of the most comprehensive and relevant bodies of public information on the social and political implications of the new information technology.

The Science Policy Research Division of LRS has provided professional staff assistance on "information sciences" to more than 150 member offices and 30 committees and subcommittees, and the number of interested parties continues to grow. Compared with other requests the LRS receives, a significantly high percentage have been for direct consultation with the congressman. In response to the interest of congressmen Robert Chartrand of the LRS has prepared a number of general studies, selected references, and annotated bibliographies, such as "The Systems Approach: A Tool for the Congress," "Applications of Automatic Data Processing in Legal Information Handling," "Automatic Data Processing and the American Political Campaign," "Systems Technology and Judicial Administration," "Information Concerning the Proposed Federal Data Center," "The Planning-Programming-Budgeting System," and "Systems Technology and the Small Businessman."

Another indication of interest is the recent series of privately sponsored Washington seminars and panels on information technology held with congressmen and staff members. Among these have been the seminars "Information Support for the Congress" sponsored by the American Enterprise Institute for Public Policy Research (June 1–2, 1967), and "Computer Applications to the Legislative Process" sponsored by the Brookings Institution, co-hosted by Congressmen Robert McClory (R-Ill.) and William S. Moorhead (D-Pa.), and attended by a half dozen computer authorities and about twenty congressmen (January 22, 1968); and two panel meetings with the Washington Operations Research Council and the Institute of Management Sciences held in the Rayburn House Office Building and open to congressional staff: "Operations Research and the U.S. Congress" (January 17, 1968) and "Improving Congressional Operations" (April 23, 1968).

Although programs of this type give most congressmen and their staff only a brief introduction to information technology and its potential, it is nonetheless an important beginning. The real change in congressional attitude and skills will probably not be felt, however, until a new generation of political talent with practical experience with computers — through universities and the private sector — begins to enter Congress. This change will come sooner than most realize. One freshman congressman, formerly employed by the International Business Machines Corporation and a candidate for the Doctorate in Business/Government Relations from the Harvard Business School, Donald W. Riegle, Jr. (R-Mich.), caused somewhat of a stir in Washington in the fall of 1967 by sending former Secretary of Defense Robert McNamara a request for a matrix of 85 specific data items for which he (Riegle) had written a computer program.[114] Another freshman senator, with a combined engineering and law background, Howard H. Baker, Jr. (R-Tenn.), lectured to the Association for Computing Machinery about the impending nuclear power breakthrough in breeder reactors that could produce power at almost zero fuel cost and the need for a much broader congressional overview and plan for the technological and social revolution that this implied. Senator Baker has been an articulate spokesman for a new Senate Select Committee for Technology and the Human Environment.[115]

[114] Column by David Broder, *Washington Post*, November 7, 1967, p. A-17.
[115] See text of address by Senator Howard H. Baker, Jr. (R-Tenn.) before Association for Computing Machinery, August 30, 1967 (Washington, D.C.: mimeo); and U.S. Senate, Subcommittee on Intergovernmental Relations, Committee on Government Operations, *Hearings: Establish a Select Senate Committee on Technology and the Human Environment*, 90th Congress, 1st Session, 1967.

Prospects for congressional acceptance of the projected information technology of 1975. The widespread congressional interest we have summarized suggests a greater receptivity toward computers and information systems than might have been anticipated. It is still likely, however, that Congress will lag behind the Executive in fully accepting the new technology.

How great a lag will exist by our projected date of 1975 — assuming that Congress permits the Executive to implement the new technology without hindrances? We may posit three points on a continuum from (I) *congressional resistance* to computer technology, notably the failure to fund any central computational facility for use by the Congress, the failure to budget any allowance for congressmen to utilize other facilities, and the failure to provide analyst staff for the use of the committees and members; through (II) *limited congressional acceptance* of computer facilities and analyst staff with access tightly controlled by the individual committees or party leaderships; to (III) *open congressional acceptance,* with all members enjoying free use of computer facilities and full access to staff and data resources. According to our assumed projection, Congress could have moved all the way to situation III by the mid-1970's. A more realistic and conservative estimate would place it somewhere between situations II and III. Ultimately, in our estimate, Congress will operate in situation III, although the exact institutional *form* in which it organizes and applies these new resources remains to be determined.

As an organization, Congress is a relatively open system, and it is unlikely to escape such fundamental changes as the computer will introduce in American society, social organization, and education itself. A number of competitive dimensions in Congress are likely to accelerate acceptance of innovations in decision making developed in the private sector or Executive branch: the built-in tension between authorizing and appropriations committees both eager to control program decision; the publicity incentive for committee and subcommittee chairmen generally to identify themselves with innovations and to push for their implementation; the perennial fear of Congress that it is yielding initiative and authority to the President; party competition; and the generational divide between activist and high-seniority congressmen. While there are many factors that will reinforce traditional ways of making decisions within Congress, change is inevitable if for no other reason than that Congress cannot afford *not* to follow the rationalization of Executive decision making.[116] Even if the congressional establishment adamantly refused to accept program budgeting and similar innovations, the Executive could proceed with internal program rationalization on its own. In time, as more versatile, relatively low-cost information systems and professional analysis became financially feasible for individual or groups of congressmen, perhaps in conjunction with political party organizations or interest groups, the impact of improved information and analysis would be felt in the legislative process itself.[117] Another possibility would be for teams of congressmen loyal to the program objectives of the President to tap Executive branch resources.

As Congress moves toward limited acceptance of information technology (situation II), some of the old internal dilemmas of organizing congressional power will be exposed in a new and more acute form. A number of decisions about the allocation of the new information resources, especially the right of access to information, will be made either consciously or by default. These decisions will confer important, although in some cases temporary, power advantages on some members of Congress.

Allocation decisions may also exert a determining influence on the institutional forms that evolve as Congress moves into a situation of open access to information. Will the centralized leadership or party policy committees be equipped with facilities for information retrieval and staffed with professional analysts? Or will the standing committees control the major information resources? Will individual members be able to use time-shared facilities through remote terminals in their offices, and will they have access to committee and general governmental data banks? Will Congress choose to build data-processing and analysis capabilities in "institutional staff arms" such as the Leg-

[116] Richard Fenno concludes, "The Congress as a whole cannot afford to slip far behind the executive branch in its ability to comprehend systems analysis, operations research, cost effectiveness analysis and the planning programming budgeting system. If no one in Congress can understand what the executive is doing, the legislature as a whole will suffer and surrender still more power to the executive branch." Yet he feels that traditional congressional techniques for appraising the budget will not be replaced by PPBS. See "Executive-Legislative Appropriations Interface," Chartrand, Janda, and Hugo (eds.), *op. cit.*

[117] One current example of independent sector initiative in developing special ADP-assisted analyses is the work of the American Enterprise Institute utilizing its own computer facility for analysis of federal budgetary data on magnetic tape. See *Program Priorities in the Budget for Fiscal 1969* (Special Analysis No. 1, 90th Congress, 2nd Session; Washington, D.C.: American Enterprise Institute, 1968).

islative Reference Service or the General Accounting Office? Will it
turn to new joint committees, such as the Joint Committee on the
Budget, proposed by Senator John L. McClellan (D-Ark.), and the
Joint Committee on the Social Report advanced by Senator Walter F.
Mondale (D-Minn.)?

We are less interested in which of these alternatives Congress
adopts during this transition phase than we are in the ultimate form
of information systems in a situation of open access. Two biases are
likely, however, in this process of adaptation of information systems
by Congress.

First, the growing experience with information systems in industry
suggests that "managerial philosophy in the structuring of organizations to use computers may be more important than the technology itself." There is documented evidence of managerial resistance "when
the computerized information system is not geared to the reward system, or when unrealistic timetables are set to introduce a new system." [118] The implications for congressional adaptation are clear: the
managerial philosophy of Congress or, more appropriately, the group
norms of the congressional system will shape the application of the
new information technology in Congress. Accordingly we may reasonably expect to see such results as increased specialization through the
standing committee system and the continued independence of the
member of Congress from disciplined, central control. But since, as
we have suggested, Congress has resisted a single mode of representation or model for organizing power, it will be difficult to discern any
coherent managerial philosophy as a general guide to reform.

Second, the new information technology itself will introduce a bias
entirely consistent with democratic theory — toward the free exchange
of information and ideas. Davidson, Kovenock, and O'Leary suggest,
"The maximization of opportunities for free competition of interests
and values should be a prime value in thinking about the future of
Congress." [119] We suggest here a few of the more intriguing possibilities for a Congress based on the free exchange and availability of information (i.e., situation III).

The contributions of the individual legislator would be enhanced.
We have noted the contribution of individual legislators to congressional initiative in legislation and investigation. Although only a
minority of congressmen will choose to play the role of legislative

---

[118] Myers (ed.), *The Impact of Computers on Management*, pp. 7–8.
[119] *Op. cit.*, p. 171.

inventor or watchdog, the effectiveness of such members will be enormously increased by computer-assisted techniques of search and analysis. Members will be free to browse through the data archives in developing and assessing legislative alternatives. Some legislators will hire professional analysts on their office staffs or acquire analytical skills themselves. While such legislative diligence will still be the exception, one can readily foresee a congressman sitting at a console in his office pouring over computer print-out into the late evening hours or over the weekend and cutting through the paper arguments and justifications of executive programs with penetrating lines of questions. The possibility of abuse also exists, but the weight of past congressional experience suggests that most congressmen will use such new investigative power wisely. In situations that invite adversary argument, alternative positions and points of view will be more thoroughly developed and cogently presented.

Ad hoc congressional study and work groups would freely form and disperse as new and challenging tasks arose at the interstices of committee power. Warren Bennis and others have suggested that transient work groups composed of interdisciplinary teams of highly skilled specialists will replace hierarchical bureaucracy as the dominant form of organization in the post-industrial society.[120] The congressional milieu with its weak hierarchical structure offers a logical setting for such work groups. Congressmen who might lack the requisite skills or resources to tackle a legislative problem by themselves could easily pool their efforts. Such informal cooperative work groups may already be seen in Congress, and one major proposal has been advanced to give them formal congressional recognition and support. The work of such study groups would be "collateral" to that of the standing committees but would introduce a "helpful and needed resilience into the congressional posture." [121] To the extent that such work groups succeeded and posed a competitive challenge to the existing committee

[120] *Changing Organizations* (New York: McGraw-Hill Book Co., 1966).

[121] See statement of George E. Agree, Executive Director, National Committee for an Effective Congress, in Joint Committee on the Organization of the Congress, *Hearings: Organization of Congress*, 89th Congress, 1st Session, August 9, 1965, pp. 1427–41. Another type of informal ad hoc bipartisan committee was formed in May 1968 to confer with the Southern Christian Leadership Conference on "realistic legislative and administrative proposals which would help solve some of the problems and national needs of the poor." The committee has since formed subject matter subcommittees. See remarks of Senator Edward Brooke (R-Mass.), *Daily Congressional Record*, 90th Congress, 2nd Session, May 23, 1968, p. S6329.

structure, they might serve to improve the quality of committees generally. Standing committee leaders might seek to co-opt able young members, according greater weight to subject-matter expertise. They might also advance talented members to subcommittee chairmanships faster than might otherwise have been the case. The committee system of Congress would still be organized according to the norms of specialization and reciprocity, but specialization would be much less dependent on a member's initial committee assignment and accumulated seniority than it would be on his motivation and time commitment to mastering a given area of substantive policy and appropriate instruments for analysis.

While information systems afford new possibilities for specialization and increased committee power — especially in the area of legislative oversight or control of the executive bureaucracy — they should also afford democratization of committee power. Where limited information previously conferred important advantages on those few individuals who had the legislative seniority and central committee positions to accumulate such information, now availability of information and program analyses would enable junior committee members and interested congressmen not on the committee to gain a better understanding of the issues involved. The majority would have greater opportunity to influence committee action and to prevail against the committee on the floor when its action was not representative of the views of the entire membership.

Generalized information systems should enable Congress to satisfy both the necessity for specialization and the goal of comprehensive policy review. Where information on executive activities has been compartmentalized within the executive budget and the congressional committee system, it would now be available on a comprehensive basis. The "special analyses" of the federal budget already being developed by the Bureau of the Budget are a prototype of the kind of comprehensive information that congressional committees would be able to tap.[122] Individual congressional committees, no longer limited to information within their agency jurisdiction, could become important points for government-wide program review and coordination. Where the President alone has had the information to develop a mea-

[122] Bureau of the Budget, *Special Analyses, Budget of the United States, 1968* (Washington, D.C.: U.S. Government Printing Office, 1967). See also John S. Saloma III, *The Responsible Use of Power: A Critical Analysis of the Congressional Budget Process* (Washington, D.C.: American Enterprise Institute, 1964), pp. 83–87.

sure of agency coordination, congressional committees would now share that information, *and* the authority to use it, subject to the majority support of Congress. Alfred de Grazia's critique of "executive-force" gains plausibility in this context:

> The presidency is a corporate body distinct from the President in some ways. Congress should consider whether the presidency forms a better topping off of the administrative pyramid of government than some new kind of organizational concept. It is not at all certain, for example, that the committees of Congress should abstain from direct policy-making as a matter of right and efficiency — something that many tend to engage in anyhow. . . .[123]

If the trend toward free exchange and availability of information becomes an accepted feature of American government in the future, we can anticipate these and other developments in system politics.

A NEW CHALLENGE TO THE CONCEPT OF SEPARATION OF POWERS. While the application of information technology in government will have its greatest immediate political impact *within* the Executive (with important secondary consequences for the Congress), the longer term consequences of better information in government raise fundamental questions about the American system of separated powers. Congress and legislative bodies generally need *not* lose power to the Executive. The potential advance in information technology is theoretically equally accessible to *both* the President and Congress, with *Congress* standing to enhance its powers over the Executive.[124] The central dilemma of American politics — how power should be organized in the American political system — will be faced once again,

[123] Arthur M. Schlesinger, Jr., and Alfred de Grazia, *Congress and the Presidency: Their Role in Modern Times* (Rational Debate Seminars; Washington, D.C.: American Enterprise Institute, 1967), p. 66.

[124] Anthony Downs feels that with the introduction of governmental information systems, legislators will lose power to administrators and operating officials. "The latter are generally more sophisticated, have more technical training, are equipped with larger staffs, devote more time to their . . . jobs, can focus more intensively upon narrow specialties, are in a better position to control the design and operation of . . . data systems, and are more likely to receive continuous reports from those systems by virtue of their positions." "A Realistic Look at . . . Urban Data Systems," p. 208. These may be short-term effects, but legislators retain important long-term advantages: the ability to question officials in both legislative and appropriations hearings, the power of appointment together with personnel controls, appropriations, audit, investigations, creating or augmenting specialist staffs.

but this time many of the ambiguities and contradictions of the dual system will be painfully evident as never before.

Compared with parliamentary systems, the American political system has been unique in its elaborate structuring and rationalization of political authority. We have developed a dual system of representation, embracing two popular majorities, legitimizing two autonomous centers of political leadership. The necessity to govern has required interdependent action, but within the ambiguities of the constitutional settlement and the precedents of American political history, a substantial measure of autonomy has been preserved. While the limits of autonomy were severely tested during the nineteenth century, the relatively low level of political demands on the system — sufficiently low as *not* to require an executive budget until 1921 — enabled the luxury of either presidential or congressional government. The first major rationalization of authority, beginning roughly with the Budget and Accounting Act of 1921 and including the establishment of the modern executive bureaucracy, the executive staffs to the President, and the Legislative Reorganization Act of 1946, required a specialization of roles — executive leadership and congressional review or oversight. The model of "executive-centered" government during this period, while tending to enhance the power of the President and reduce the autonomy of Congress, was based on a rationale that differentiated roles for President and Congress. Simply stated, the President set the agenda for legislation; the Congress reviewed, amended, and passed legislation; the President supervised the execution of the laws by the federal bureaucracy; and the Congress reviewed administrative performance. Executive-centered government, however, conferred important relative information advantages on the President. The President was closer to the day-to-day operations of the executive bureaucracy. He had access to the detailed information generated by the budgetary cycle and the numerous intelligence activities of the federal bureaucracy. Moreover, the budgetary process and supporting central staff gave him a continuing framework for decision.[125] While the President still faced the problem of controlling the bureaucracy, congressmen were even more frustrated. Even within more limited specialized fields, committee members viewed governmental agencies

---

[125] For a discussion of presidential information requirements and techniques for gathering and using information, see Richard E. Neustadt, *Presidential Power: The Politics of Leadership* (New York: John Wiley & Sons, 1960), Chap. VII.

as "impenetrable mazes" posing major hazards for the inexpert congressman. A kind of bureaucratic curtain insured that the executive bureaucracy would enjoy autonomy from congressional oversight and that Congress would have difficulty in communicating its intent clearly. The typical congressman's complaint was, "Most of us just don't know enough about it to even begin to ask intelligent questions." [126]

A second major rationalization of authority has begun with the new emphasis on program budgeting and information systems in government. As this rationalization proceeds, many of the assumptions underlying specialized roles for the President and Congress will have to be re-examined. The distinction between executive decision making and broad policy oversight by Congress will become increasingly blurred as the time perspective of governmental decision makers is lengthened. As improved information systems yield better indicators of performance, reduce the time of the management information cycle, and permit realtime monitoring of governmental activities, the congressional role of oversight (review after the fact) will be supplemented by new possibilities for control (legislative decision or activity prior to the relevant administrative action).[127] The policy or control functions of the President and Congress will become less distinguishable as both develop the capacity to ask program questions and undertake analyses of data from the same generalized information systems or specially developed systems for their own use. One restraint on a fully developed congressional policy role in the past has been the unwillingness of Congress to build a parallel legislative staff bureaucracy. As a result, Congress has often had to second-guess the Executive without the information to back its hunches. Now, as technology extends the availability of information, Congress can tap into executive-based information systems, establish quality controls, and develop more limited information systems for its own specific requirements. Program budgeting suggests the potential leverage that may accrue to Congress. The executive bureaucracy, under the direction of the President and Budget Bureau, will structure program choices and undertake analysis of various alternatives. Congress will be presented with a program budget which may easily be rearranged by traditional

[126] See Seymour Scher, "Conditions for Legislative Control," *Journal of Politics*, August 1963, pp. 526–37.

[127] The distinction is developed by Joseph P. Harris, *Congressional Control of Administration* (Washington, D.C.: The Brookings Institution, 1964), p. 9.

line-item categories or into other desired formats. Congress will review program choices, evaluate analyses with its own analyst staff, and determine its own priorities. The process of making choices and analyses more explicit enables Congress to participate much more intelligently and vigorously, with a *limited* staff, in the decision-making process. In fact, there may even be a danger of too vigorous participation. Industrial experience suggests the need of top decision makers to practice forbearance in control:

> Because of the computer, there is a very definite danger of over-control from the top, since top management can get detailed reports on the operations. It is easy for top management to misuse these reports and not allow managers at lower levels to develop properly through the experience of making their own decisions.[128]

The question remains whether the President will permit Congress to have access to the information resources and analyses of the Executive branch. He will have to, insofar as analyses are used to justify his program requests. Other background analyses and alternatives may not be presented to Congress. In such a case, these would have to be duplicated by congressional analysts. (Congress would want the capacity to go beyond alternatives presented by the Executive in any event.) But in general, as Charles Dechert concludes, "Congress' information problem is not primarily one of access to information in the Executive."

> There is every indication that, with the exception of requests for data tendentiously serving partisan political objectives, or which could be used to the detriment of individuals (such as investigative files) or of the national security, members of Congress and congressional committees could get the information they need if they had appropriate facilities to define their needs, routinize transmission, and impose appropriate sanctions upon unwarranted refusal of information by the executive.[129]

[128] Witt I. Langstaff, "The Effect of Computers on Members of Management," unpublished M.S. thesis, Sloan School of Management, M.I.T., Cambridge, Mass., 1965, cited in Myers, "The Impact of EDP on Management Organization and Managerial Work," p. 36.

[129] "Availability of Information for Congressional Operations," in Alfred de Grazia (ed.), *Congress: The First Branch of Government*, p. 211.

In fact, the effectiveness of implementation of the right of Congress to information will be a critical test in the future of the degree of congressional autonomy within a system of separated powers.[130]

We can only speculate on the new definition of the separation of powers that will evolve. If we assume the political trends that we projected earlier, distinctive presidential and congressional biases may soon develop in the decision-making process. We might expect the Executive to overemphasize the benefits of cost-effectiveness analyses in program formulation and administration, to overvalue economic and technical criteria of performance. If, as some observers anticipate, the new information technology leads to "an increasing separation between operating missions, life styles, and social roles for those institutions and individuals involved in rationalized activities compared to those involved in nonrationalized ones," [131] Congress, representative of a society embracing both life styles, would inherit the difficult task of mediating the impact of the former on the latter and restraining the tendency toward irrational and frustrated response. Congress would add political considerations of human costs and benefits to the decision-making process.

In this context, one rationale for the separation of powers — "systemic dissonance," or the planned discordance of political voices — takes on new significance.[132] We have suggested through this discussion that the revolution in information technology represents an almost immeasurable potential increase in man's knowledge, especially in his understanding of, and ability to control, his environment. The intelligent use of that knowledge and the power it confers is an awesome responsibility. In a political democracy, emerging technological possibilities and consequences must be considered from multiple perspectives. The multiple perspectives of the American system — the numerous points of access for developing, testing, and advancing ideas — may ultimately prove to be one of the greatest assets of American democracy in the future.

[130] Katz and Kahn define the test of organizational autonomy to include "power to stipulate sources of input rather than accepting sources prescribed by the supersystem." *Op. cit.*, p. 59.

[131] Michael, *op. cit.*, p. 29.

[132] Bertram Gross suggests the importance of such dissonance in developing economic and social indicators. Gross and Springer, *op. cit.*, pp. 14–19.

CHAPTER EIGHT

Congress and the New Politics: The Challenge to Congressional Excellence

But my vision had always been that all of a sudden a million people would march on Washington, singing "A Mighty Fortress Is Our God," and the government would come tumbling down. I would feel much more identified with that than if a million people marched on Washington singing "The Internationale." . . . If I let down all my defenses, I would wind up being Billy Graham or Elmer Gantry. That would be my first impulse, to say, "That's immoral." . . .

. . . [I]n January [1965] — at the opening of Congress, that was — they tried to unseat the Mississippi delegation. People thought, "Well, we couldn't do it at the Democratic Convention, but the Congress won't fail us. It's illegal." Those kids really worked their tails off to get reams and reams of legal evidence. Everybody felt a good deal of confidence that this was going to happen. That's a good example of the kind of feeling . . . where people have been promised time and time again that the white folk in the North would come through. "The support will come through, the Society will be able to provide for you," this is the same thing that [Martin Luther] King was saying. . . . Of course, it didn't happen that way. It caused a very serious setback to us all.

. . . I felt . . . kind of the ideology of the alienated: "The old values have been destroyed; the old structures and institutions of the past no longer fit our needs; therefore we must rebuild." That's how I personally connected into it.[1]

[1] From Kenneth Keniston, *Young Radicals: Notes on Committed Youth* (New York: Harcourt, Brace & World, 1968), pp. 31, 204–5, 109.

As significant as information technology may be for the future of decision making in government, it would be misleading to suggest that it will be the dominant factor in shaping the Congress of the future. Technological change is one of the easier dimensions of the future to forecast. Congress, as a popular representative assembly, stands at the intersection of numerous currents of change in American society. The objective of this concluding chapter is to project some of the major contours of a new *political* era, of the 1970's and beyond, and to relate these to the challenges Congress will face.

The political dimensions of change are obviously more volatile than the technological. While a few political observers — men like Peter Drucker, Samuel Lubell, and Max Ways — have imaginatively probed the political future, insufficient attention has been given to the subject to yield anything approaching a consensus.[2] The presidential politics of 1968, once again, has underlined the element of contingency in politics and the uncertainty of political prediction, even for the short term.

Yet behind the noise of sometimes unexpected political events, quiet, clearly discernible trends are evident in American politics. Some of these trends are working in support of the technological breakthrough in decision making outlined earlier. Others are potentially disruptive. Congress, as a central participant in the definition of social policy, cannot escape the responsibility of choice in supporting or resisting various demands for change, in striking some balance among contending forces. Congress shares in the responsibility for defining and developing the American political future.

CONGRESS AND THE CHANGING POLITICAL CONTEXT

The term "new politics" has been popularized, on the one hand, as a new radical commitment in politics embodied in the New Left and, on the other, as a rationalization of old-style, ward-boss, party-organization politics, made possible by a new political technology of professional campaign management, mass media utilization, and opin-

---

[2] See, for example, Peter Drucker, "New Directions for American Society," *Harper's*, February 1965; Samuel Lubell, "The Changing U.S. Electorate," *Fortune*, July 1964; Max Ways, "1964: A Chance to Look at Ourselves," *Fortune*, October 1964; and The Ripon Society, *From Disaster to Distinction: The Rebirth of the Republican Party* (New York: Pocket Books, 1966), Chap. V.

ion polling.[3] Our use of the term comprehends both of these. If one takes the 1960's as a decade of political transition, connecting the Eisenhower years with the 1970's, several important contrasts can be made in the politics of two eras. Throughout the 1960's new and old forms and styles have confronted one another. The new politics embraces, in our definition, all that is new and sufficiently permanent to be part of the political world after 1970: changes in major institutions, demographic shifts, new values and ideologies, and technological advance.

Each of the following political trends constitutes an aspect of the new politics. Each has important consequences for the Congress of the future. Besides the new style of decision making considered in our discussion of information technology, the trends are: (1) the increased nationalization of politics and the decline of southern power; (2) the growth of a sophisticated electorate and corresponding new forms of political organization; (3) metropolitan growth and the rise of a new urban cleavage; (4) future trends in American federalism — centralization or decentralization?; (5) the impact of the cultural revolution — the post-modern style; (6) the new power centers of the post-industrial society; and (7) new challenges to the American political consensus — radical movements and the American party system. As a final topic in this discussion of the new politics, some general observations on the Congress of the future are presented.

The increased nationalization of politics and the decline of southern power. As America continues to develop a more national culture, so too will its politics, under the influence of mass media and jet transportation, become more national. Congress, based on ever enlarged and more complicated individual constituencies, will increasingly shift from parochial to national concerns. Stephen K. Bailey predicts that the congressional system will change "from one that accommodates the gaps between parochial and national interests to one that emphasizes their commonalities." [4] The independence of the

[3] The term in the first sense was used by the "New Politics Convention on 1968 and Beyond," held in Chicago, August 29 to September 4, 1967. For a discussion of the "new politics" in quite a different sense, see James M. Perry, *The New Politics: The Expanding Technology of Political Manipulation* (New York: Clarkson N. Potter, 1968).

[4] *The New Congress* (St. Martin's Series in American Politics; New York: St. Martin's Press, 1966), pp. 14–15. See also Donald E. Stokes, "Parties and the Nationalization of Electoral Forces," in William Nisbet Chambers and Walter Dean Burnham (eds.), *The American Party Systems: Stages of Political Development* (New York: Oxford University Press, 1967), pp. 182–202.

congressman from local constituency interests will be offset by his increased dependence on the President or national party organization. The sum effect will be a broader-based Congress with an expanded potential for national policy roles.

One casualty of the trend toward nationalization has been the one-party regional base of southern Democratic power. The leverage that seniority and committee control have afforded southern Democrats in Congress, particularly in the decades since World War II, is already markedly on the wane.[5] As a generation of southern tacticians such as Senator Richard Russell of Georgia and Congressman Howard W. Smith of Virginia passes from the congressional scene, new congressmen — especially northern, midwestern, and western urban Democrats — will move into power. The nascent two-party system in the South, given added impetus by congressional reapportionment, will preclude the easy accumulation of new southern seniority. We are already past the point where the Congress can be described as a southern-dominated institution. The South may continue to play coalition politics in the electoral college and Congress, but its power stakes have declined to the point where it can no longer set the tone of national political institutions.[6]

The growth of a sophisticated electorate and corresponding new forms of political organization. The steady maturing of the American electorate (toward an educated, politicized, sophisticated, and socially integrated middle class) has resulted in "a new differentiation and pluralism of political organization."[7] The new voter finds the two major parties too omnibus to be effective political instruments. He is increasingly unwilling to make a blind commitment to the party as such, and is more selective in investing in individual candidates and causes. He may consider himself an Independent or simply split his ballot at elections.[8]

[5] See Raymond E. Wolfinger and Joan Heifetz, "Safe Seats, Seniority, and Power in Congress," *American Political Science Review* (APSR), June 1965, pp. 337–49.

[6] See Drucker's analysis of the decline of the South, "Notes on the New Politics," *The Public Interest*, Summer 1966, pp. 17–20. This will constitute one important loss for Congress, since southern chairmen, while often autocratic and immovable, "endowed Congress with a solid backbone of expertise such as no other parliamentary body in the world possesses."

[7] Frank J. Sorauf, *Party Politics in America* (Boston: Little, Brown & Co., 1968), p. 430.

[8] The concept of the "ticket-splitter" has been developed by Walter DeVries and Fred Currier of Market-Opinion Research Company. See Perry, *op. cit.*, Chap. IV, "Scientific Polling: The Romney Experience in Michigan," pp. 77–

The American party system is entering a new stage in its development corresponding to these more complex and sophisticated political demands.[9] Several new forms of organization are already evident, and these should develop further as new political technology is diffused. Among these are entrepreneurial forms of political organization that sell professional political services (campaign management, polling, advertising, research, media skills, fund-raising, political intelligence, and even precinct organization) to candidates and party organizations;[10] personal candidate organizations functioning independently from the formal party organizations and appealing directly to the electorate via the mass media;[11] ideologically based electoral interest groups that seek intermediate power between the politically active individual and his party and whose power base is the ability to raise money from a public constituency to aid endorsed candidates (for example, the National Committee for an Effective Congress);[12] and organized "pools" of potential party activists or cadre whose participation in party politics is contingent on the ideological emphasis of the party.[13]

The full impact of these and related organizational innovations will not be felt until the potential of the new information technology has been substantially adapted for political use. One would expect the professional political firms to increase their influence rapidly through first-hand familiarity with the political uses of data banks, although a stable "cartel" arrangement might evolve between the key firms and

---

106; and Fred Currier, "Some Remarks on the Ticket Splitter," paper prepared for the Harvard Seminar in Practical Politics, Cambridge, Mass., February 21, 1968.

[9] Sorauf, *op. cit.*, pp. 413–16, 426–30.

[10] See Perry, *op. cit.* The first comprehensive listings of campaign management and polling firms are available in "Campaign Management Grows into National Industry," *Congressional Quarterly*, Weekly Report No. 14, April 5, 1968, pp. 706–14, 720; and "Political Pollsters Head for Record Activity in 1968," Weekly Report No. 18, May 3, 1968, pp. 992–1000. Walter DeVries, currently a Fellow at the Kennedy Institute of Politics, is preparing a book on American political campaigns that will include applications of polling and new campaign techniques.

[11] See Gene Wyckoff, *The Image Candidates: American Politics in the Age of Television* (New York: The Macmillan Co., 1968).

[12] For an analysis of these new "pseudoparties" see Harry M. Scoble, *Ideology and Electoral Action: A Comparative Case Study of the National Committee for an Effective Congress* (San Francisco: Chandler Publishing Co., 1967).

[13] A vivid case study of an ideological party cadre is found in F. Clifton White with William J. Gill, *Suite 3505: The Story of the Draft Goldwater Movement* (New Rochelle, N.Y.: Arlington House, 1967).

national party organizations.[14] The current generation of political entrepreneurs, recruited largely from public-relations and market-research backgrounds, would be replaced by men with training in the social sciences and computer systems (a new profession of political analysts). Both electoral interest groups and activist cadres would extend their base and membership communications through new information systems in a way that might considerably enhance their power in relation to more apathetic, less well-organized constituencies. The possibilities afforded radical movements and ideologies are discussed below.

These related developments will affect Congress in at least two ways. First, congressional campaigns will become increasingly sophisticated and, accordingly, dependent on professional skills that the candidate will purchase himself, be allocated by the national party organization (with priorities set by target states and target districts), or receive from electoral-interest groups or quasi-party groups.[15] The issue of campaign financing, particularly for media, may become a critical problem. Second, the congressman's personal constituency campaign organization will become increasingly differentiated from the local and state party organization. Information technology will enable the incumbent congressman to integrate much more effectively his day-to-day case work and constituency service with his campaign for re-election. The differential resources of the incumbent and a challenger may become so inequitable that Congress will have to find ways to subsidize or compensate new candidates. On balance, however, the incumbent in Congress will have the advantage.

Metropolitan growth and the rise of a new urban cleavage. As urbanization continues in the United States, the old rural-urban cleavage in American politics already reduced by reapportionment will become increasingly anachronistic. The Bureau of the Census reported in 1960 that 63 per cent of all Americans lived in 200 metropolitan areas (Standard Metropolitan Statistical Areas) and that the rate of population growth over the previous decade had been almost four times as great in metropolitan areas (26.4 per cent) as in non-metropolitan areas (7.1 per cent). Three great megalopoli, stretching from Boston to Washington, Chicago to Pittsburgh, and San Fran-

---

[14] See "Republican Campaign Groups Name 'Purchasing Agent' for Extensive Polls," *Congressional Quarterly*, Weekly Report No. 18, May 3, 1968, pp. 998–99.

[15] *Ibid.*

cisco to San Diego, will dominate American culture by the end of the century.[16]

As the urban metropolis becomes dominant, a new tension — between the core-city and suburbs — is likely to appear in national politics and in Congress. Peter Drucker has characterized two emerging political styles in metropolitan politics. Ethnic blocs, notably in the Negro ghetto and neighboring white ethnic communities, will persist and even intensify in the core-city. An "economic" politics of the have-nots (seeking welfare benefits, unemployment compensation, medicare, etc.) is also likely to survive in the core-city — an exception to the politics of the affluent society. Drucker observes, "The core-city is increasingly likely to present yesterday's politics, yesterday's issues, and yesterday's alignment." [17] In contrast, the suburbs, representing the new, educated, prosperous middle-class, the residential base of the new power centers of American society, will evolve a new future-oriented politics of issues and problems. Drucker concludes that it is conceivable that tomorrow's political parties will primarily be characterized by having a "core-city" or a "suburban" temperament.

These trends are already discernible in the Congress. Urban Democrats and suburban Republicans even now are close to forming the center of gravity of their respective parties. Ironically, the safest seats in Congress and the surest routes to committee power may soon be the increasingly Negro and Democratic urban districts of the North. The cleavage will most likely be expressed in the House of Representatives. Both United States senators and candidates for the Presidency will have to generalize their electoral appeal to include both sections of the metropolis.

Future trends in American federalism — centralization or decentralization? The prediction of some of the futurists that computers will lead to greater centralization in decision making and social planning, control, and regulation is not certain by any means, particularly in a system as diverse and complex as American federalism. The degree of centralization in the federal system of the future will depend on three general factors. First, it will depend on the degree of mobilization of governmental resources required by international and domestic crises. A relatively stable international order and domestic

[16] See Herman Kahn and Anthony J. Wiener, *The Year 2000: A Framework for Speculation on the Next Thirty-Three Years* (New York: The Macmillan Co., 1967), pp. 61–62.

[17] "Notes on the New Politics," pp. 22–23.

society will obviously require far less centralization than one involving large American troop commitments abroad, an accelerated arms race, or severe racial unrest or social disorders at home. Assuming no serious exogenous disruptive factors, we can probably achieve the desired mix of economic policy objectives for the future, given our level of economic understanding, *without* any necessary further centralization of federal power. Improved economic indicators, analysis, and forecasting (particularly through the availability of data for micro-analysis from a national data system) will permit more selective, timely, and appropriate public economic policy decisions, many at a level of current administrative discretion. Furthermore, continued economic growth will afford new possibilities for a redistribution of tax resources to state and local governments and a decrease in federal taxes.

Second, the degree of centralization will be a political decision, between the central decision makers (President *and* Congress) and the peripheral units of power (public and private). The latter constitute powerful political forces toward decentralization. The extraordinary fiscal resources of the federal government will gain increasing importance as "the primary source of discretionary public expenditure" for all levels of government.[18] The President and Congress, through the budgetary process, will control this power in the bargaining process with peripheral units, and hence will be able through conscious central political decision to influence the shape of the federal system, especially innovations in metropolitan and regional government. The type of political decisions will, of course, reflect the different representational systems of the President and Congress.

Compared with the crisis and political factors, the third influence on the degree of centralization — computer technology — seems less significant. The experience of large business corporations and financial institutions that have introduced computer systems has been that certain functions — especially those that afforded significant economies through central record maintenance, scheduling, and ordering — were centralized. An optimal mix of functions in terms of comparative economic advantage of central management and decentralized units seems to have been achieved in several cases, although experts in management organization are reluctant to make hard and fast generaliza-

---

[18] Daniel Moynihan, "The Relationship of Federal to Local Authorities," *Daedalus*, Summer 1967, p. 802. See also Walter W. Heller, *New Dimensions of Political Economy*, Chap. III, "Strengthening the Fiscal Base of Our Federalism."

tions.[19] If, as some suspect, organizational adaptation is a function of the capabilities of the computer system, new and more versatile generations of computers may be fit to a wide variety of organizational configurations with marginal differences in economic benefits. Similarly, as computers become more widely available and utilized, virtually every level and unit of government will have its own computer "utility." In a political system where information is a form of power, the rules governing access to and the use of information have important political consequences. Improved computer technology, through linking networks of data banks in a federal system, will *generalize* the availability of information. Political rules will *specify* limits to its use. Thus in a stable general environment the issue of centralization versus decentralization stands to become an increasingly political issue, as economic growth increases the base for discretionary spending and technological innovation eliminates many of the nonpolitical barriers to access to information. The future shape of American federalism promises to be one of the major issues of the new politics.

The impact of the cultural revolution — the post-modern style. Another change in American society that has profound implications for the future direction of our politics is in our values, beliefs, and attitudes. One dramatic facet of this change is the so-called "generational revolution" in American politics. Half of our population is already less than 26 years old, and by the presidential election of 1972 more than half of all Americans eligible to vote will be under 32 (i.e., born during the span of years between 1940 and 1951). Even more significant than the shift in chronological age is, according to Drucker, "a shift in outlook, perception, and formative experience. The world this new generation of Americans considers as 'normal' is one of long years of advanced education, of very high job security, of affluence, a world dominated by science and technology." [20] Students of computer technology suggest that a similar divide will occur between those who have been educated in direct association with or in the environment of computers (students below the age of 15 in 1965) and those who have not.

What will be the politics of this young generation? What are its

[19] See, for example, the differing viewpoints expressed in Charles A. Myers (ed.), *The Impact of Computers on Management* (Cambridge, Mass.: The M.I.T. Press, 1967).

[20] "Notes on the New Politics," p. 27.

political expectations and what commitments will it make to the political process? How will it use its affluence, its education, and its leisure time?

Some tentative answers to these and related questions have been suggested by studies of the American student population. Several types of students may be identified in terms of their dominant value commitment.[21] Of these, two appear to be most significant in defining competing emphases in the new politics. The *professionalists*, born of upper-middle-class and professional parents, aspire to a life pattern of achievement, expertise, and *noblesse oblige*. They are highly motivated to advance through graduate study to the key professions and leadership positions within society. Politically, they are "cool," seldom excited by issues and ideas, conservative to middle-of-the-road in outlook, and oriented toward the status quo. The *radical-activists* of the left have a basic commitment to personal involvement in action — to reforming American society. Their family backgrounds are also prosperous, middle class, but liberal in political orientation. Their outrage at perceived hypocrisy and injustice is translated into a passionate commitment to politics. (The response of the current hippie movement is a pessimistically apolitical withdrawal.) Radical-activists probably number no more than 2 per cent of the college population. According to one estimate, "the overwhelming majority of American college students are politically apathetic — caught up in their vocational, academic, or hedonistic pursuits." [22]

The impact of the professionalists and of related student types like the vocationalists, who generally come from working-class backgrounds and specialize in engineering, education, business, and other technical specialities, will be expressed through the new power centers discussed in the following section. It is to the radical-activists (and the hippies) that we turn for an insight into the political values and style of the future.

The "post-modern style," as Kenneth Keniston defines it, is the product of rapid social change, automatic abundance, and a preoccupation with the issue of violence.[23] Its most visible and influential current expressions are found in the hippie world and the New Left.

---

[21] For a summary of research on the subject, see Richard E. Peterson, "The Student Left in American Higher Education," *Daedalus*, Winter 1968, pp. 293–317. The following discussion draws on Peterson's classification of eight student types.

[22] *Ibid.*, p. 312.

[23] An excellent analysis of the "post-modern style" is developed by Keniston, *op. cit.*, pp. 272–90.

The post-modern style is a *way* of relating to a world where radical change is the rule. It is an open style, characterized by fluidity, flux, change, movement. Post-modern youth are generally nondogmatic and anti-ideological. They identify with a generational movement, rather than a cross-generation organization or nongenerational ideology, and are highly inclusive — both in an interracial and an international sense. They stress the quality of personal relationships and the potential of each man for self-expression and self-actualization. A corollary for the New Left is participatory democracy and the creation of new institutions that enable men to influence their own lives. Post-modern youth accept the benefits of technology but reject its dehumanizing consequences.

The radical-activists, in their commitment to political action, combine a confusing mix of political attitudes. They reject the manipulation, power relationships, and control that characterize exploitative, old-style politics. They feel that existing political institutions have failed to solve the great social problems of racism and poverty, not to mention the problems of the international order. At the same time, radical-activists lack effective political organization and any detailed program of reform. Instead they have evolved new tactics of political action that seek to increase the social and political awareness of Americans — a politics of dialogue, participation, and confrontation.

What is the significance of this new political style for American political institutions and especially the Congress? The presidential campaign of Senator Eugene McCarthy (D-Minn.) is one suggestion. The involvement of McCarthy activists in congressional races and continued reform efforts in state party organizations is another. Temperamentally, the new generation will identify more readily with the problem-solving, program-defining capacity of the Executive. It is likely to be impatient with the Congress. Not having the time to master the congressional system, the new generation will be on unequal terms with the older political professionals. With sufficient numbers, however, it might soon be in a position to topple congressional traditions like seniority. The Democratic Study Group in the House of Representatives has been carefully laying out the preliminaries for such an assault.[24]

The most important effects of the new generation on Congress may be indirect. Already it staffs key positions within the Executive and

[24] See Davidson, Kovenock, and O'Leary, *Congress in Crisis: Politics and Congressional Reform* (Belmont, Cal.: Wadsworth Publishing Co., 1966), pp. 129–42.

will increasingly set the tone of the new professionalist emphasis in government. The apportionment decisions have opened unprecedented opportunities for young Americans to enter politics at the level of state legislatures. In time, this should have important consequences for recruitment patterns in the national Congress. Congress, however, is unlikely to become the "advance guard" of the new generation simply because it is such a broadly based and elaborately structured representative institution. The Presidency or at least nomination for the Presidency is a more amenable target. Yet Congress cannot long be isolated from such a significant generational shift in American politics and the cultural change this implies.

The new power centers of the post-industrial society. The same economic and technological advances that have moved America into the post-industrial society have effected fundamental changes in the structure of power.[25] The coalition of interests that backed the New Deal social and economic reforms of the 1930's — labor, agriculture, the ethnic minorities — has achieved most of its policy goals. These older blocs, with the exception of the Negro, are now conservative forces. The entire nature of interest-group politics has changed as America has become a pluralized society of large, integrated organizations. Bigness, Max Ways observes, has inculcated "a common style of action among business managers, government officials, and university professors" with a free circulation through all three of these formerly walled-off worlds.[26] The ascendancy of Big Government, Big Business, and Big Education is rooted in the new base of power of the post-industrial society, theoretical knowledge. The knowledge worker — the mathematician, the economist, the social scientist, the computer programmer, and the scientific and engineering community in general — will be the dominant figure of the coming decades. The knowledge industry, based on the new university city and the complex of private research corporations and laboratories that will link government, the universities, and big business, will become the driving force of the new society.

> What has become decisive for society is the new centrality of *theoretical* knowledge, the primacy of theory over empiricism, and the codification of knowledge into abstract systems of

[25] For one definition of "post-industrial," see Kahn and Wiener, *op. cit.*, pp. 24–25, 186–88.

[26] *Op. cit.*, p. 95. Also see Theodore H. White, "The Action Intellectuals," *Life* magazine, June 9, 1967, pp. 43–58 ff; June 16, 1967, pp. 44–56 ff; June 23, 1967, pp. 76–78 ff.

symbols that can be translated into many different and varied circumstances. Every society now lives by innovation and growth, and it is theoretical knowledge that has become the matrix of innovation.[27]

How will these new power centers influence the direction of the new politics? John Kenneth Galbraith indicates that the mature corporation or "technostructure" of the new industrial system will increasingly be a passive force in politics, scrupulously nonpartisan.[28] At the same time the technostructure will enhance its position of influence as a virtual extension of the arm of the bureaucracy from which it can help shape the highly technical choices of public policy and the larger climate of belief within which public goals are projected. Galbraith feels that the industrial system will support its own needs, especially education, but will ignore the qualitative or aesthetic dimension of American life. The educational and scientific estate, which has also grown in influence by supplying the system its critical factor of production — qualified talent — has greater political options if it chooses to use them. It has grown enormously in numbers, maintains privileged access to scientific innovation, and will continue to exercise an almost unique role in social innovation. Where individual members of the technostructure are inhibited in regard to political action, members of the educational and scientific estate have no similar ties of organization and are handicapped only by the belief that their role is professionally passive.

The university, accordingly, becomes a critical focus of the new politics. On the one hand it is pulled in the direction of professionalism as a supplier of the intellectual capital of the major organizations of the system (including itself).[29] On the other hand it is urged by members of its own community, radical-activist students and professors, to "speak truth to power" and to take an active role in social reform. Galbraith, noting that "only a strongly creative political hand" may be needed to shape a new and "decisive instrument of political power," identifies the future of modern society with the de-

[27] Daniel Bell, "Notes on the Post-Industrial Society: I," *The Public Interest*, Winter 1967, p. 28. See also Stephen R. Graubard, "University Cities in the Year 2000," *Daedalus*, Summer 1967, pp. 17–22.

[28] Galbraith, *The New Industrial State* (Boston: Houghton Mifflin Co., 1967), pp. 296–317.

[29] See Christopher Jencks and David Riesman, *The Academic Revolution* (Garden City, N.Y.: Doubleday & Co., 1968).

gree of willingness and effectiveness of the intellectual community to "assume responsibilities for political action and leadership." [30]

The identification of the educational and scientific estate with the capacity for social invention has further implications for Congress. The politically active members of the new power centers appear to be gravitating toward the Executive branch and toward the federal and urban tiers of government. Congress has made some contacts with the scientific community through its science, space, and atomic energy committees and has sought the counsel of social scientists in its studies of poverty and the urban crisis. The Joint Economic Committee has won the respect of a critical element of the knowledge community, the professional economist.

If Congress is to maintain a vital partnership with the Executive in defining social policy, it will have to broaden its contacts with the new power centers. We noted in our discussion of information technology the natural tendency of Congress to be cast in a questioning or adversary role to the new technocrats and policy analysts in the executive bureaucracy. This does not preclude, however, the development of rich and constructive associations with the intellectual community and its roots of social criticism and innovation.

New challenges to the American political consensus — radical movements and the American party system. How will the various forces we have noted — affluence, urbanization, technological advance, organizational power — be translated into the dialogue of politics? What do they imply for the future of the American party system? How will they influence the content and passions of our future politics?

We can develop a set of general observations from several apparently contradictory trends. First, consistent with the forecast of those social and political historians who have foreseen an "end to ideology," the pragmatic, problem-solving approach of the "social engineer" and a new emphasis on the rational discussion of problems will characterize the politics of the educated, affluent, middle-class suburbanites.[31]

[30] *Op. cit.*, pp. 294–95, 381. Galbraith states, "Political action requires that legislators be persuaded or replaced by those who do not need persuasion. There is no alternative to having effective friends of these ideas occupy the relevant elective and appointive public offices and to having them held firmly to their duty by a watchful and determined constituency" (p. 386).

[31] For a classic statement of this interpretation, see Raymond Aron, "The End of Ideology and the Renaissance of Ideas," *The Industrial Society: Three Essays on Ideology and Development* (New York: Frederick A. Praeger, 1967). Aron believes that total systems of interpretation are in decline, but the ambiguity inherent in the concept of "ideology" inevitably colors the idea of an end to the ideological age.

Beginning with the new problems of metropolitan growth — the core-city, governmental reform, open-housing, mass transportation, air and water pollution, open spaces — middle-class politics will follow an essentially technocratic agenda of reform. The very success of effective management of the economy and systematic allocation of resources to solve public problems, however, will produce new, longer-range problems of affluence and alienation.

Second, the tension that already exists between pragmatic social reform and radical activism will be accentuated. The radical-activist student population, although a minority, will continue to grow in numbers and political sophistication. Kenneth Keniston anticipates student criticisms of American society to continue and intensify on two grounds: "first, that it has excluded a significant minority from its prosperity, and, second, that affluence alone is empty without humanitarian, aesthetic, or expressive fulfillment." Moreover, American students, sympathetic to unfulfilled aspirations of those abroad, may seek to "internationalize" American foreign policy.[32]

Third, the social structure of the future affluent society and the alienation it produces may prove fertile ground for extremist movements and new ideologies. Herman Kahn and Anthony Wiener project an American society in the year 2000 with three major social strata: (1) an upper-middle and middle-middle class earning from 20,000 to 100,000 dollars a year; (2) a lower-middle class earning generally from 5,000 or 10,000 to 20,000 dollars a year on a greatly reduced work week; and (3) lower-class minorities, concentrated largely in the big cities and receiving a comfortable government welfare allowance.[33] While the upper-middle classes would staff the command posts of industry, government, education and science, maintaining current work-oriented, advance-oriented, achievement-oriented norms in an otherwise leisure society, the attitude of the average American toward an economic and political system that seemed increasingly beyond his control might become one of "cynicism, emotional distance, and hostility."[34] Extremist groups and even racially based movements or minor parties might flourish in the militant black communities of the ghetto, which will grow both in size and black population concentration. The lower-middle classes, enjoy-

[32] *Op. cit.*, pp. 320–25. Keniston notes two styles of dissent: universalistic-activist and romantic-alienated. "A sense of ineffectuality, especially if coupled with repression of organized dissent" could discourage student activists and leave dissent to the alienated.

[33] *Op. cit.*, pp. 202–8.

[34] *Ibid.*, p. 200.

ing the income and leisure benefits of the post-industrial society, would resist the political demands of the relatively poor nonworking class and would likely provide "the primary support for both conservative national policies and political jingoism." [35] Yet Kahn and Wiener believe a partly alienated, affluent, humanistic, leisure-oriented society might be quite stable, with a large majority of Americans becoming relatively elitist in education, skills, and tastes, and a large minority competing to be "an elite of elites."

Fourth, new political technology may make the American polity more susceptible to the radical enthusiasms it has successfully resisted in the past. Daniel Bell, commenting on the media transmission of shock effect in the Selma march, sees dangers in the too rapid communication of political influence:

> In effect, our society has become more "permeable" and open
> to plebiscitarian pressures. One may applaud the fact that the
> nature of mass media increases the likelihood of a spectacular
> rise in "participatory" democracy, but these instances are also
> more likely to be on emotional issues, so that the loss of "in-
> sulating space" itself may permit the setting off of chain reac-
> tions which may be disruptive of civil politics and reasoned
> debate.[36]

In this situation, Congress may gain importance as an institutional buffer providing a new kind of insulating space as the speed of political decisions accelerates through technological innovation and the intensification of political ideologies.

What do these observations imply for the future of the American party system? Political parties have tended to coalesce or to realign themselves significantly only infrequently in our political history.[37] We have cited the cyclical nature of party majorities as one major

---

[35] *Ibid.*, p. 207.

[36] "Notes on the Post-Industrial Society: II," *The Public Interest*, Spring 1967, pp. 109–10.

[37] For a historical and theoretical analysis of realignment in American political parties, see William N. Chambers, "Party Development and the American Mainstream" and Walter Dean Burnham, "Party Systems and the Political Process," in Chambers and Burnham (eds.) *op. cit.*, pp. 3–32, 277–307. Chambers notes that the comparative ideological stress of the 1960's may foreshadow the emergence of a new party alignment. Burnham concludes, "The period since 1950 may legitimately be described as one of great confusion in American party politics, a period in which the classic New Deal alignment seems to have evaporated without being replaced by an equally structured ordering of politics" (p. 304).

factor affecting the legislative performance of Congress. The 1960's have initiated a period of party realignment, although in view of the events of the past few years, few would be so brash as to predict the outcome of the realignment. It does appear that a political coalition that incorporates the new power centers and that articulates a coherent, unifying political philosophy can gain a dominant position in American party politics that could last for most of the remaining century.[38] We can anticipate, then, a new political realignment that may be scarcely recognizable in terms of our current party programs and leadership. With this realignment, Congress will likely inherit a new legislative agenda and new priorities.

We can also anticipate, on the basis of current trends, a more ideological form of party politics, with the possibility of new radical and conservative minor parties. Two factors may be working toward a radicalization of party issue-positions. First, as the economic incentives of the old style of politics, such as patronage and party services, continue to decline, an increasing number of party workers, or activists, will find their incentives in ideological and psychological rewards.[39] Second, the politically aware strata in the country have typically held more polarized views on domestic economics and social welfare policy than the average voter.[40] With increasing affluence and education, it is logical to expect a higher level of issue partisanship. One result of these trends might be the control of the national party organizations by new middle-class professionals with relatively strong ideological commitment.

Some highly emotional issues may strain the traditional two-party system to the breaking point; for example, foreign policy, more especially the use of American power, affluence, and technology in the world, both because of the decline of middle-class interest in many domestic economic issues and because of the growing incongruity

[38] Both Lubell (before November 1964) and Drucker have suggested that the Republican party was in the better strategic position to achieve such dominance, although it has shown little predisposition to follow their prescriptions for electoral success. The near future, at least, appears to have eluded the political seers.

[39] See Frank J. Sorauf, *Political Parties in the American System* (Boston: Little, Brown & Co., 1964), Chap. V, "The Structure of Incentives," and James Q. Wilson, *The Amateur Democrat: Club Politics in Three Cities* (Chicago: University of Chicago Press, 1962).

[40] Herbert McClosky, "Consensus and Ideology in American Politics," APSR, June 1964, pp. 361–82; and Herbert McClosky, Paul J. Hoffman, and Rosemary O'Hara, "Issue Conflict and Consensus Among Party Leaders and Followers," APSR, June 1960, pp. 406–27.

between American wealth and technological problem-solving capacity at home and declining American influence in the international arena. The political and economic development of countries like China, Indonesia, and Brazil will lead to the disintegration of "the American sponsored system of world security" that developed in the decades following World War II. The consequences of "the loss of empire" for American politics could be highly disruptive. At the same time, American politics will have to come to terms with a new world ideology of equality that will challenge the right of the United States to determine for itself the use of its own wealth and power.[41]

As Congress becomes involved in the national articulation and mediation of these pressures, it will of necessity develop a greater capacity to participate in the formulation of foreign policy. This will generate a major new source of tension in legislative-executive relations.

In domestic policy, the issues of race and social justice could affect the American party system. Racial politics could move in several directions: toward one or two genuinely multiracial national parties based on an ideology of social justice; toward a dominant conservative, white political party based on a program of racial separation; toward a balance between a moderate (on racial policy), predominantly white, middle-class, suburban party and a radical, multiracial, urban-based party; or toward a fragmented or unstable party situation with a mixture of militant, racial, separatist parties and moderate multiracial parties. The only sure prediction that one can make is that race will inevitably interject dissonance into the middle-class American dream.

Congress may become the national forum for the discussion and resolution of racially explosive issues, although the role Congress will be called upon to play will be largely shaped by the alternatives presented to it by the party system. If a conservative, white political party were to capture the Presidency in the wake of widespread urban violence and middle-class reaction, Congress might play a highly significant moderating role.

As American politics becomes increasingly concerned with moral and aesthetic values, with the consequent need to find meaning and

---

[41] See Samuel P. Huntington, "Political Development and the Decline of the American System of World Order," *Daedalus*, Summer 1967, pp. 927–29; and Ithiel de Sola Pool, "The International System in the Next Half Century," *ibid.*, pp. 930–35.

structure in a world of revolutionary change, the great game of politics can become the most dangerous game of all. Irving Kristol has warned against turning to organized political-ideological action to cope with the current American crisis in values, but he doubts that there is any way of removing the issue from politics.

> I cannot persuade myself that a democracy whose notions of public and private virtue are slowly being emptied of their substance can sustain itself. Democracy, after all, means self-government; and such self-government is, in the long run, utterly impossible without adequate self-definition, self-certainty, self-control. All of modern life and modern culture have combined to make the self a question to itself. I regard it as utopian to expect that people will not turn to politics for answers. And I regard it as certain that they will take vicious answers rather than none at all.[42]

Further observations on the Congress of the future. These various trends, taken together, suggest the bewildering change that Congress faces in its political environment. In comparison, the problems of congressional adjustment to an information technology that can be adapted to internal specifications by Congress seem minor. We can suggest several possible changes or adjustments of Congress to the environment of the new politics:

1. As a major national institution, Congress should share generally in the enhancement of power of Big Government, Big Business, and Big Education in the post-industrial society. Its members and committees will enjoy access to various knowledge elites and may develop continuing forms of institutional liaison. The resources available to Congress should increase impressively.

2. The congressional career will become increasingly professional in its demands through the combined effect of the new technology of decision making in public policy and the political technology of elections. Both should favor the survival and advancement of the more competent congressman, as will the continued growth of a more sophisticated electorate. The new political technology may work, however, to strengthen the incumbent in Congress quite apart from the competence of the individual candidates. (The recent successes of the practitioners of the new politics in surprising incumbent congressmen and senators, especially in party primaries, may be a short-term,

[42] "New Right, New Left," *The Public Interest*, Summer 1966, p. 7.

transitional effect.) National campaign commitees will steadily update campaign technique based on the pooled experience of candidates in the previous (and current) election.

3. Congressmen will face demands for increasing ethical standards in a society where value questions will steadily replace "life and death" economic issues. An entire new range of political issues will be opened up, for example, by the possibilities for the biological manipulation of man. The accelerating changes in knowledge and technology are propelling not only Congress but all large organizations in American society into "an era in which ethics must become a dominant concern if we are to survive." [43]

4. Congressional parties may become more partisan and ideologically coherent as committed activists seek election to Congress.[44] A breakdown of the two-party system, with the addition of militant third or fourth parties, would lead to a multiparty organization within Congress, with added tension and delay in the legislative process.

5. Congress will need to evolve new forms of mediation and conflict resolution as our society encounters new tactics of social protest and the politics of confrontation. If Congress is to maintain its broad legitimacy as a representative body, it must learn to understand and communicate in the languages of the new politics. As our politics and party system enter a period of turmoil and adjustment to unfamiliar issues and concerns, Congress can serve perhaps its most crucial role in affording a continually open *national forum* for rational deliberation and decision.

6. Although it will be technologically feasible in coming decades to take instantaneous polls of the public on any policy issue, it is highly unlikely that Congress will become a "push-button legislature." The congressional resistance to electronic roll-call votes is one indication that Congress will be anything but hospitable to plebiscitarian pres-

[43] For an excellent discussion of the changing public expectations of congressional standards of conduct, see the testimony of Dr. Franklin P. Kilpatrick in U.S. House of Representatives, Committee on Standards of Official Conduct, *Hearings: Standards of Official Conduct*, 90th Congress, 1st Session, 1967, pp. 18–25. See also Robert S. Getz, *Congressional Ethics: The Conflict of Interest Issue* (New Perspectives in Political Science; Princeton, N.J.: Van Nostrand, 1966).

[44] This trend has been evident in the congressional Republican party during the 1960's. See Frank S. Meyer, "Conservatism," in Robert A. Goldwin (ed.), *Left, Right and Center: Essays on Liberalism and Conservatism in the United States* (Rand McNally Public Affairs Series; Chicago: Rand McNally, 1965), pp. 1–17.

sures that replace the congressman's judgment.[45] Congress, and especially the House of Representatives, has been and will continue to be responsive to public opinion at the same time that it has served as a buffer to it.

7. Congress can work to counter the tendency toward alienation in the affluent post-industrial society through the diffusion of the middle-class ideal of participation. Besides maintaining an openness to dissent and encouraging citizen initiative in the study-investigating, hearing processes, Congress could stimulate opportunities for participation through innovations in the federal system generally, and help restore the value of community in American politics.[46]

TOWARD CONGRESSIONAL EXCELLENCE

We anticipate that the Congress of the future will have a considerable degree of freedom in determining what it shall be, both internally in structuring its activity, and externally in its relationship to the President and executive bureaucracy. The framework of alternative evaluations that we have suggested may serve as either a guide for congressional choice or a means for interpreting the consequences of choices as they are taken.

Beyond outlining a broad framework for evaluating congressional performance, we have avoided a more personal statement or evaluation of Congress. The careful reader will have noted, however, certain emphases.

1. In suggesting multiple perspectives and criteria for evaluation, we have frequently called into question stereotyped, partial, limited interpretations of Congress. Much of the commentary on, and analysis of, Congress unfortunately has been of such a nature. Our intention has been not to exclude any value premises but to enlarge the range of perspectives and criteria. We have also argued that value criteria

---

[45] See Davidson, Kovenock, and O'Leary, *op. cit.*, pp. 112–13.

[46] Daniel Moynihan suggests that many of the "traditional disadvantages" of American political structure, notably the diffusion of power and the multiplicity of governmental jurisdictions, may become virtues by providing opportunities for people to keep busy. *Daedalus*, Summer 1967, p. 684. For a less sanguine view of the incentives for political participation in the post-industrial society, see Philip Reiff's discussion of "anti-politics" and the revolt against "community" in *The Triumph of the Therapeutic: Uses of Faith after Freud* (New York: Harper & Row, 1966), pp. 238–46.

should be explicit and that evaluations should be consistent with relevant data.

2. By considering the historical development of congressional functions, we have suggested that there are some modal characteristics or aspects of the American political system, such as dual representation and congressional control of administration. This, in turn, implies that some of the alternative models for evaluating congressional performance are more relevant to the American system as it has functioned in the past than are others. The Burkean presumption in favor of institutional continuity is written into the Declaration of Independence — "prudence, indeed, will dictate that governments long established should not be changed for light and transient causes." Our emphasis, however, has not excluded the statement of alternatives.

3. Finally, by projecting our analysis into a future that assumes significant technological and governmental advance, we have suggested that Congress faces a new range of problems and possibilities in organizing itself to exercise power. The current descriptive, behavioral interpretations of Congress may give us a limited view of potential congressional performance in an environment of improved information and rationalized decision making. Once again our intention has been to enlarge the base of understanding for interpreting or evaluating Congress.

A PERSONAL INTERPRETATION OF CONGRESSIONAL PERFORMANCE

Congress has demonstrated considerable innovative response and adaptation. The popular critical image of Congress as a static or decaying institution with archaic forms is, in our estimate, highly inaccurate. While scholars have structured and restructured power in Congress, much of their analysis has ignored the steady, incremental thrust of change within Congress itself. In an important sense, much of the reform literature on Congress has been detached from reality. It has posited some reforms that have dramatic appeal in limited circles but that appear utopian to most congressmen, while missing significant change not announced as reform. Virtually unnoticed, the Library of Congress Legislative Reference Service adds a science policy unit, the Senate Majority Leader announces a new policy in appointing junior Democratic senators to major committees without regard to seniority, a congressman begins updating and codifying the precedents of the House, a senior southern Democrat moves to permit joint sponsorship of bills in the House to economize on printing, a committee staff experiments with a symposium format for soliciting expert advice (a kind of congressional teach-in), an ad hoc committee of House and Senate Republicans begins an intensive survey of professional staff on congressional committees and the requirements for increased minority party staffing, the Clerk of the House informs members that they may obtain almost unlimited, toll-free, long distance telephone service, evenings and weekends through the Federal Telecommunications System, and an Appropriations subcommittee votes funds for an additional top-level staff aide for each member. We have suggested in our review of the control or oversight function that virtually no data exist in one of the most significant areas of recent congressional change.

One obvious conclusion is that we need to be much more aware of and focus more explicit research on the processes of evolutionary change within Congress: Congress *is* a dynamic, innovative institution. Once we have recognized this point, we can ask more appropriate questions about the *adequacy* of change within Congress. First, if incremental change takes place experimentally or in relatively isolated contexts within the Congress, one might reasonably assume that innovations at the committee level are not adequately understood or evaluated by the Congress as a whole. One function that a standing Joint Committee on the Organization of Congress might provide is a comparative analysis of such innovations. What forms of the legislative veto and limited authorization, for example, have proven the most useful in what legislative situations? What staffing patterns best meet the requirements of committee members? What alternatives have been attempted to bring expert technical advice to bear on committee decisions? Obviously, innovation in itself is not a measure of congressional excellence, but rather innovation directed toward perceived congressional needs and reviewed and evaluated in the broadest congressional context. More fundamental is the issue of whether such evolutionary change, even if it meets the preceding qualitative test, is adequate to the demands for congressional performance. Is Congress adapting itself to a changing policy environment rapidly enough? Different people will of course have different expectations of the degree and form of congressional response required. The Burkean conservative may interpret the current degree of change as a sign of the vitality of Congress. The black radical will probably discount it as insignificant.

We feel that the amount of congressional innovation is impressive in comparison to most academic estimates of the congressional capacity for change. As to the adequacy of change, Congress can and should give more explicit attention to the impact of diserete and uncoordinated innovation undertaken by its Houses, its committees, and its individual members. Finally, Congress needs to accelerate innovations in program analysis and information systems to help it better understand the impact of governmental programs on society at large and to determine whether governmental programs are meeting the needs and expectations of various sectors of the public.

The representative character of Congress is both one of its greatest strengths and one of its greatest weaknesses. At several points in our analysis we have suggested that Congress may perhaps be *too* representative of the American people. Midway through the 90th Congress with the Johnson legislative program at a near standstill, with the Congress confused and sullen in the face of an indefinite commitment in Vietnam, mounting spending and inflation at home, and a requested tax increase, Senate Majority Leader Mike Mansfield (D-Mont.) volunteered to the Washington press corps that the Congress reflected the American mood of "unease and frustration." "What the House does, whether we like it or not, represents fairly accurately what the people feel, the mood of America. Congress usually follows. It seldom takes the lead. This has always been true." [47]

The representative character of Congress enables it to mediate between governmental decision and public opinion. A representative legislature permits an important degree of popular control and oversight over public policy in both its legislative and administrative phases. Moreover a popular assembly performs an important legitimating function. This mediating function of Congress will become even more critical as governmental decision making becomes more rationalized through information technology.

While Congress may be representative, is it responsive to the needs for governmental action? Again, the answer depends on one's definition of needs. The author believes that congressional responsiveness can be increased without sacrificing the representative character of Congress. Congress should give careful attention to a more comprehensive and penetrating definition of needs, i.e., legislative priorities. This requires the development of the investigative or study function of Congress. New techniques of analysis will contribute to this de-

[47] *New York Times,* November 11, 1967, p. 20.

velopment, but the critical factor is likely to remain the enthusiasm and dedication of its members. To the extent that ignorance is an excuse for inaction or shields an inadequate or inappropriate public response, more thorough congressional study should improve the fit between stated objectives and program results.

Increased congressional responsiveness to policy needs also implies the development of the educative function of Congress. Certain policy needs, especially in foreign policy and in broader national or metropolitan constituencies, require clear statement by policy leaders. Congressmen can play an important supporting role to the President in articulating these broader policy requirements and interpreting them to their constituencies.

In summary, Congress must assert itself more in its investigative and educative roles — in such critical areas as government of the urban complex; equal opportunity in education, employment, and housing; American foreign aid and trade programs; arms control and disarmament — if it is to be a responsive as well as a representative institution. The success of the American experiment in self-government will depend in no small measure on the congressional capacity to lead as well as to follow popular opinion.

The congressional system exhibits significant slack in virtually all of its functions. Any review of the functional performance of Congress, such as this, is likely to expose the reviewer to more congressional activity than he originally anticipated. This is not surprising for a vital institution of 535 members supplemented by committee, institutional, and personal staffs. We have questioned, for example, the view that Congress exercises no initiative in the contemporary legislative process and we have underlined the growth of control and constituency service activity.

Yet impressive as the range and extent of congressional activity may be, considerable slack (in the form of utilized resources) remains in almost all that Congress does. The participant observer on Capitol Hill quickly notices what is left undone — the committee meetings not attended, the committee staff positions that are not filled or added, the minority views not filed, the investigations not initiated, the committee reports and hearings not followed through, the legislative decisions not made. In the pressurized policy atmosphere of contemporary Washington, the Congress preserves a certain leisureliness in its committee and floor proceedings.

Work within Congress, as one might expect, is distributed unevenly. Some insiders estimate that no more than 50 to 100 members bear the major burdens of legislative work. These are the wheel horses of the congressional system: the leadership, the hierarchy of the standing committees, and the subject-matter experts within the rank and file. Much of the slack in the system is accounted for by the rest of the membership's lacking either the motivation or the access to staff and other resources to contribute more effectively.

In our estimate, Congress functions considerably below its potential. Existing slack leaves room for a significant enhancement of congressional performance within the present institutional framework of the Legislature. Again, how slack should be removed depends very much on one's perspective. From the Whig perspective there is too much slack in the control function of Congress; from the presidential perspective there is not enough. Our preference, consistent with the arguments developed above, is for Congress to reduce the slack in its investigative or study function first, and then, armed with greater information and understanding, to give more attention to its other functions.

It is not our intention to present here a comprehensive agenda or strategy for congressional reform. Strengthening the investigative function of Congress, as we have already noted, will require enlarged professional staff resources for Congress. It will require serious debate of the costs and benefits of strengthening partisan adversary roles within Congress and in control and oversight of the executive bureaucracy. It will require further innovation in the standing committee system, perhaps to include the use of ad hoc bipartisan study groups. Above all, it will require rapid assimilation and adaptation of information technology.

To summarize this personal assessment, Congress is more innovative and representative than most of its critics are willing to acknowledge. However, in performance Congress falls considerably below its potential. By developing its investigative or study function, Congress can become both more responsive to policy needs and more effective in realizing its intent in legislation and administration.

PROSPECTS FOR THE FUTURE: THE PROBABILITIES FOR SUCCESS. Can Congress achieve these standards of performance or excellence? We believe so, for the following reasons.

The direction of reform suggested is consistent with the views of congressmen. An enhancement of congressional functions, such as we have suggested, appears to be consistent with the normative assumptions of the great majority of congressmen.[48] The sentiment for strengthening congressional effectiveness extends across party lines and between Houses; reform proposals that would strengthen the Executive (consistent with the presidential-responsible party or presidential-pluralist models of legislative-executive relations) have much less chance for success. Reforms of the former type can generally be introduced through an incremental strategy. Slack within the system should permit considerable development without a direct frontal challenge to the existing organization of power within Congress. Reforms of the latter type, especially party reform, constitute a much more immediate threat to the existing committee and congressional hierarchy.

The suggested reform should be greatly facilitated by the breakthrough in information technology. We have already outlined the possibilities for greatly improved governmental decision making afforded by the new information technology. Although one must consider the intervening time period until low-cost information systems are widely and effectively adopted for governmental use, we are generally optimistic that technology will significantly increase the options for development and reform open to Congress. The rationalization of governmental decision making should increase the quality of public policy and raise the standards of congressional excellence.

We have discounted the possibility of prolonged effective congressional resistance to the new technology for several reasons. Again, the basic concern of most members for strengthening Congress will require some congressional response to rapid change within the Executive branch. Moreover, the openness of the congressional system and the numerous built-in dimensions of competition favor the dissemination of innovation. How rapidly Congress responds, however, will affect the level of congressional performance.

Congress should be able to recruit and develop the requisite member and staff talent and skills. Over the past decades, Congress has steadily upgraded the quality of its membership. The job of a con-

---

[48] Davidson, Kovenock, and O'Leary, *op. cit.*, pp. 69–73, 163–76. See also Congressman Morris K. Udall's (D-Ariz.) letter to Democratic members of the House of Representatives announcing his candidacy for Speaker, *New York Times*, December 27, 1968, p. 19. "The House if properly organized and led, can restore its influence and can again become the independent, constructive force it once was; we need not simply react to the plans and programs of the executive. The House can and should be a source of innovative programs to meet national problems."

gressman has developed into a profession. Within the past two decades, the concept of professional staff has further extended the work
potential of a congressman. We have also discussed the possibilities
of the new politics further enhancing the quality of congressmen
elected.

Will Congress be able to recruit *sufficient* talent, however, to match
the potential for reform? Isn't the motivation and skill of the individual congressman the critical limiting factor? Admittedly, Congress
will have a finite pool of talent, of human resources, upon which it
can draw at any one time. How limiting a factor this will be will depend on how flexible Congress is in assigning members with highly
specialized skills and interests to specialized tasks. A flexible system of
committee assignments could easily be supplemented with ad hoc
study or work groups. It will also depend on how innovative Congress
is in developing and utilizing specialized institutional staffs to assist
the member and existing professional staff. We believe the congressional efforts to develop member and staff skills in economic policy,
atomic energy, and space, for example, support a moderately optimistic estimate of the future.

Ultimately, Congress alone possesses the power to reform itself. If
congressional reform, such as we have suggested, depended on executive approval or the development of widespread popular support, we
would be much less optimistic about the chances for success. The
Executive (and his constituency in the political science profession)
has not generally been favorably disposed toward reforms to strengthen
congressional effectiveness. It is unlikely that reform proposals of any
variety could excite sustained and wide public interest. But this is beside the point since Congress alone has the responsibility for the
staffing levels it accepts, the organizational and staff innovations it en-
courages, and the information requirements it specifies. It may make
good copy to blame the President, but in the last analysis Congress
itself must answer for its performance.

There is no easy assurance that Congress can attain this or any similar definition of congressional excellence. It is in the nature of the
American experiment that power should be organized so that mortal
men might achieve an immortal dream. The test of that experiment
and of that part of its design which is the Congress of the United
States will always be tomorrow.

Index